AF291709

ART CLASS
Flowers and Foliage

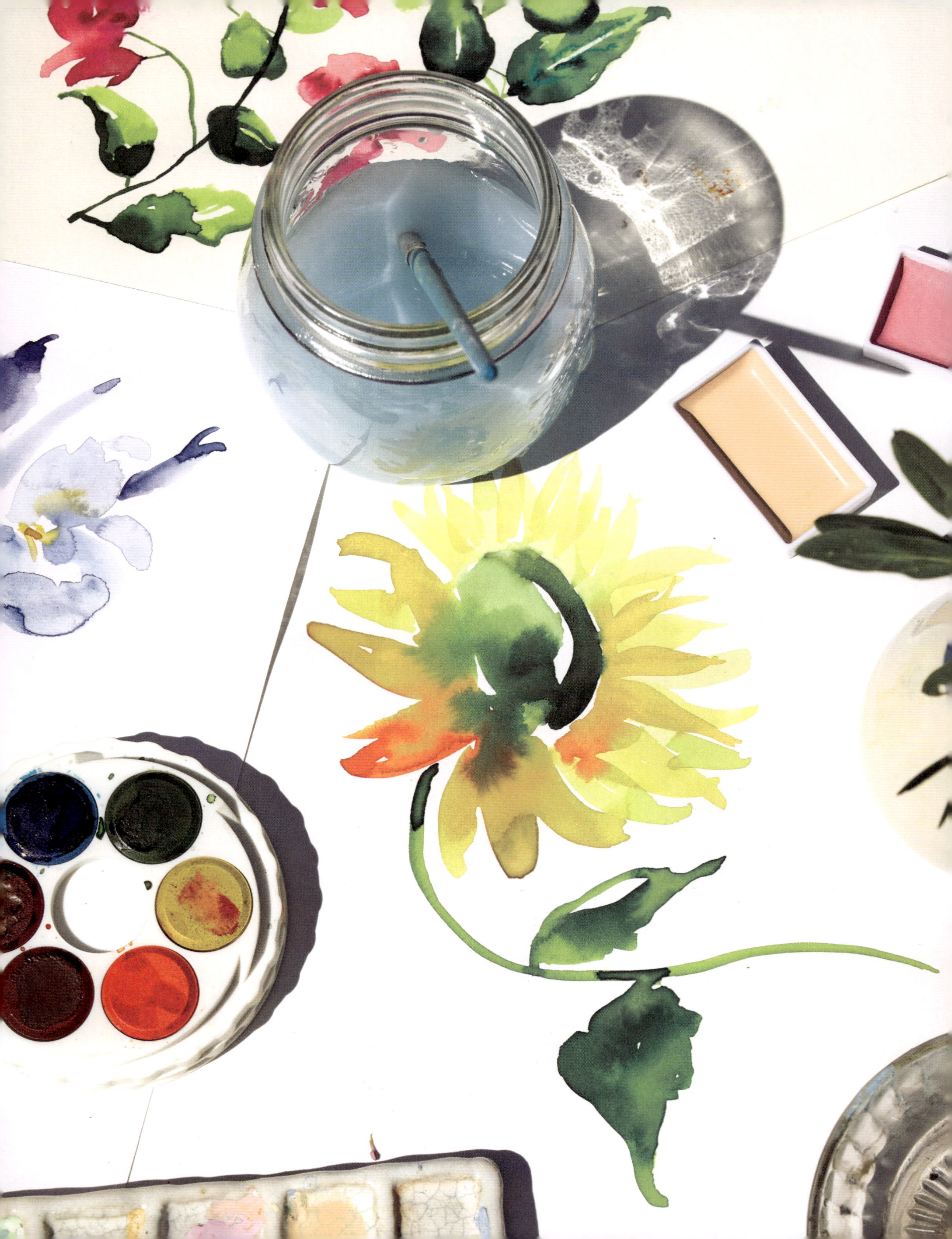

ART CLASS

with Sarah Hankinson

Flowers and Foliage:
Creating contemporary botanical art

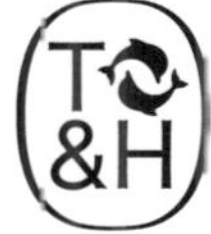

Contents

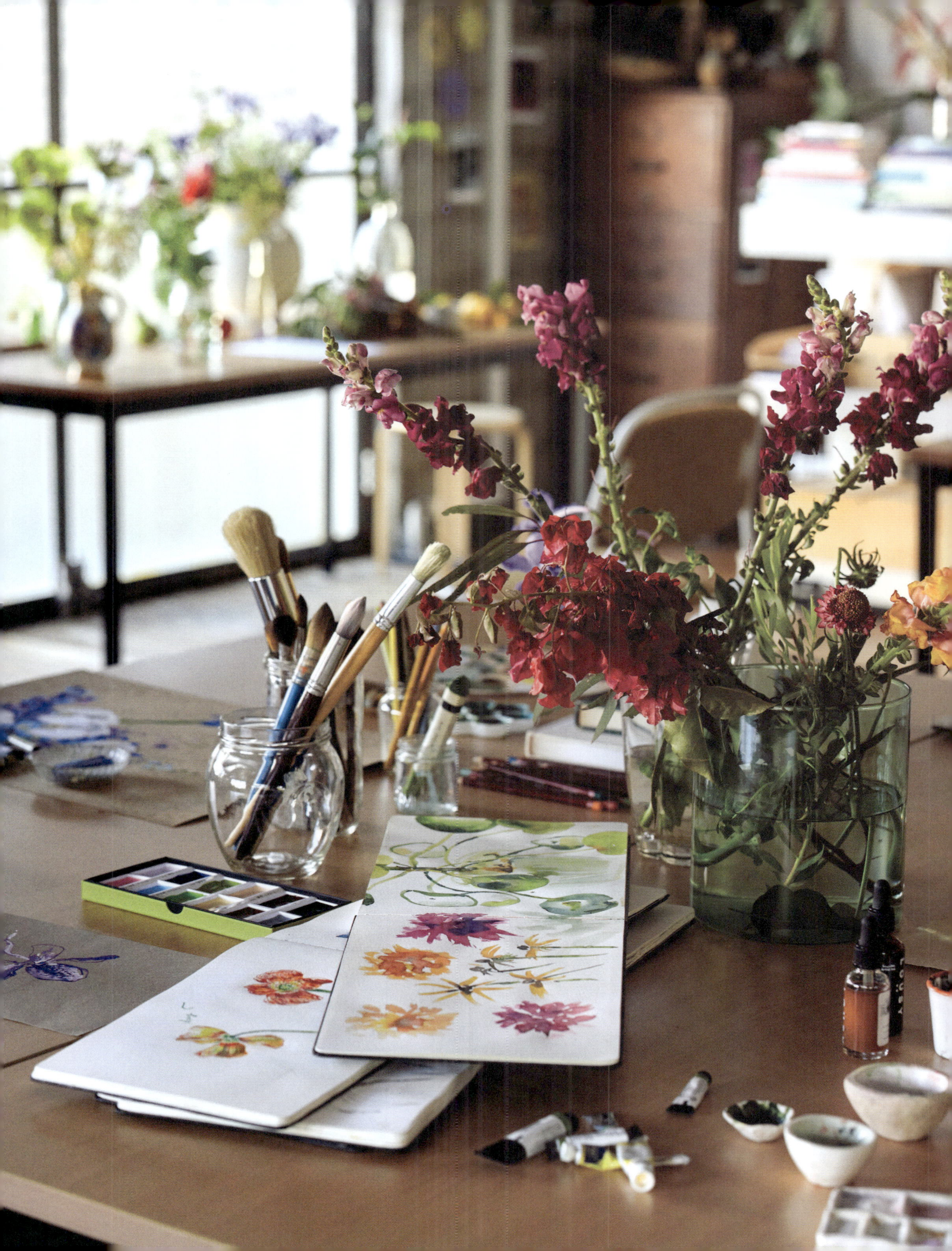

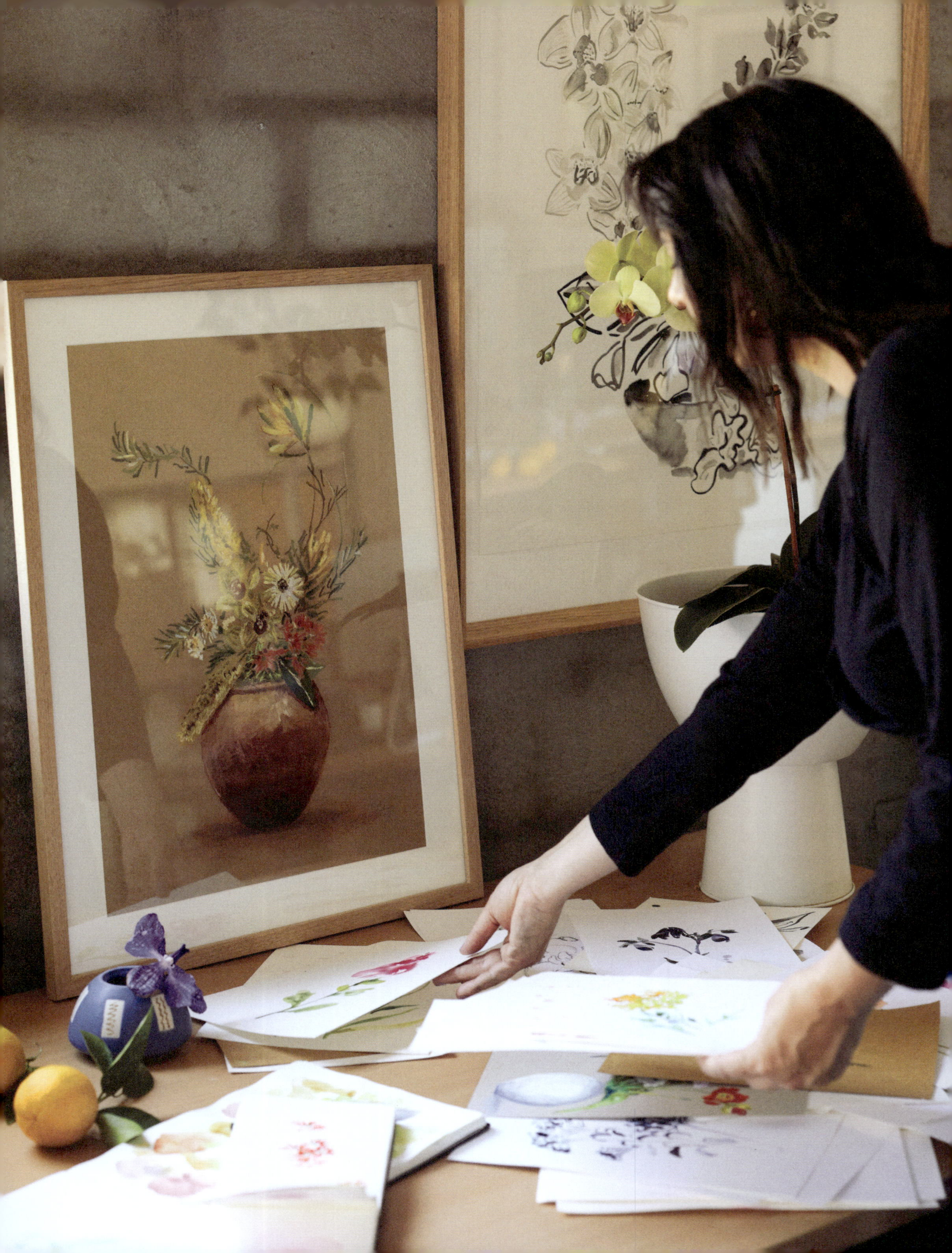

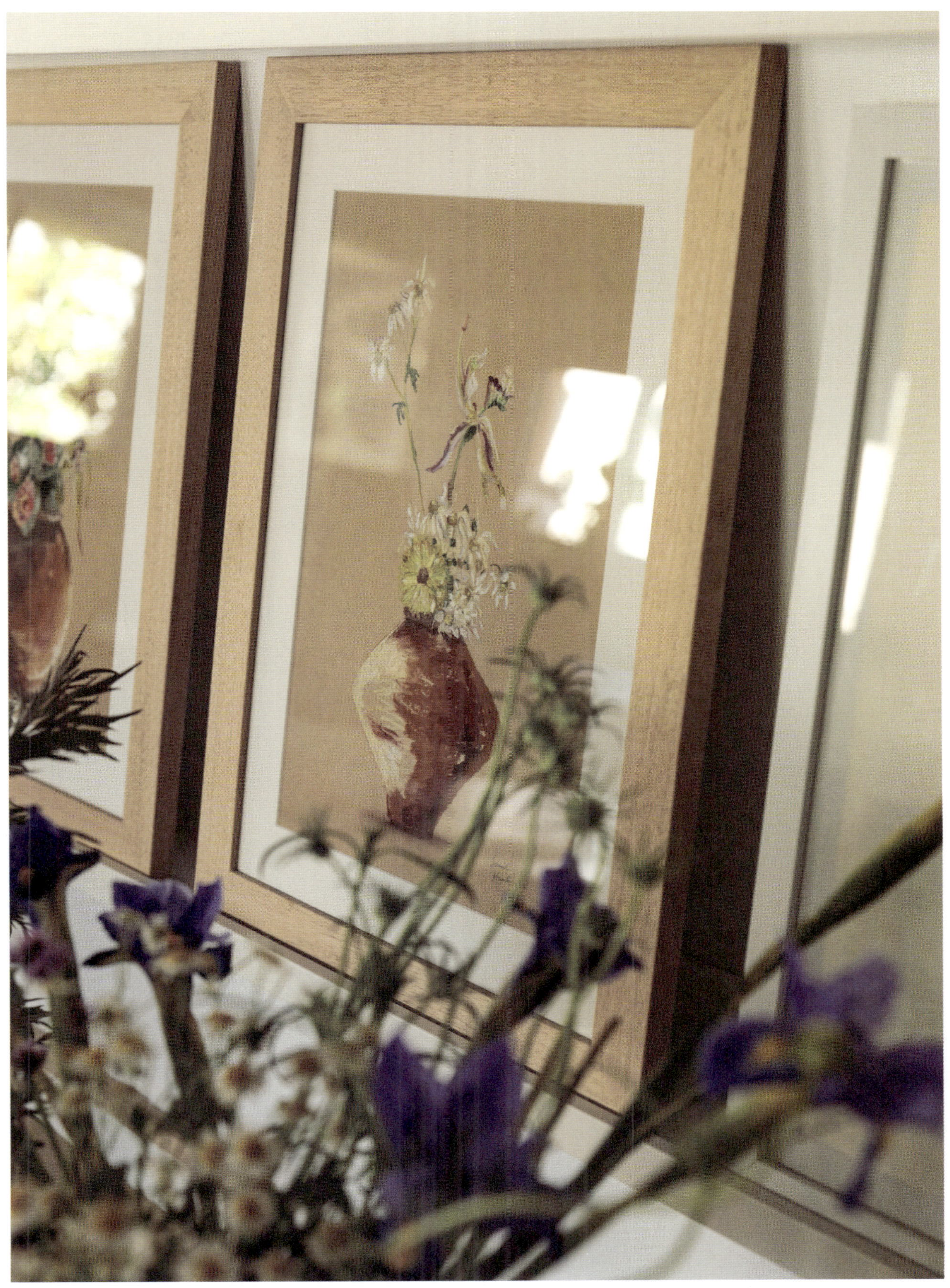

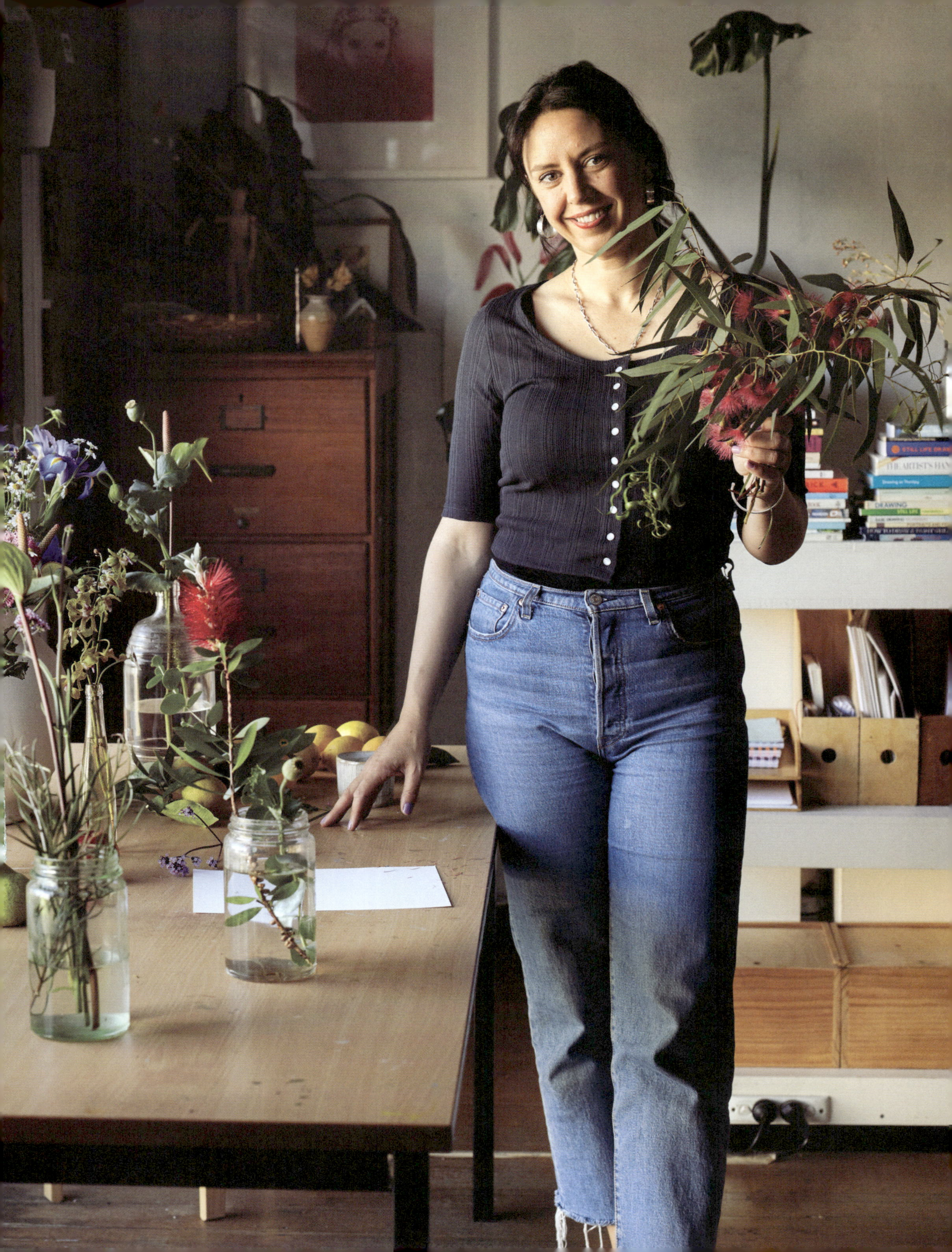

Introduction

Botanical art has a long history. Before the advent of photography, accurate hand-drawn illustrations of plants were important for documentation, identification and classification. Nowadays, the genre of botanical art thrives as a celebration of and an ode to the natural beauty of all botanical subjects, including flowers, plants and fruit.

Flowers make fascinating artistic subjects. They all have their own individual histories and unique meanings; delving deeper into these can lead us to the folklores of different cultures and beliefs about the varied healing and magical powers of botanicals. Flowers can also evoke memories, as they are often associated with rites of passage and some of life's most important events. Different flowers remind me of important times in my life: the violets that Mum bought me after the birth of my first son, the dahlia I grew at the first home I shared with my partner, the smell of geraniums that will always take me back to running around my nana's backyard.

Creating botanical art can help us take notice of, appreciate and engage with the incredible beauty that is all around us. There's a tranquillity to be found in the sensory bounty of nature, and engaging with nature through art can be deeply therapeutic and can have a profound, positive impact on mental health, offering solace and joyful mindfulness. I love the practice of looking, seeing and recording when I make art, capturing and expressing an environment, making sense of it and sharing how I experience and feel the world. Art making is a wonderful opportunity to be completely present, to really see your subject and to feel a moment more deeply than you would otherwise. I have found nothing more nourishing than being absorbed in the flow of creating, tuning in to my subject, getting lost in the work and translating my ideas into tangible works of art. There is magic in making something from nothing, bringing to life a scene, idea or feeling on blank paper.

This book is designed to teach you how to create botanical art with a contemporary approach, whether you are a beginner or a practised artist looking to expand your skillset. You will begin with some practical warm-up exercises that introduce the basics of botanical art making; techniques to loosen up and hone your observation and drawing skills; and new ways of looking, absorbing and documenting. Then, using various mediums and images of flowers arranged by Sour Sunflower, you will be guided by step-by-step instructions to create your own artworks.

I encourage you to think of your own botanical art practice as play, connection and an unfolding of ideas. Most of all, enjoy it. Reject the concept that the work you create is either good or bad; rather, it is an experimentation. Embrace vulnerability and take risks. If you can hold a pencil, you can draw: we are all artists. The act of making art should not be reserved for select people, because it is such an accessible, rewarding and mindful way to connect with the world around us. It's a joy to capture the richness of botanicals, the enigmatic beauty that makes life full and complex.

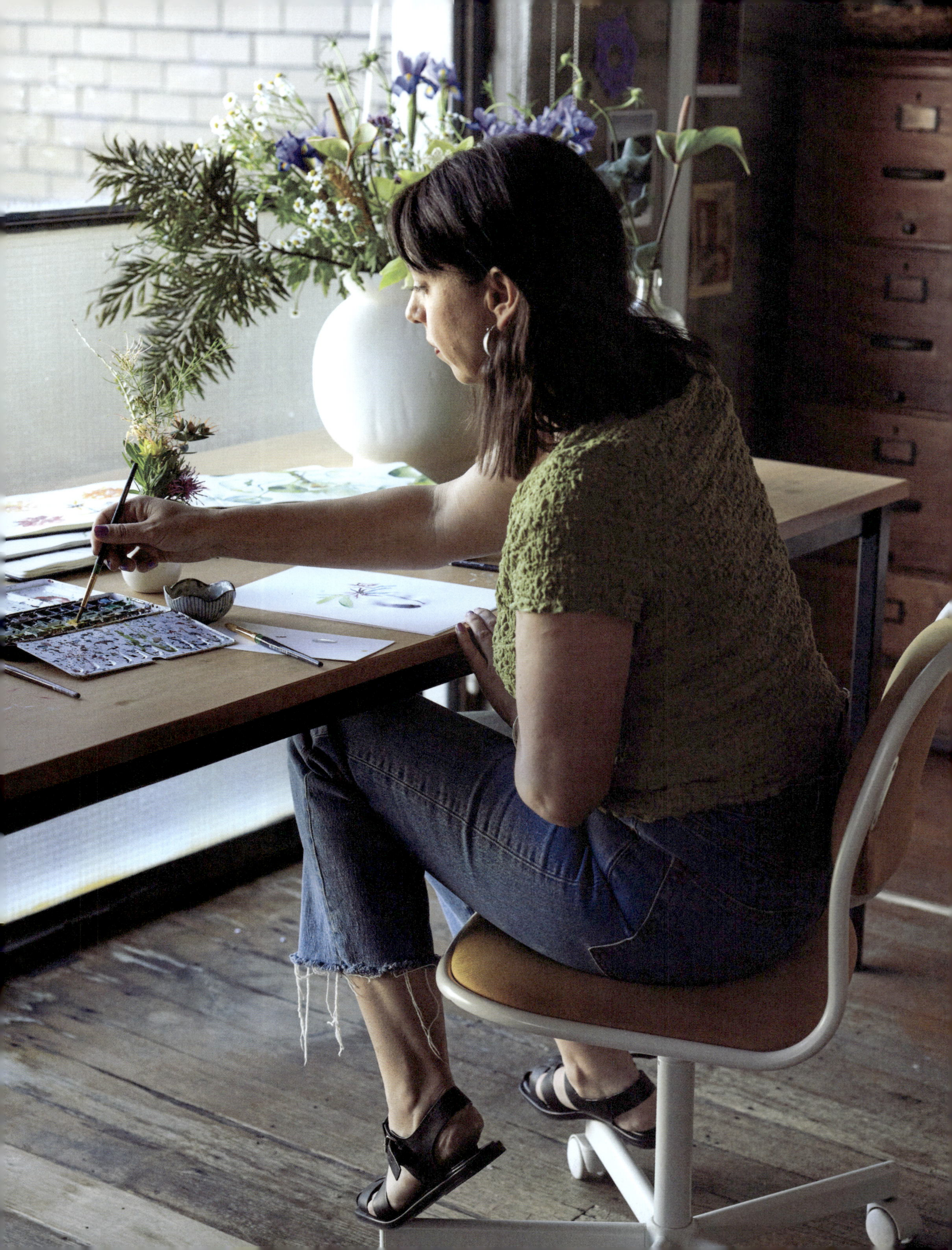

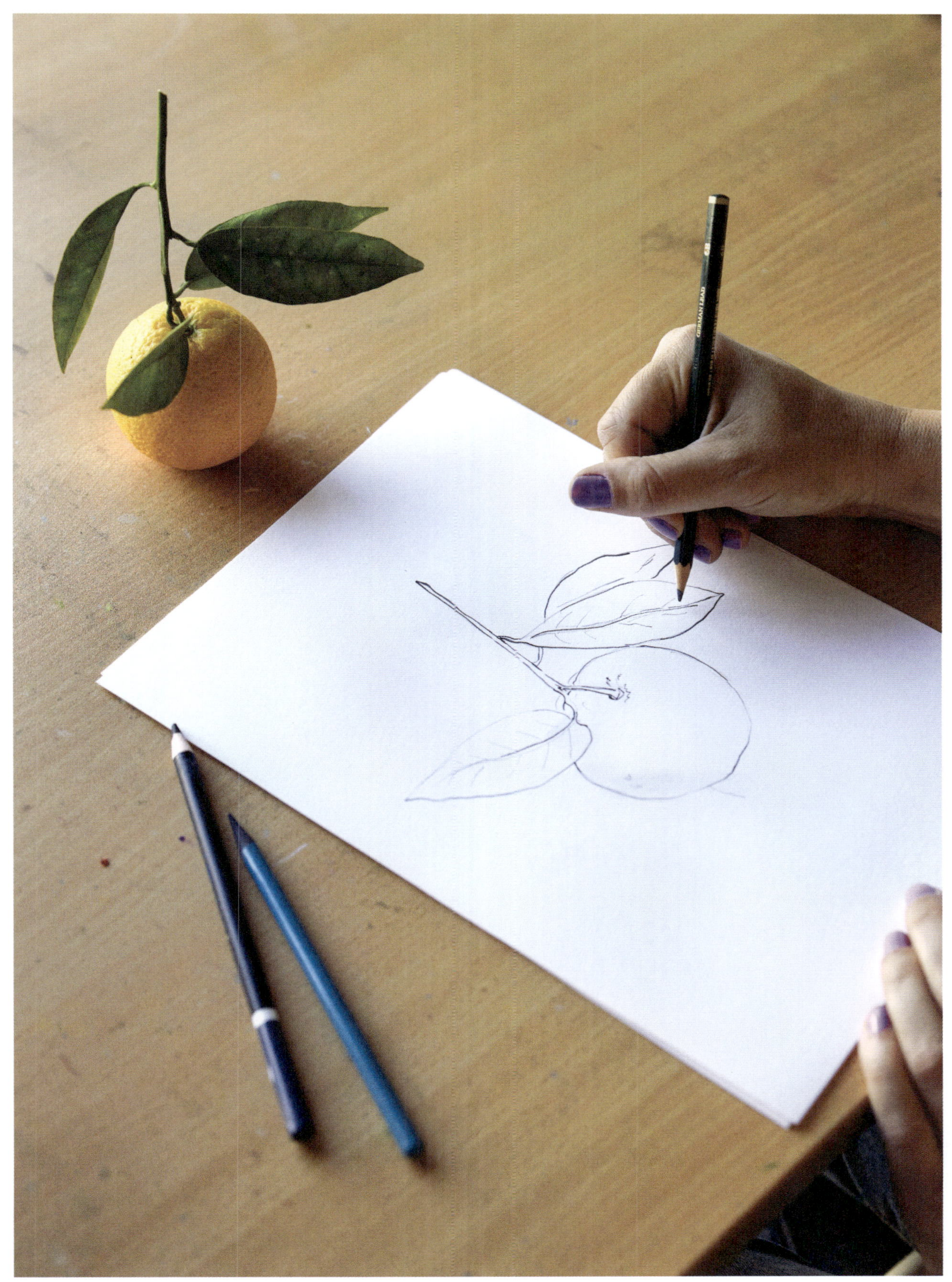

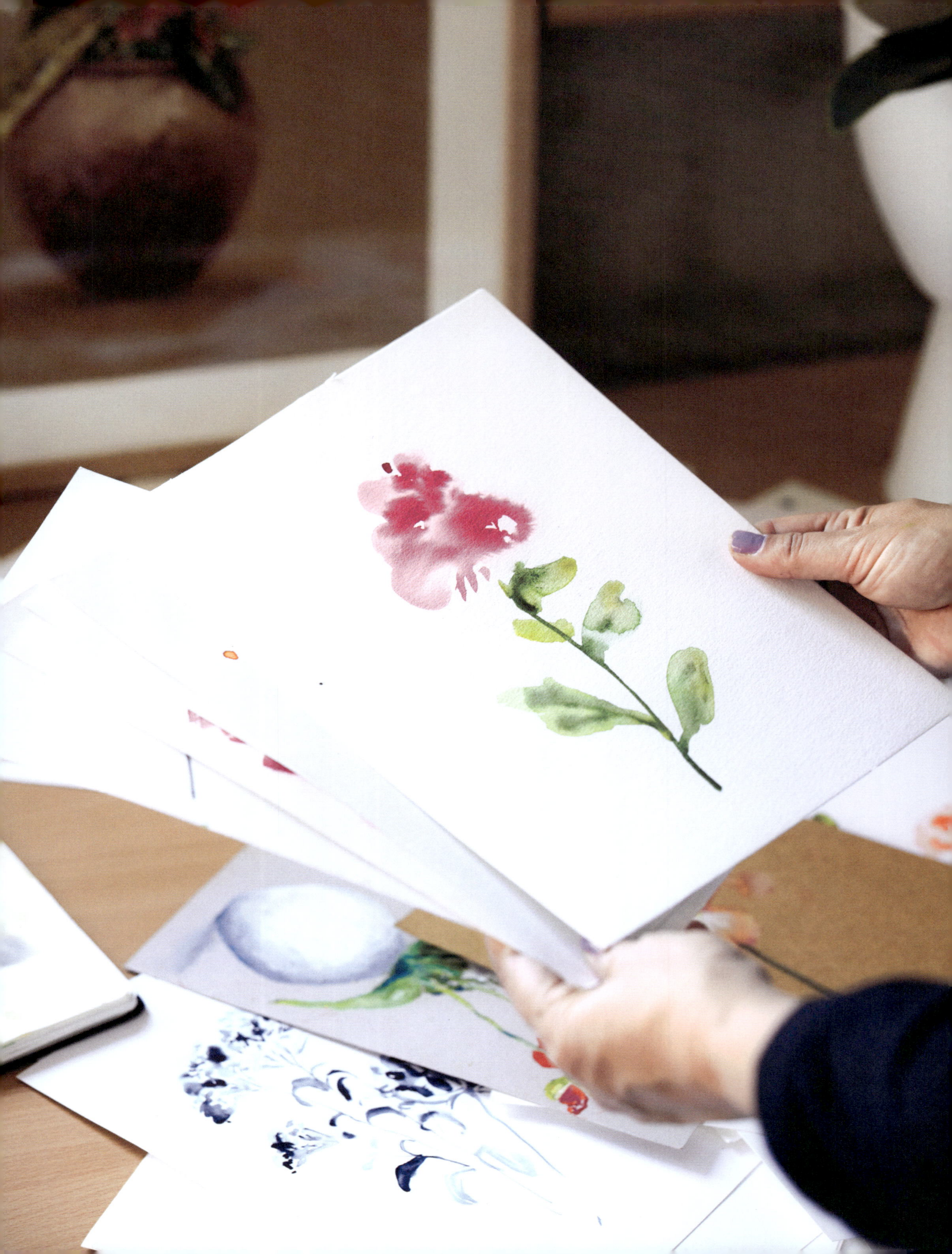

• THE BASICS •

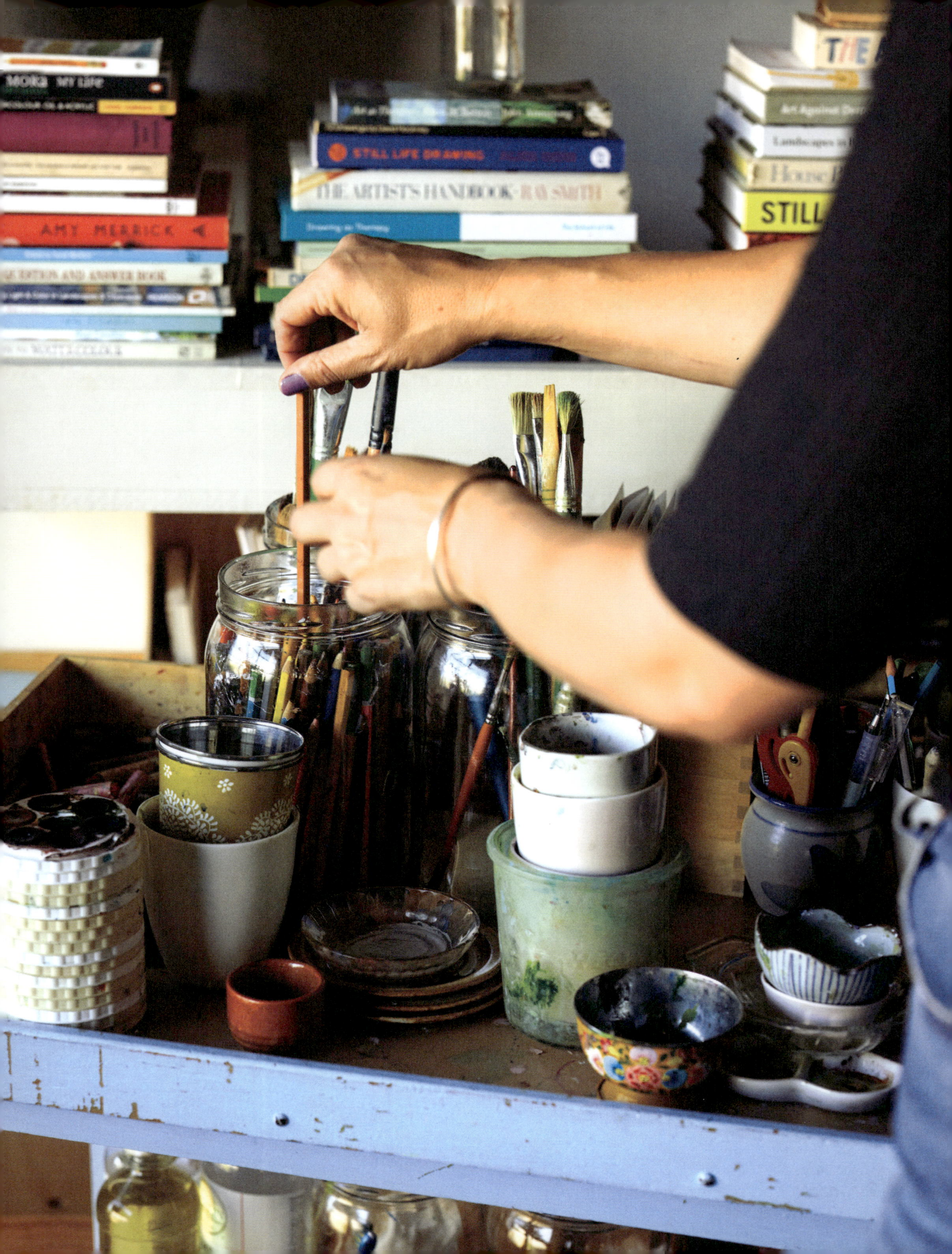

Materials

Artists' energies, personalities and expression can be seen in their artworks, and specific materials can help to convey them. Each material suggested in this book will work uniquely to give life to the botanicals you are illustrating, so immerse yourself in experimenting and becoming familiar with each of their distinctive properties.

I use a diverse array of materials, depending on the subject matter and which medium, surface and tools I feel will best depict it. The projects here introduce you to a few of the many and various materials available by using a range of the most common and popular mediums: graphite pencil, charcoal, coloured pencil, oil, soft pastel, watercolour and ink.

It is also useful to experiment with different types of papers, as mediums vary in appearance depending on the surface they are applied to. I use Kraft paper as an option with pastels, and watercolour paper with most other mediums. Kraft paper provides an earth-toned surface with a slight sheen which contrasts against the matte appearance of pastels. The natural tone of Kraft means white pastel or pencil can be used without disappearing like it does on white paper. Watercolour paper is sturdy, weighted and a great material to start with, because it can be used with all mediums. It is available in smooth, medium and rough, and each type has its benefits.

SMOOTH WATERCOLOUR PAPER • This is paper that has been hot pressed. It is better for pencils, as it can handle fine detail. Colours appear more vivid on hot-pressed paper, as the light reflects from the flat white surface. Paint can also be moved and manipulated more easily before it's absorbed.

MEDIUM WATERCOLOUR PAPER • The textured surface of this type of paper, which is cold pressed, suits the fluidity of watercolour. Pigments sink into the rivets in the paper, and this makes colours softer in appearance. Cold-pressed paper is more absorbent than hot-pressed, giving a quicker drying time but slightly less time to manipulate paint on the surface of the paper before the pigment it absorbed. It is the most popular type of watercolour paper, due to its durability and versatile surface texture; it provides a balance of absorbency and texture that accommodates various painting techniques.

ROUGH WATERCOLOUR PAPER • This type of paper is very textured. It is good for ink and watercolour, as it provides good water retention and colour dispersion. It also allows you to create pronounced, loose and expressive brushstrokes.

When working with wet mediums, such as watercolour and ink, it's important that your paper is a minimum of 300 grams per square metre (gsm), so that it will absorb water without warping. If you're not sure where to start, I recommend medium paper as a good middle ground between smooth and rough.

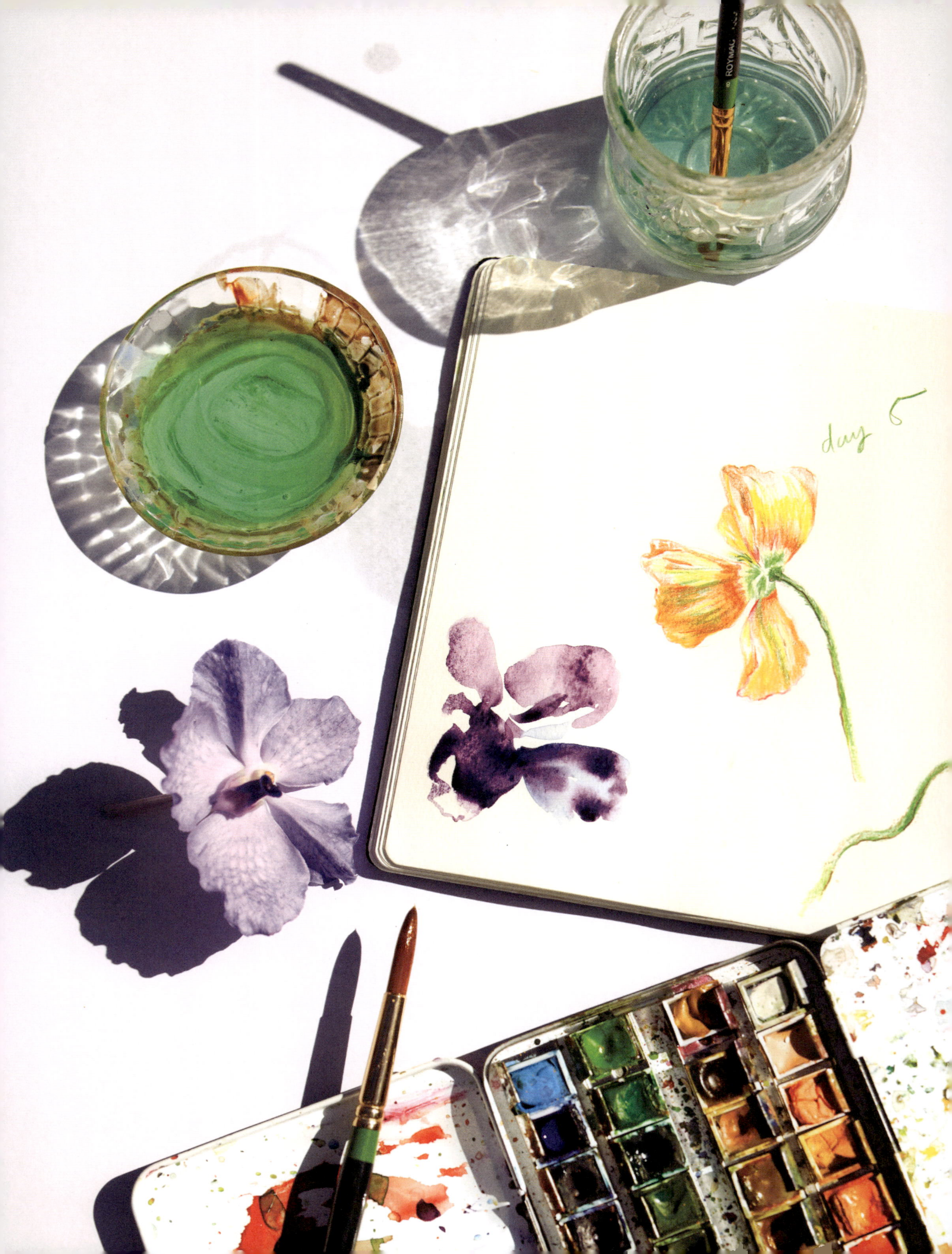
day 5

For working with watercolour paint, a good all-round brush is a soft, smooth, tapered, synthetic round in a size 12. This is big enough to hold a good amount of liquid for gestural washes but will keep its pointed tip. For more intricate areas, you could use a soft, smooth, tapered, round brush in a size 8. For filling larger areas, I use large, round brushes up to size 36. Sable brushes are lovely to use, but there are so many reliable, artist-quality synthetic alternatives available, which are designed to mimic the feel and function of sable and are much more affordable. You will have a good brush for years and years, so take care of it: don't leave it brush-end down in water, which will result in warping, and after use, rinse it in soapy water.

When I work with ink, I use a big, soft mop brush in a size 20 or 24. The bigger your brush, the more pigment and water it will hold, which allows for more working time before having to re-wet the brush. If my artwork requires finer detail, I use a round brush in a size 14 or 16.

Keeping a sketchbook for botanical art practice is a must. By having your artworks in one place and dating each page, you're able to track your progress over time and look back on all your creations. There are many sketchbooks to choose from in a variety of paper types, including sturdy watercolour paper in different textures.

Colour and value

Colour is an intrinsic element of art and can be broken up into three components: hue, saturation and value.

HUE • is the colour itself, like green, blue, red or orange.

SATURATION • measures how intense the colour is, ranging from highly saturated, such as bright yellow, to barely saturated, such as ochre.

VALUE • determines the lightness or darkness of a colour and is often considered one of the most crucial components of an artwork.

Flowers come in a wealth of colours, so they make perfect subject matter for playing and experimenting with hue. Try layering coloured pencils and pastels or mixing watercolour shades to match your botanical subjects. If you have a limited range of premixed colours, you can mix your own with just the primary colours of red, blue and yellow. Mixing two of the primaries will give you the secondary colours of green, orange and purple. Then you can mix one primary with one secondary colour to create the six tertiary colours of red-orange, yellow-orange, yellow-green, blue-green, blue-violet and red-violet. Adding black or white to your colour will change your hue even further.

Aside from the flowers, generally, the most dominant colour in nature is green. In each coloured medium I have a vast array of green shades, and green is always my most used and replaced colour. It pays to really look at the greens in your botanical subjects and to note the hue variations, ranging from earthy brown-greens, to vibrant yellow-greens and darker blue-greens. Your skills of observation and analysing are crucial when using colour. Look for shadows, highlights, gradients, blending of tones and subtle nuances. Aim to depict the brightest lights and deepest shadows within each colour. Shadows and highlights can define and clarify a complex structure within a subject without the use of line.

Value (or tone, as it can be referred to) is expressed on a scale from light to dark – for instance, from white through light grey, mid-grey and dark grey to black. The best way to practise with value is to work in grey, using charcoal, graphite or ink, and to utilise a range of values from very light to dark. Areas of highlight, where the light hits your subject, will have the lightest value, and shadowed areas will have the darkest. I try to use a range of values in my work to make each piece compelling, as a lack of contrast can result in an artwork looking flat and one-dimensional. Adding contrasting values brings interest, form, life and dimension to your subject – converting a three-dimensional object onto a two-dimensional page. Look at your subject matter and ask yourself: Which is the brightest area? Which is the darkest? And where are the midtones? Observe and analyse.

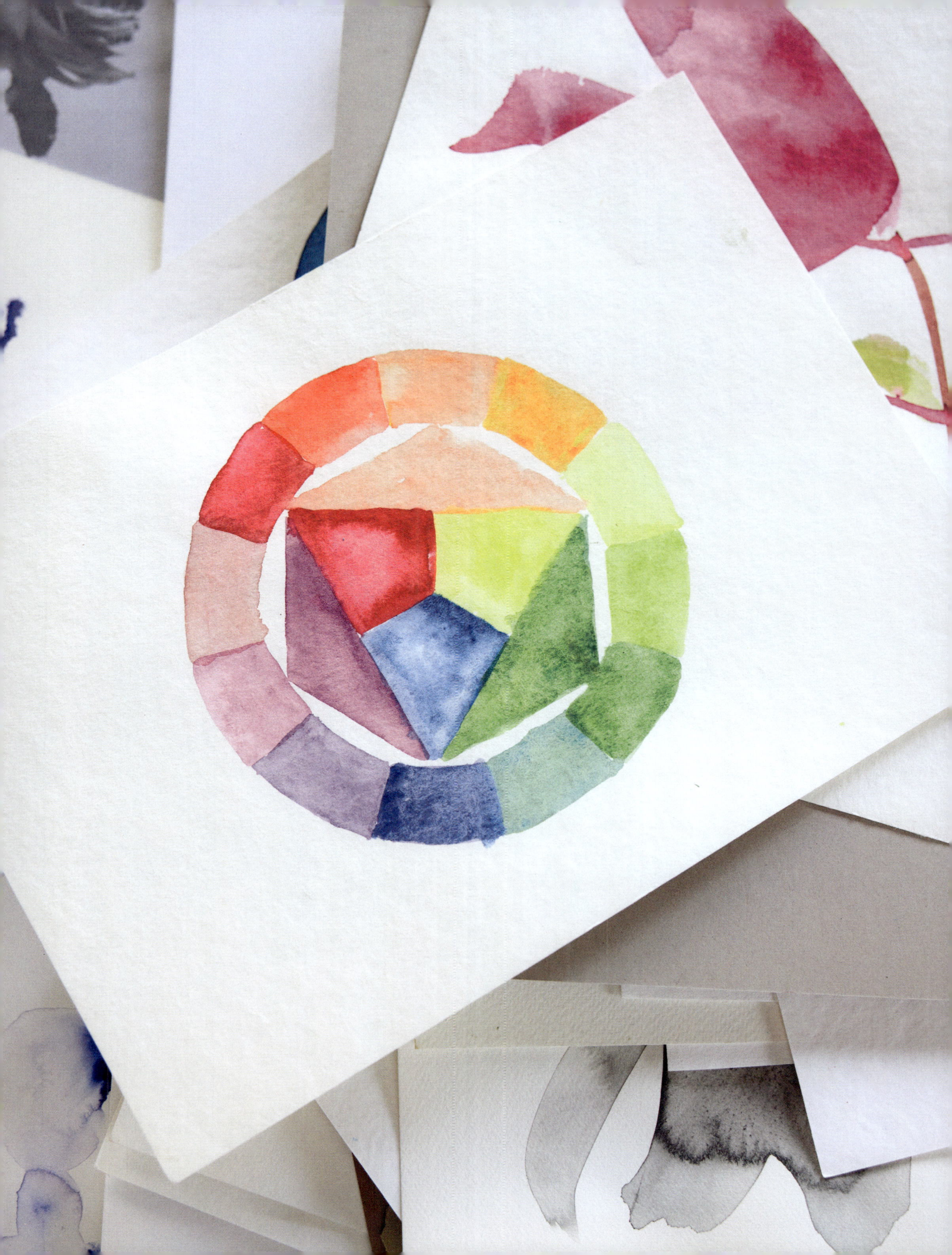

Botanical still-life arrangements

Sourcing botanical inspiration not only provides a subject matter to work from but also fosters a deeper connection with and appreciation of nature. Botanicals come in a vast array of colours, shapes and textures, and there's nothing better than to have them in front of you as a reference. You will learn so much by smelling and being able to touch the flowers, observing them close up and appreciating their intricate beauty. There are various ways to gather inspiration; here are some ideas.

To make a flower arrangement, first you need some flowers! Florists, of course, can create everything from small posies to enormous architectural displays, if cost isn't an issue for you. But there are many less expensive alternatives. You may have your own flowers growing in your garden or on a balcony. Or, if a neighbour has an amazing garden, you could ask for permission to take a flower or two. (But do be mindful not to forage from public or private land without consent.) You can also make some lovely arrangements with a few carefully selected supermarket flowers: daffodils, orchids, snapdragons and poppies are affordable and cheerful choices. Try to include flowers with a variety of textures, to add interest, and enhance the selection's natural appearance with some foliage, in the form of leaves and other greenery.

When you have collected the flowers and foliage for your art project, arrange them in a vase or jar naturally, as they would grow from the earth, overlapping and at different angles and heights. There is beauty in a seemingly haphazard, organic arrangement. You can also position extra botanical elements around the vase, like fruit and vegetables, a branch of citrus leaves and fruits, seed pods or gum nuts. Consider the season and add elements that reflect it, such as autumn leaves or sunflowers.

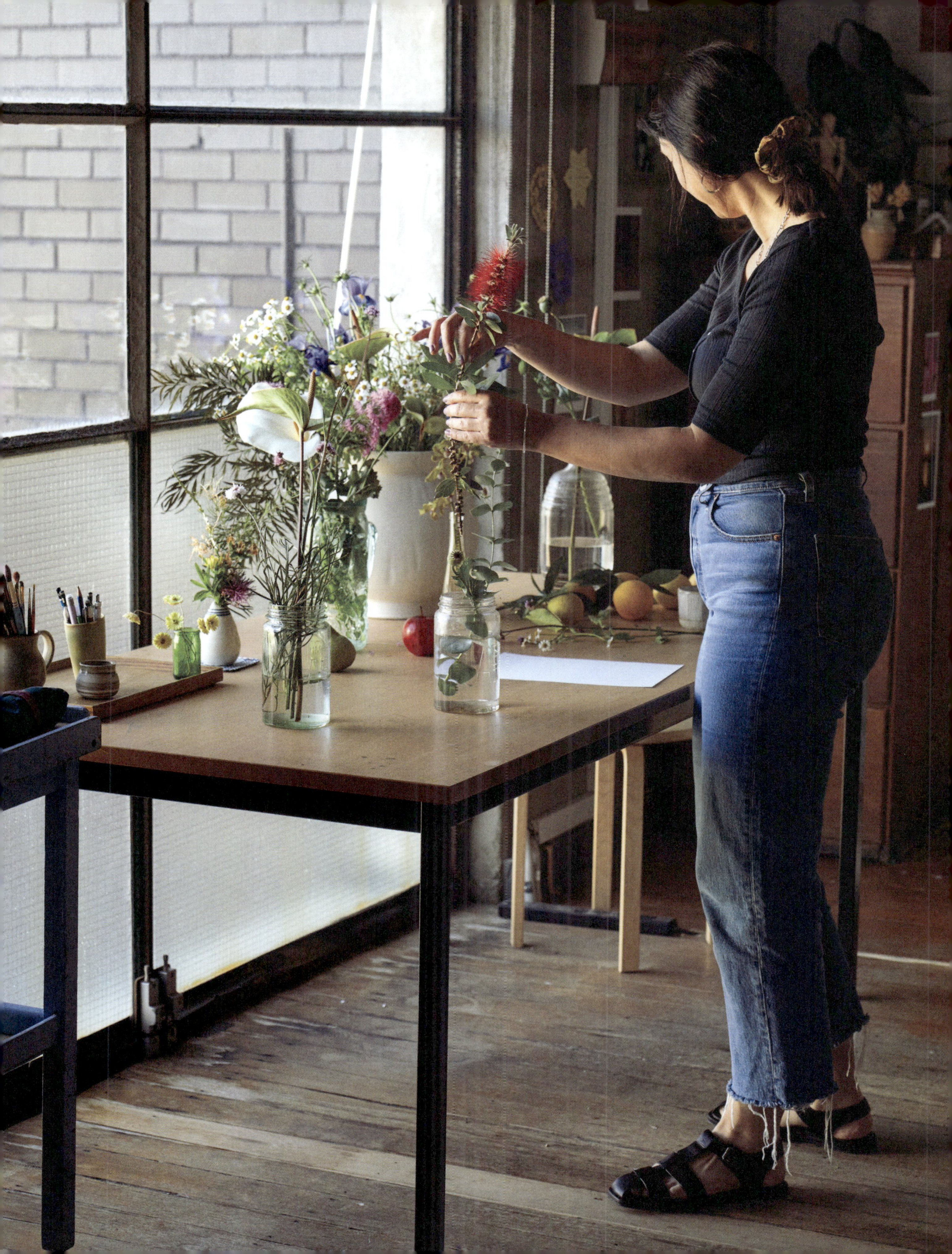

It can help to shine a lamp onto your subject, with the light directed from high up on one side, to imitate the sun's rays and to act as a consistent light source. This will cast shadows, add reflected areas of light and emphasise contrast. Light and shadows are pivotal in artwork, giving dimension and imbuing mood by emphasising focal points and creating a compelling composition. Shadows help to anchor the still life, providing depth and adding drama. Including strong contrast and variation in tone will bring your art to life and make it more interesting and pleasing to the eye.

TIPS

If you plan to create botanical illustrations regularly, I recommend growing your own plants. For my arrangements, I grow flowers from seed, so that I have blooms on hand to pick, pop in a vase and draw. This practice is so satisfying and accessible. Some easy flowers to grow in pots or garden beds are cornflowers, cosmos, poppies, sweat peas, nasturtiums and sunflowers. If this seems like too much work, garden nurseries stock a wide selection of already-growing potted flowering plants for purchase. For best results, choose varieties suited to your local climate and consider factors like sunlight and water requirements.

If you prefer your botanicals to be in their natural settings, another way to find artistic inspiration is to take your materials to a botanical garden or park and immerse yourself in nature. Using living plants, trees and flowers as your subject matter is a great way to connect with nature mindfully. Listen to the sounds around you; watch how the light plays and casts shadows; feel the earth beneath your feet. Be enchanted by the wonders of nature, and draw and paint to capture the essence of your environment.

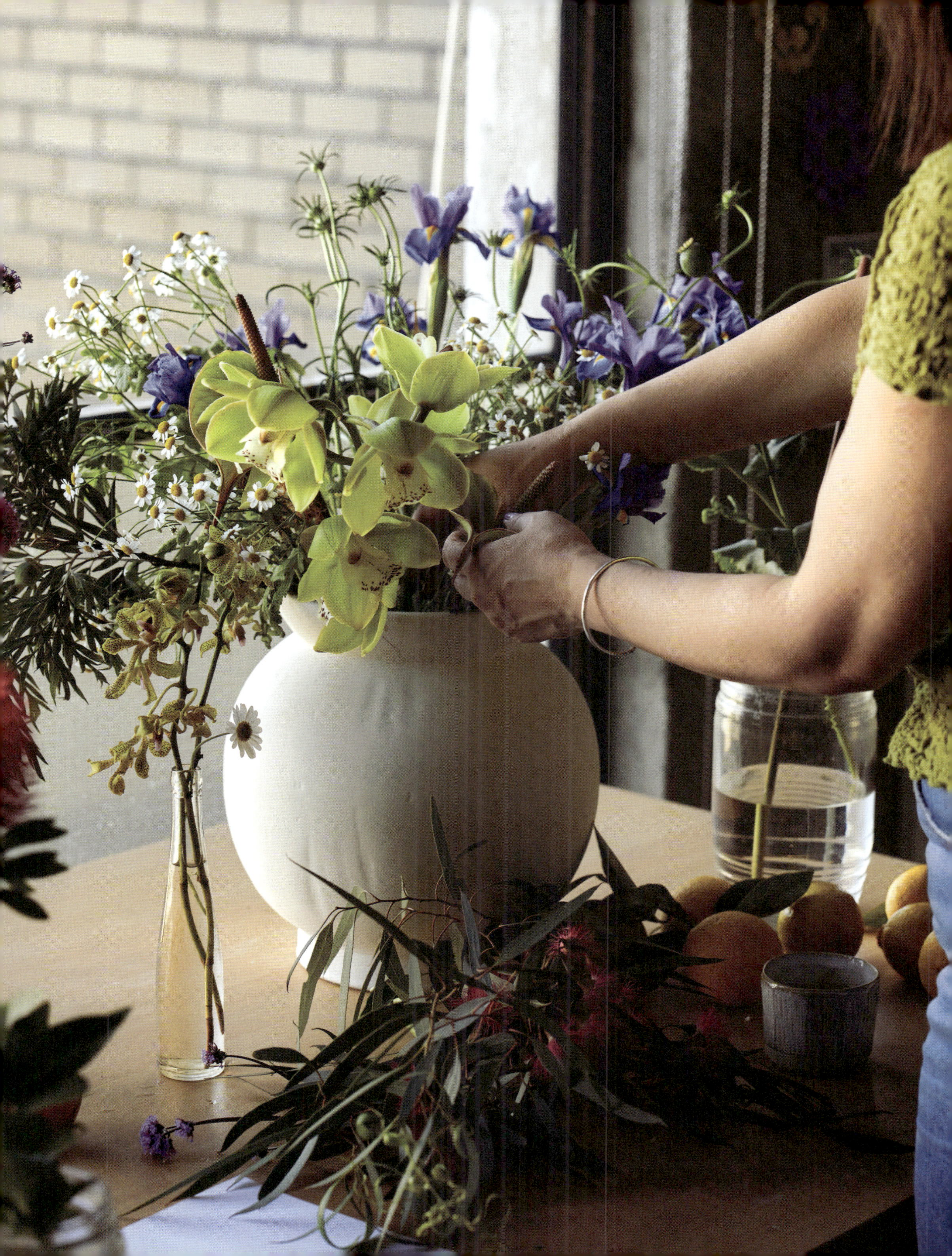

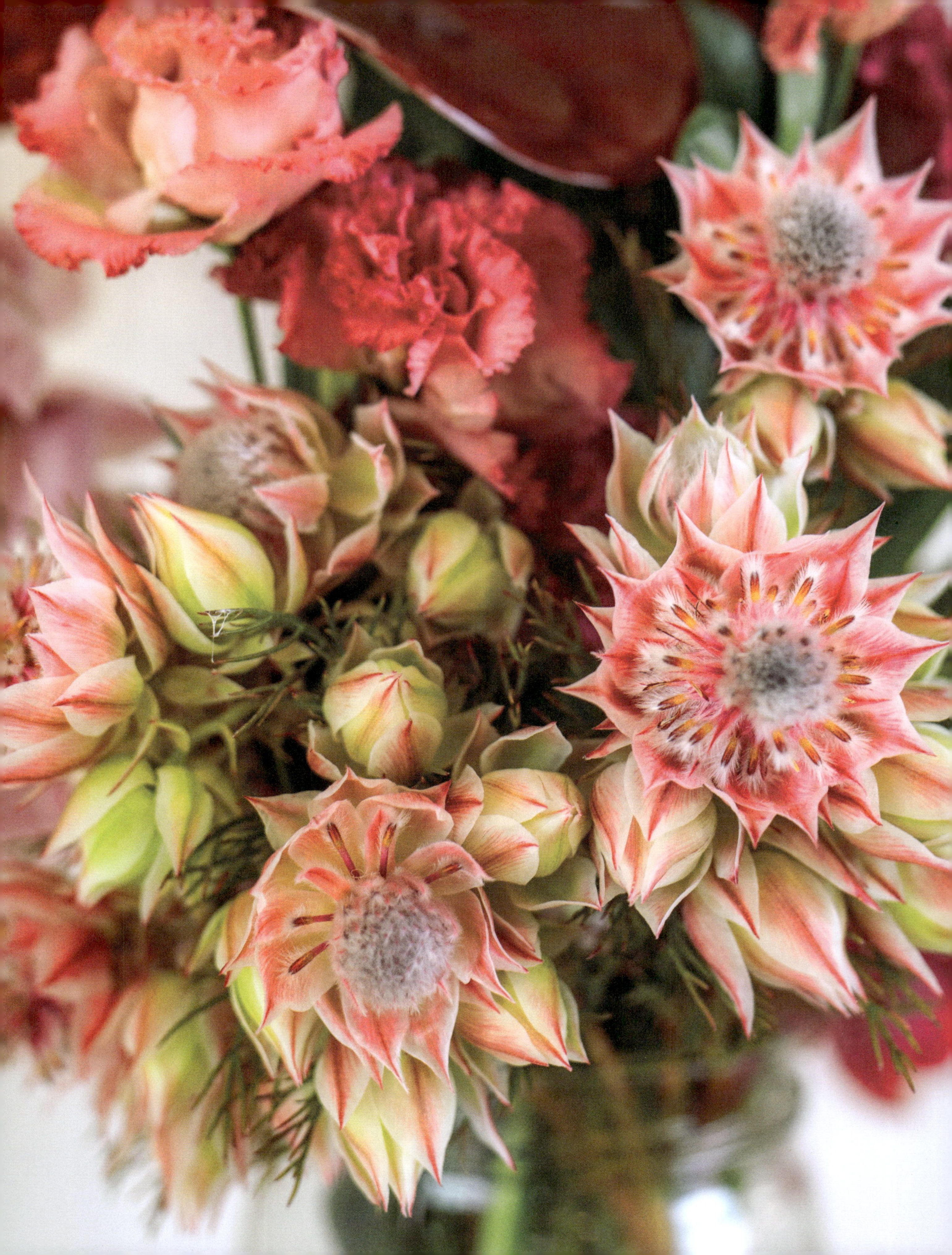

Learning to see

The most fundamental element of drawing is observation. It's not until we really look that we notice what we may never have seen before. Drawing transforms passive seeing into a more active focus and appreciation: the more you look, the more you really do see. What we actually see is different from our preconceived idea of how an object should appear. Our conditioned response to an object and our habits of seeing should be shaken up when we observe and then draw.

Before starting to draw, study your flower subject as if you have never seen a flower before. Be curious. Contemplate how each flower became – where it grew and its place in nature. The structure of a flower is the result of growing from a tiny seedling upwards and outwards. Flowers are always organically changing and transforming, like all natural processes. Get familiar with botanicals: if possible, pick up your flower and study its anatomy. If you have several varieties in front of you, you will notice they are all vastly different; focus on the intricacies that make each flower unique. Think of yourself as a botanical detective: your job is to investigate and describe what you observe. Ask yourself: What do I see? What shapes are the leaves making? Is the stem on an angle? Is there a pattern in the petals? What is the darkest area? How can I best portray the beauty of this flower? Ask yourself exactly what you are seeing – the shape, texture, surface, proportions, lines, angles and relationships between forms. Botanicals are a treasure trove of graphic shapes. Look intensely and purposefully, remembering that artistic skill is less important than awareness and observation.

Explore and clarify your observations by describing on paper what is in front of you. When drawing, focus on what your flower is doing: is it tightly closed, fully in bloom, limp or upright? Look at your subject holistically and constantly refer to it, to compare and relate smaller sections to the whole. Finding where elements connect and line up will result in a more accurate depiction. A great technique for looking is to squint your eyes to blur your vision: this helps to make the subject more manageable and breaks it down to its simplest form.

If I could give only one tip for your art-making journey it would be to look, then look again.

Enjoying play

Botanicals are an expressive and emotive subject, and the task of creating an image on a blank page can seem daunting. It's great to begin by loosening up and creating a sense of life and movement. So your first activity is fun and freeing: make a start by simply testing different mediums, brushes, and papers. Experiment. Become more comfortable with mark making. Be spontaneous, energetic, playful and gestural.

Play around with scribbling lines and painting shapes. Tune into what the materials can do. Use different amounts of pressure and weight when applying a medium and vary the speed at which you make your marks. Build up tone by layering your tool. Practise creating a gradient from light to dark with each medium. Experiment with pencil, charcoal and pastel through using the tips or sides to achieve diverse effects and textures.

Have fun with the process of following the lines you make and curating where you want to draw attention. Enjoy the simple pleasure of child-like drawing.

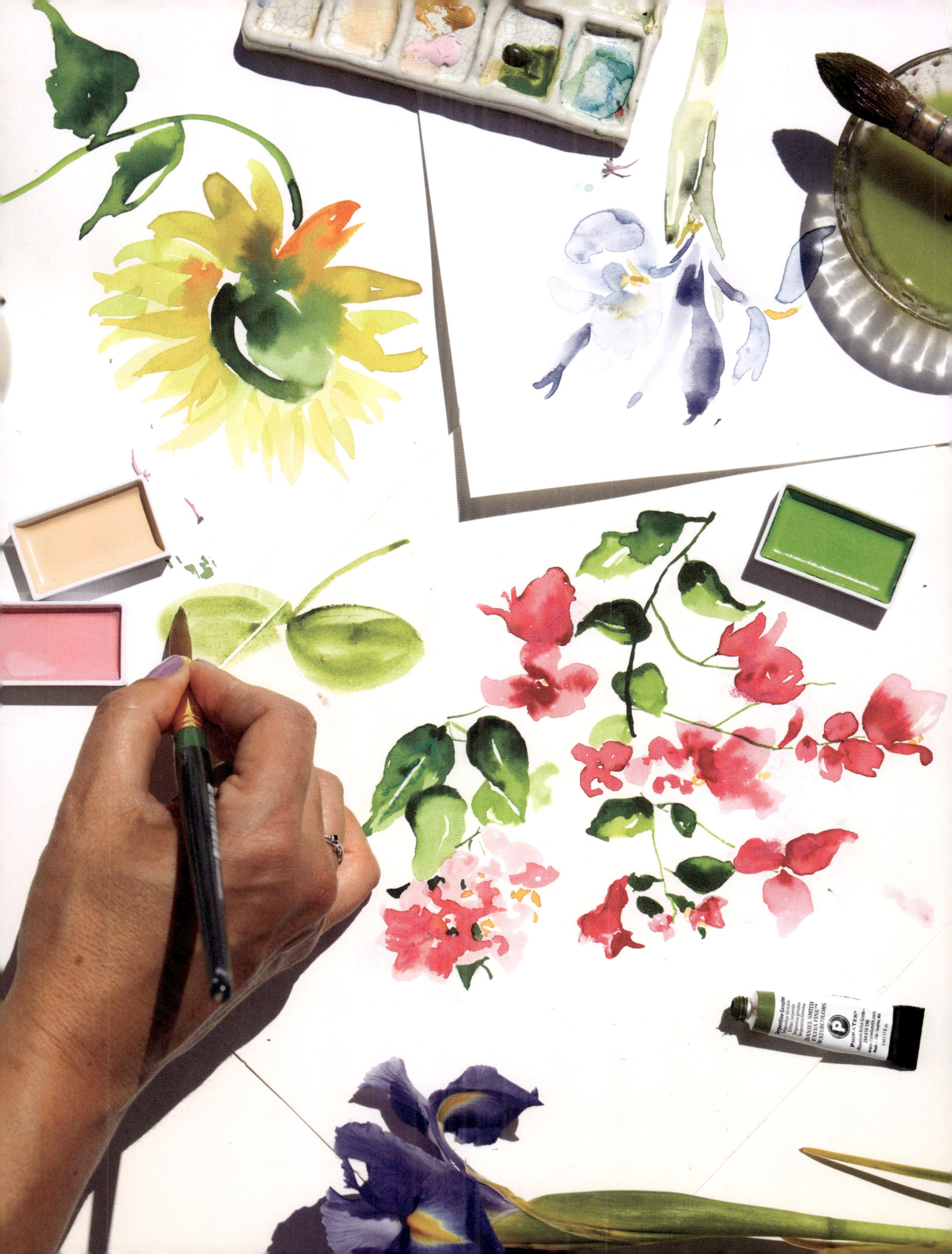

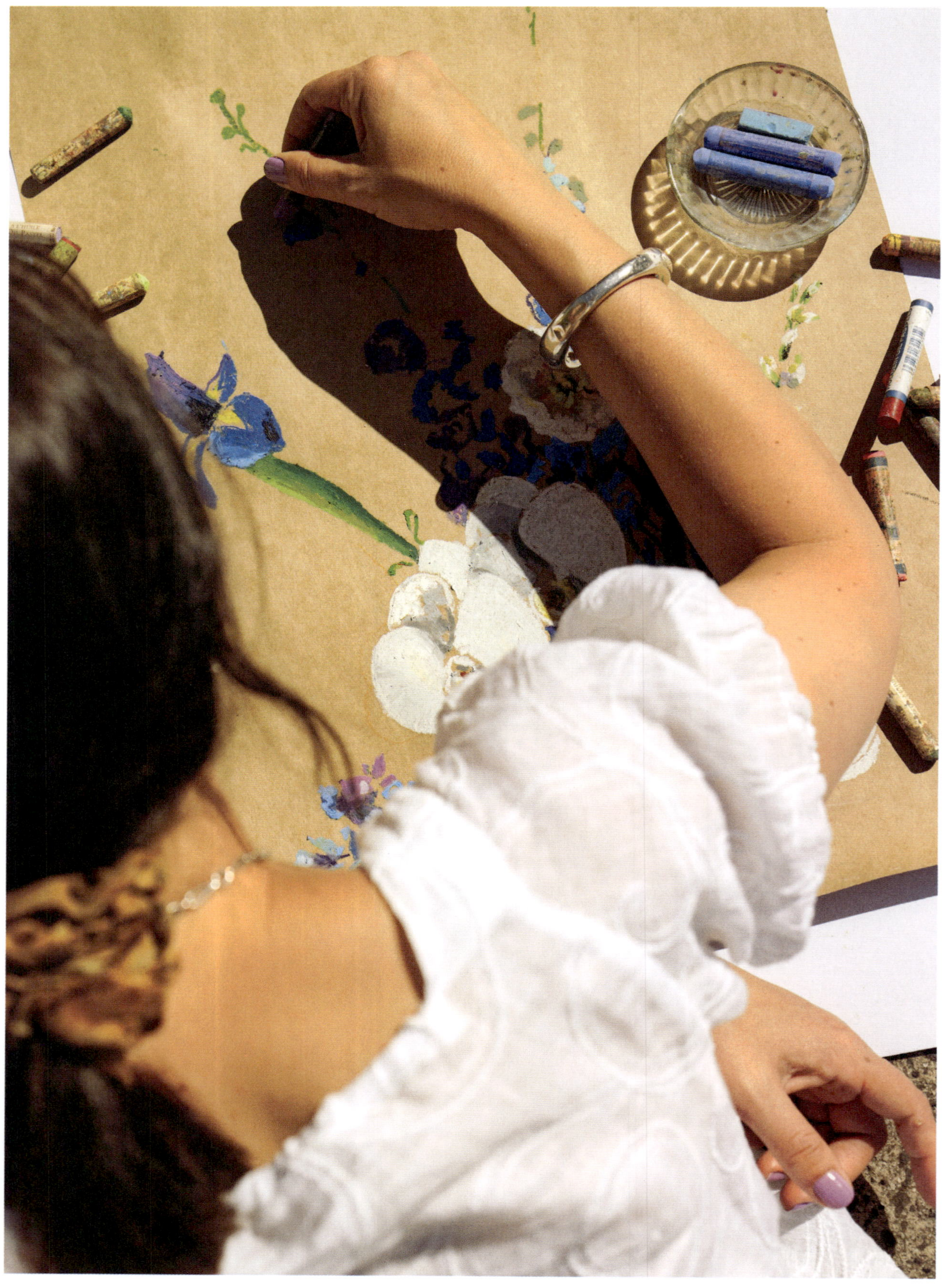

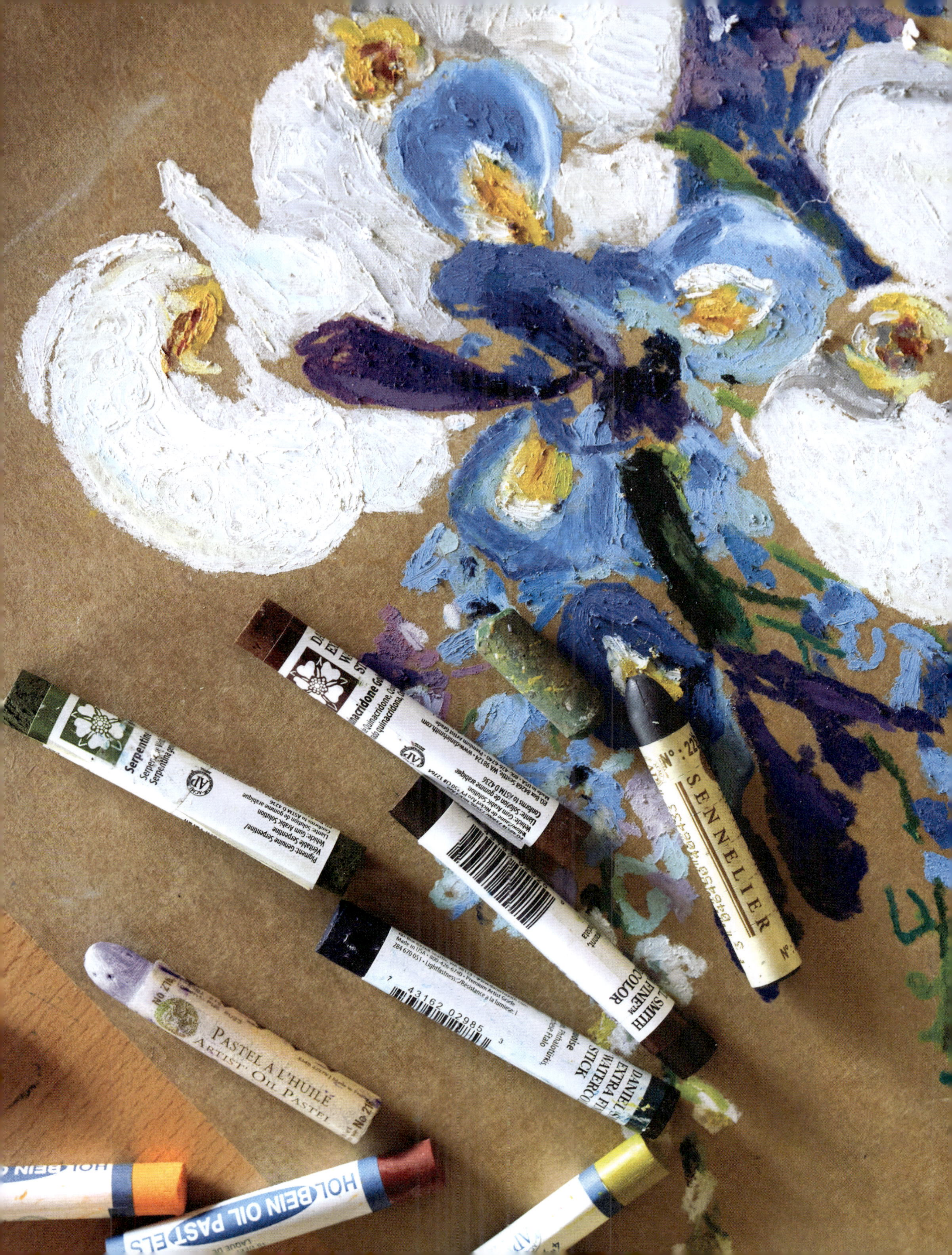
Serpentine
Serpentine
Pigment: Genuine Serpentine
Verdâtre Serpentine
PASTEL A L'HUILE
ARTIST' OIL PASTEL
SENNELIER
DANIEL SMITH FINE WATERCOLOR STICK
EXTRA FINE WATERCOLOR STICK
HOLBEIN OIL PASTELS
HOLBEIN

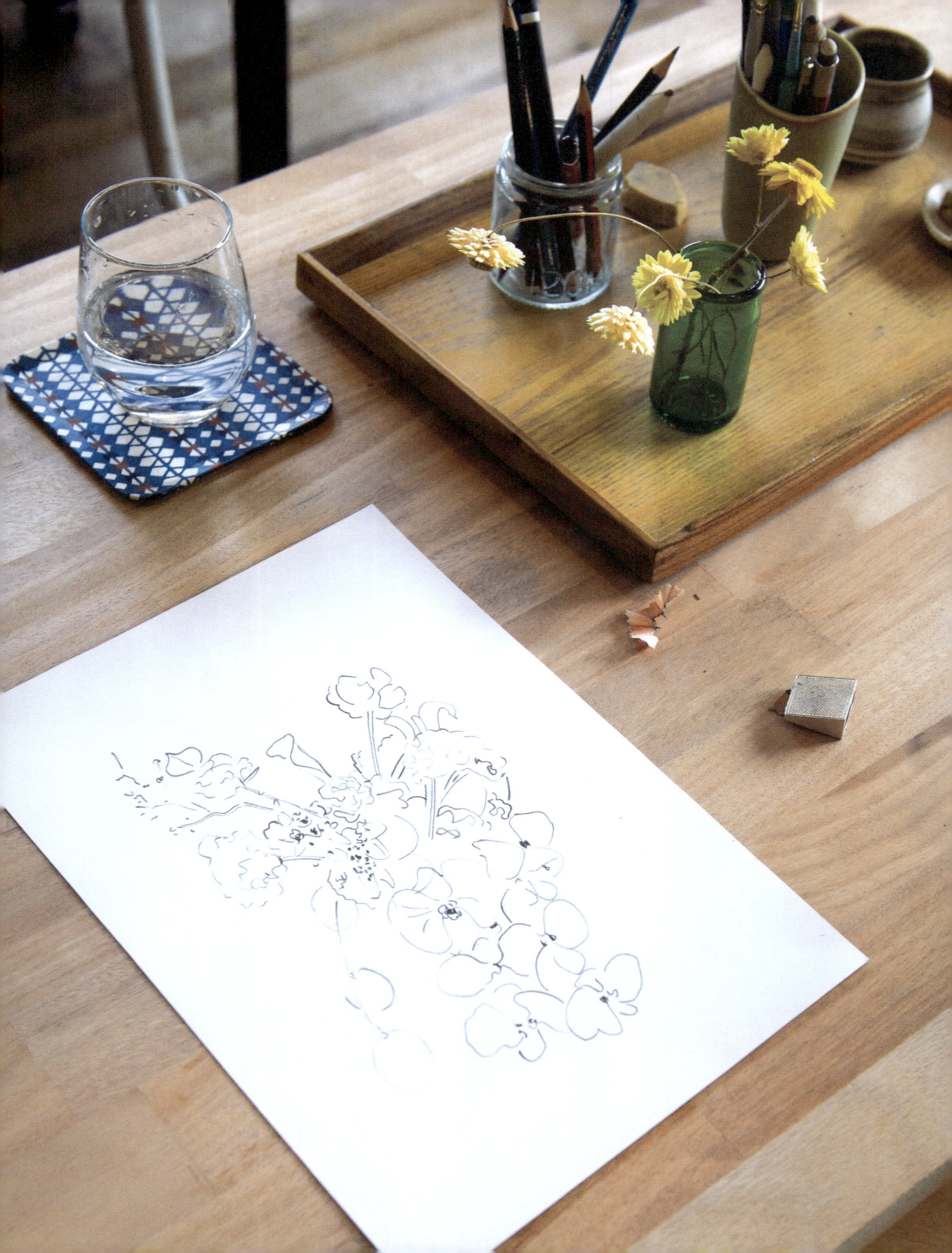

· EXERCISES ·

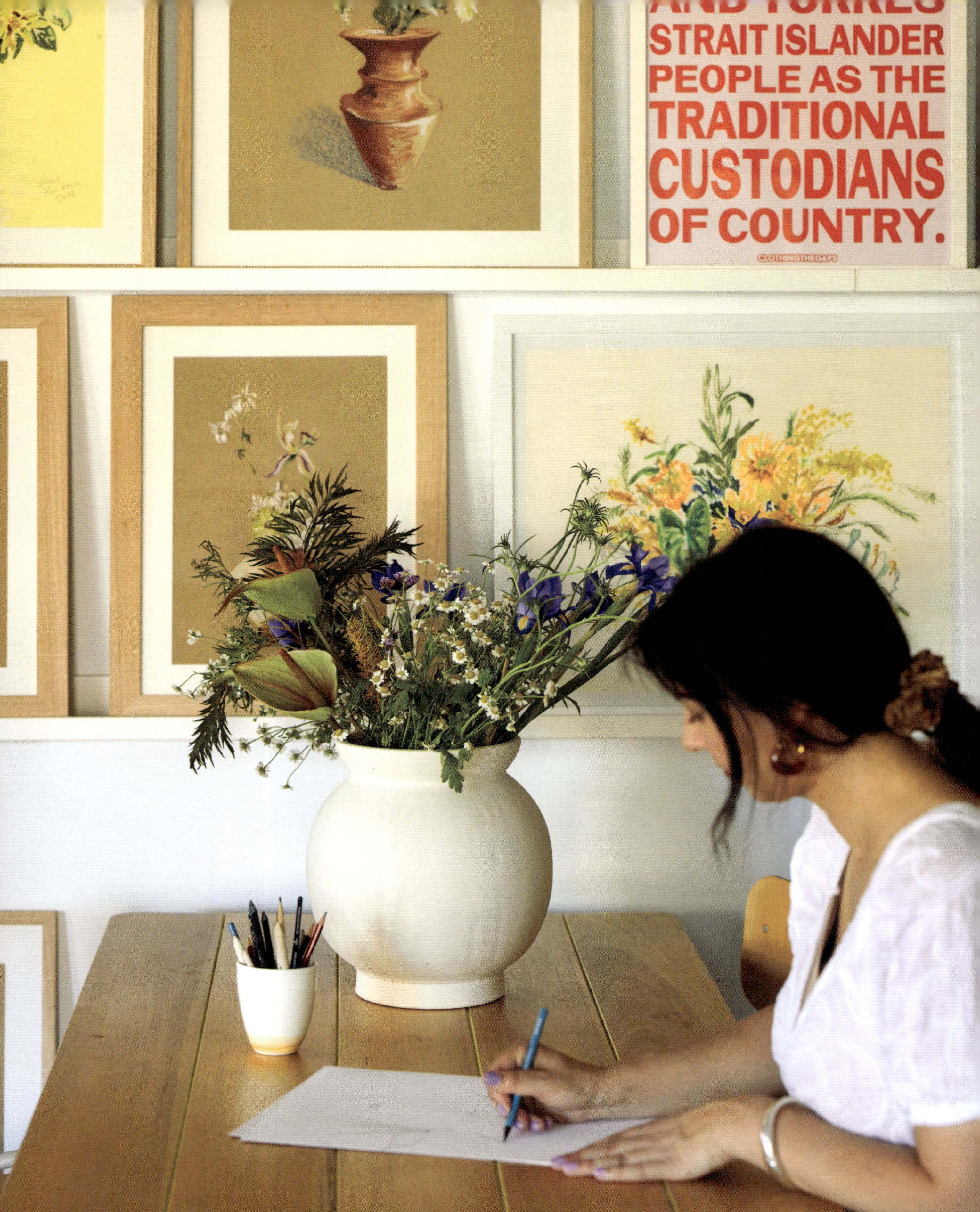
AND TORRES
STRAIT ISLANDER
PEOPLE AS THE
TRADITIONAL
CUSTODIANS
OF COUNTRY.
CLOTHING THE GAPS

**Exercises are a great way to start any art practice. They allow you
to loosen up while encouraging experimentation and growth and
promoting a natural, intuitive approach to drawing.**

The following exercises follow a series of progressive observation practices
and warm-up activities that serve as the building blocks for later projects.
They are designed to explore the art of looking, to cultivate observational
skills and to help you become confident in recording what you see. Have a
willingness to make mistakes and work with the idea of process over product
while enjoying and learning from the experience. Be unselfconscious in these
exercises and don't worry about the end result – let go of your critical mind!

I encourage you to mix and match the exercises with the photographs and
reference images throughout this book and to extend them by drawing from
your own botanical arrangement. Use a 6B–9B graphite pencil and any type
of A4 or A3 paper for these exercises.

Quick sketch

In 1 minute, sketch the sunflower arrangement in a way that captures its gesture, or essence.

Quick sketches are a great warm-up exercise to loosen up and focus on ways of looking and analysing the subject matter. In a still-life flower arrangement, there is a gesture, or essence – for example, flowers standing tall to catch the sun, drooping under their own weight or withering as they die. To convey this in a quick sketch, it's necessary to simplify the arrangement by rapidly choosing what you feel is important (such as the petal shapes, pistil and leaves) and being spontaneous with what you include and leave out. In quick sketches, you don't have to depict every tiny detail but rather the main shapes and proportions. You will find that working quickly helps you to lose inhibitions, as there is no time to overthink or be judgemental about what you are drawing.

1

Look at the subject for 10–20 seconds and discern the gesture, or essence, that you want to convey in the sketch. Observe the shapes and connecting elements within the arrangement.

2

Set a timer for 1 minute and, working quickly, sketch the arrangement, breaking it down to its simplest form. This could include the curved shape of the vase, straight lines for the stems and a roughly sketched circle flowerhead with wiggly line work to represent the petals.

3

Assess the sketch: identify what works and what doesn't.

•

MATERIALS

Graphite pencil, 6B–9B
Paper, A4 or A3

TIP

Repeat the exercise but allow yourself more time – 2 minutes for one sketch, and 5 minutes for another. With the extra time, you may want to add tone to your artwork by using your pencil to shade or darken areas. Notice the differences in your approach and the outcome that result from the additional time.

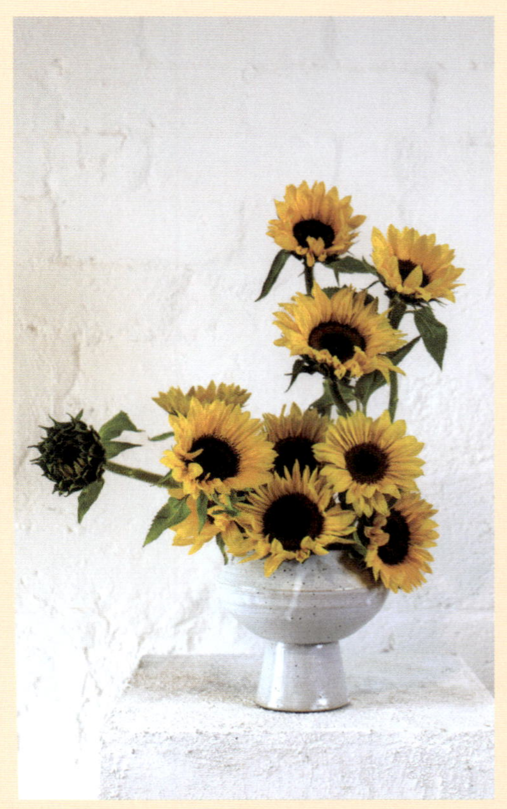

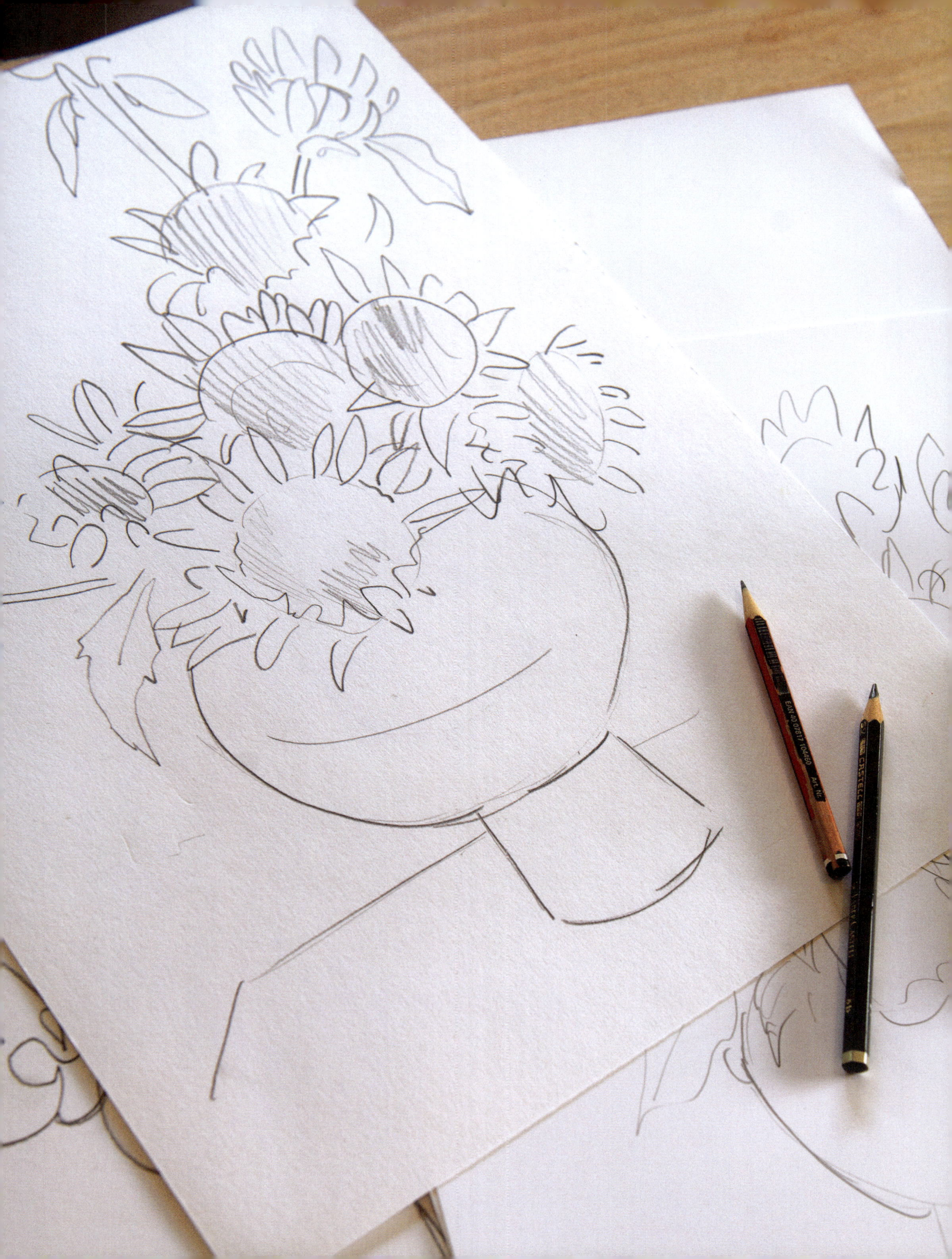

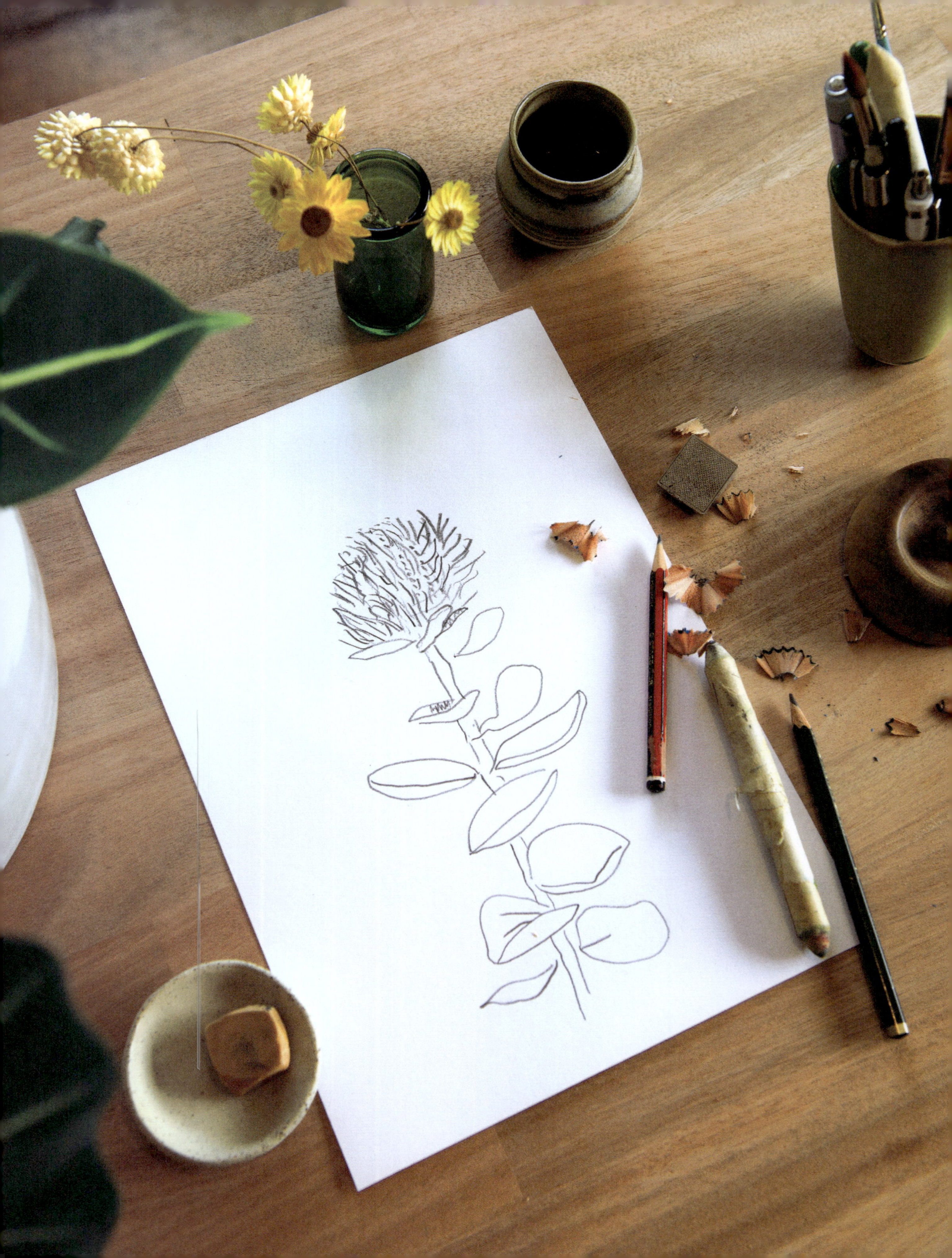

Your other hand

Use your non-dominant writing hand to draw the scarlet banksia.

This exercise will force you to draw slowly and take your time in observation. Non-dominant-hand drawing works to stimulate curiosity about your subject and focus on its forms, shapes and structure. It feels odd and will require concentration and perseverance, but sitting with the discomfort switches you out of autopilot so you can better observe the flower.

1

Take a moment to observe the scarlet banksia and break the scene down to a collection of connecting shapes.

2

Using your non-dominant hand, sketch the shapes of the flowerhead and stem, followed by the leaves.

3

Check your sketch's overall proportions; don't worry about wobbly lines.

4

As you become more comfortable with drawing with your non-dominant hand, mark in some finer details.

●

MATERIALS

Graphite pencil, 6B–9B
Paper, A4 or A3

TIP

Don't overthink what you are doing while you are working on this piece, and try to relax into the mindset of process over product. The final result of your non-dominant hand exercise isn't important.

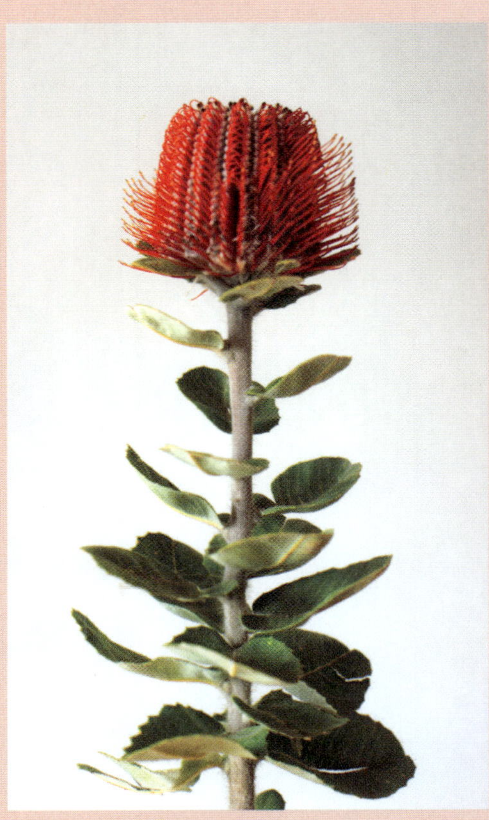

Blind contour

Draw the moth orchid reference without looking at your paper or removing your pencil from the page.

Blind contour drawing is great practice for hand-to-eye coordination and for using your senses of sight and touch. Draw as if your pencil is touching the edges of the form and describing the contour of the subject. Take your time with this exercise and work slowly and sensitively, conveying the flow of the flowers. You will be interpreting what you perceive when you look at the orchid. Embrace the inaccuracies and focus on the experience of creating your contoured, fluid line. You will see how line alone can create works that are uncannily descriptive.

1

Start by focusing your gaze on the moth orchid reference and pick a point to begin the drawing.

2

As you draw, keep your eye fixed on the reference and draw its contours in one fluid movement without taking your pencil off the page. Your pencil should be coordinated and move in sync with your eye: as your eye moves, your hand should follow.

3

Once you've completed your line, take a look at the elements of the flower you've managed to capture.

●

MATERIALS

Graphite pencil, 6B–9B
Paper, A4 or A3

INSPIRATION

Ellsworth Kelly was a master of organic contour botanical studies and is a great reference for this type of work. Kelly didn't use any shading or fine detail for these studies, using just line to represent the shapes and essence of the botanicals. He used his plant observations as the basis for some of the first abstract paintings.

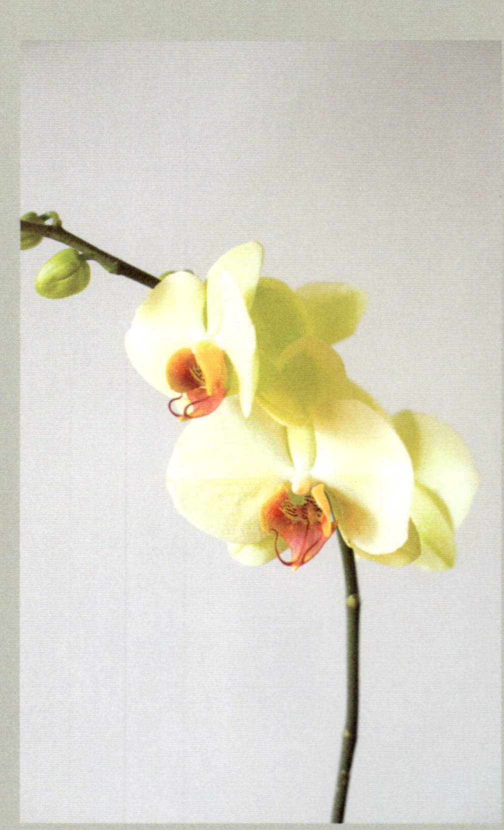

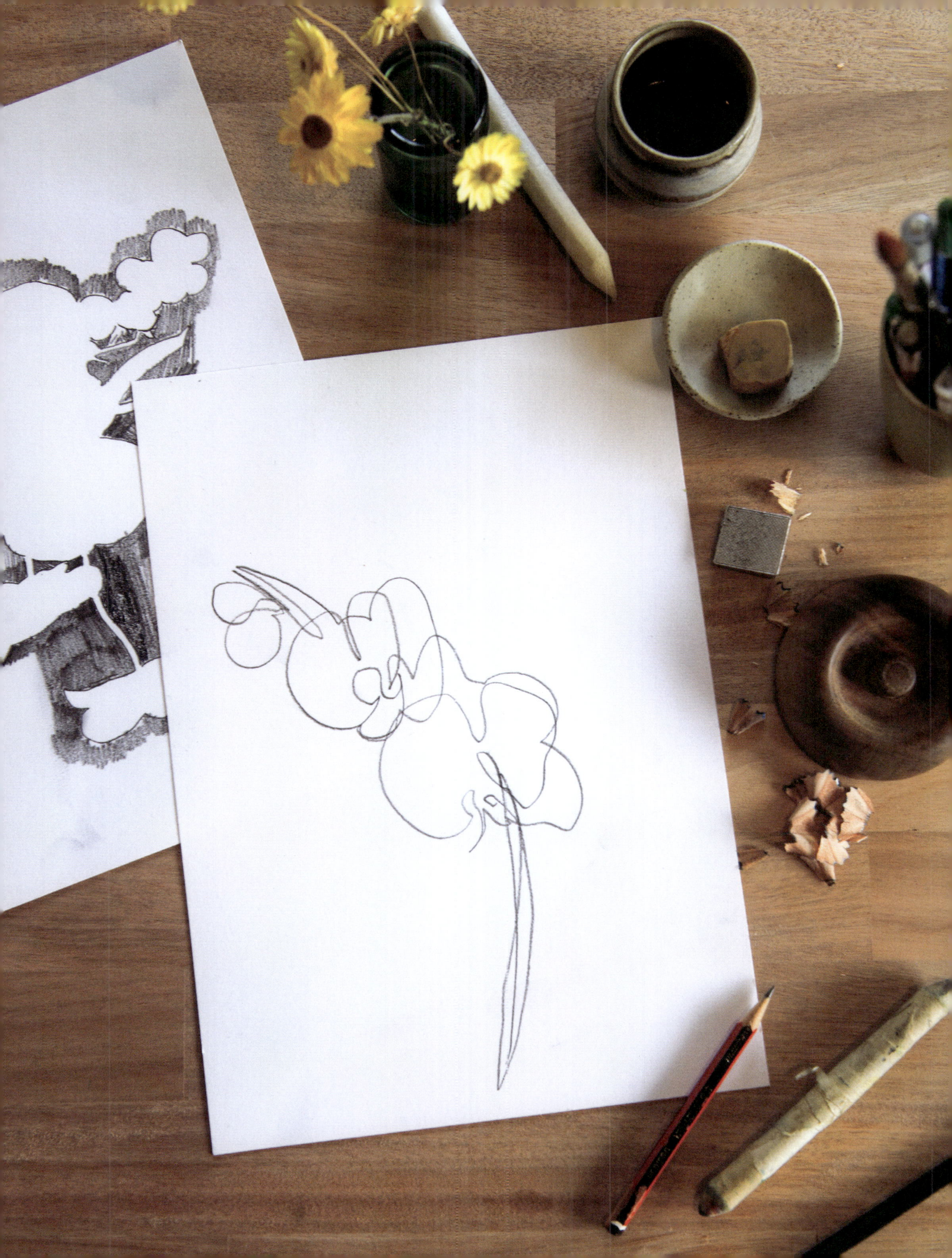

Drawing from memory

Observe the orchid reference for several minutes and then draw it from memory.

This is a timed observation and memory exercise. It will help you to translate what you see into a drawn image through actively looking at the subject and absorbing its visual information. Look at the reference to see the image as a whole as well as its individual parts.

1

Start by deeply observing the basic elements of the orchids: their shapes, textures, patterns, highlights and shadows.

2

Note the flowers' intricacies, including imperfections and colour variations: elements which will bring character, richness and interest to your drawing.

3

Look at the gesture of the orchids, how they have grown, their movement and life.

4

When you have spent several minutes observing, close this book or turn away and draw the orchids from what you remember.

●

MATERIALS

Graphite pencil, 6B–9B
Paper, A4 or A3

___

TIP

Use your senses when observing, imagining the flowers' feel, smell and weight. Look at the reference holistically, as well as the form and unity of the flowers' anatomy.

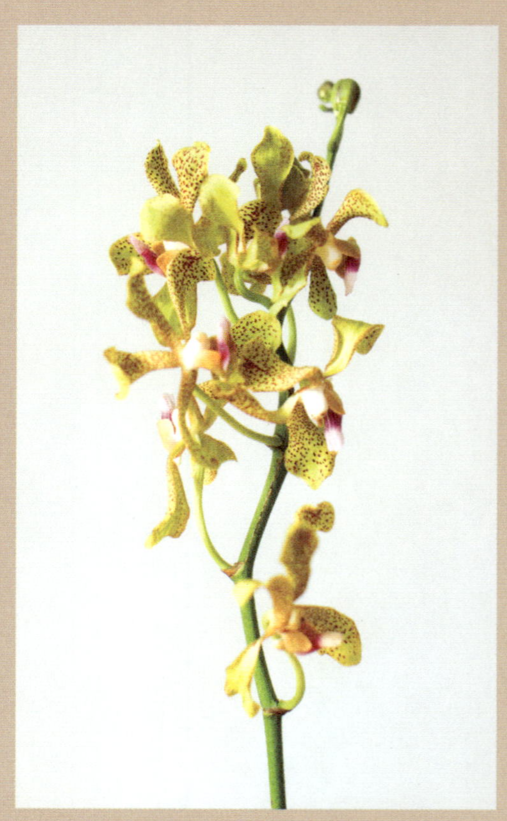

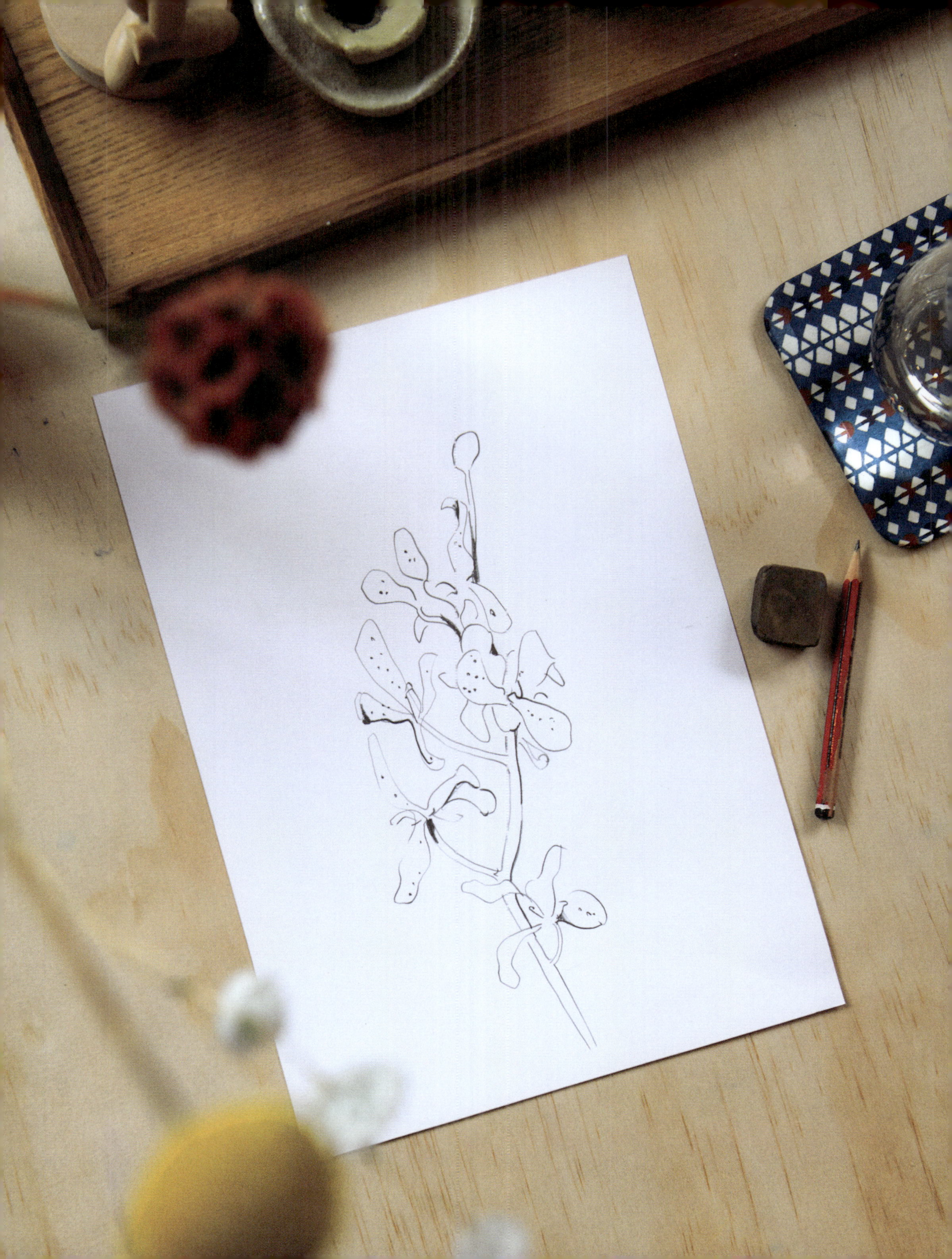

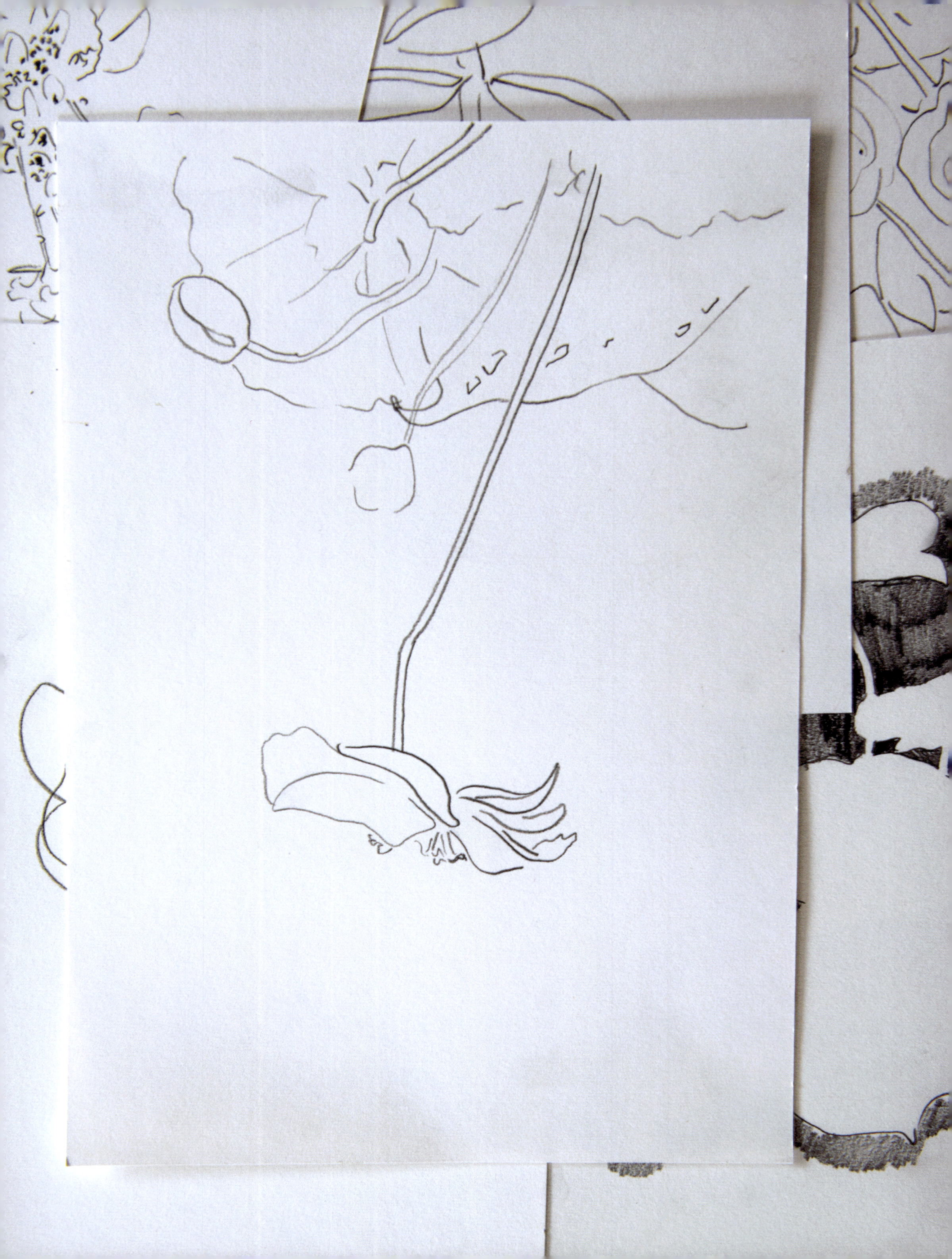

Upside-down sketch

Turn this book upside down and draw the reference as you see it, in its upside-down state.

This is a great exercise to refine observational skills, as the subject loses its initial familiarity, forcing you to draw what you see rather than your perceived idea of what a flower looks like. Strangely, making the familiar unfamiliar when drawing makes it easier to comprehend a reference image.

MATERIALS

Graphite pencil, 6B–9B
Paper, A4 or A3

1

Look at the image as a collection of lines, shapes and angles instead of a flower.

2

Draw the components that you see, rather than focusing on drawing a flower.

3

Once you have finished, flip your drawing and this book the correct way up and note how the two images compare. Don't be discouraged if your drawing isn't perfect! Working in this way will help you to observe with fresh eyes.

●

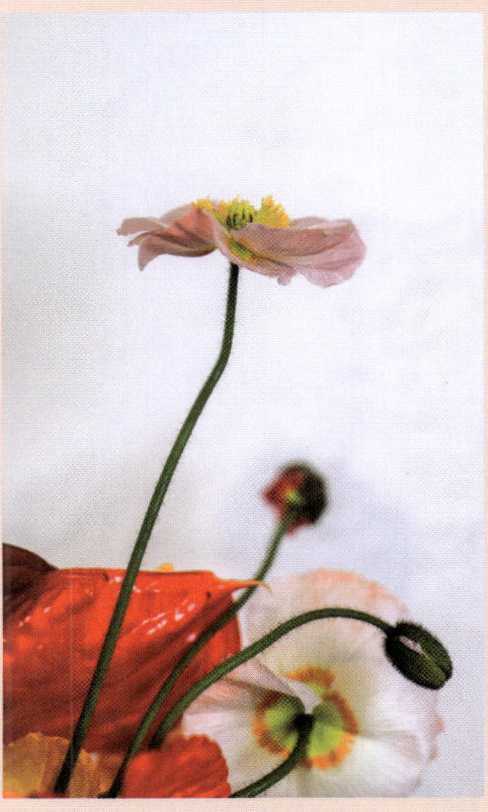

Cropped view

Choose a section of the arrangement (next page) to focus on and draw it to fill the page.

This is a great exercise to focus your attention and will help you to uncover details you otherwise may not have noticed. Don't worry about the result; instead, enjoy the practice of looking, drawing and filling the page. On the right is an example of what the composition may look like, and on the next spread is the reference image and another alternative crop.

1

Cut a rectangular hole in a piece of card and place it over the reference image so that only a section of the image is visible. Alternatively, you can cut two pieces of card into L-shapes and make a rectangle with them to isolate a section of the image that will define your composition. Choose this section with intention and clarity to create a dynamic composition with visual impact.

2

Sketch the selected area, enlarging it to fill your page. Take your lines to the edges of your paper, as though they extend past the boundaries of the page.

3

Sometimes less is more, so leave empty space within the artwork to rest the eye and provide breathing room.

4

Pay attention to fine details, textures and nuances you may not have noticed if you had been drawing the whole arrangement. Imagine you have a magnifying glass on the area you are drawing.

MATERIALS

Graphite pencil, 6B–9B

Paper, A4 or A3

TIP

Practice alternative compositions using the same arrangement as a reference – there are so many ways to look at one image.

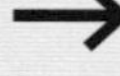

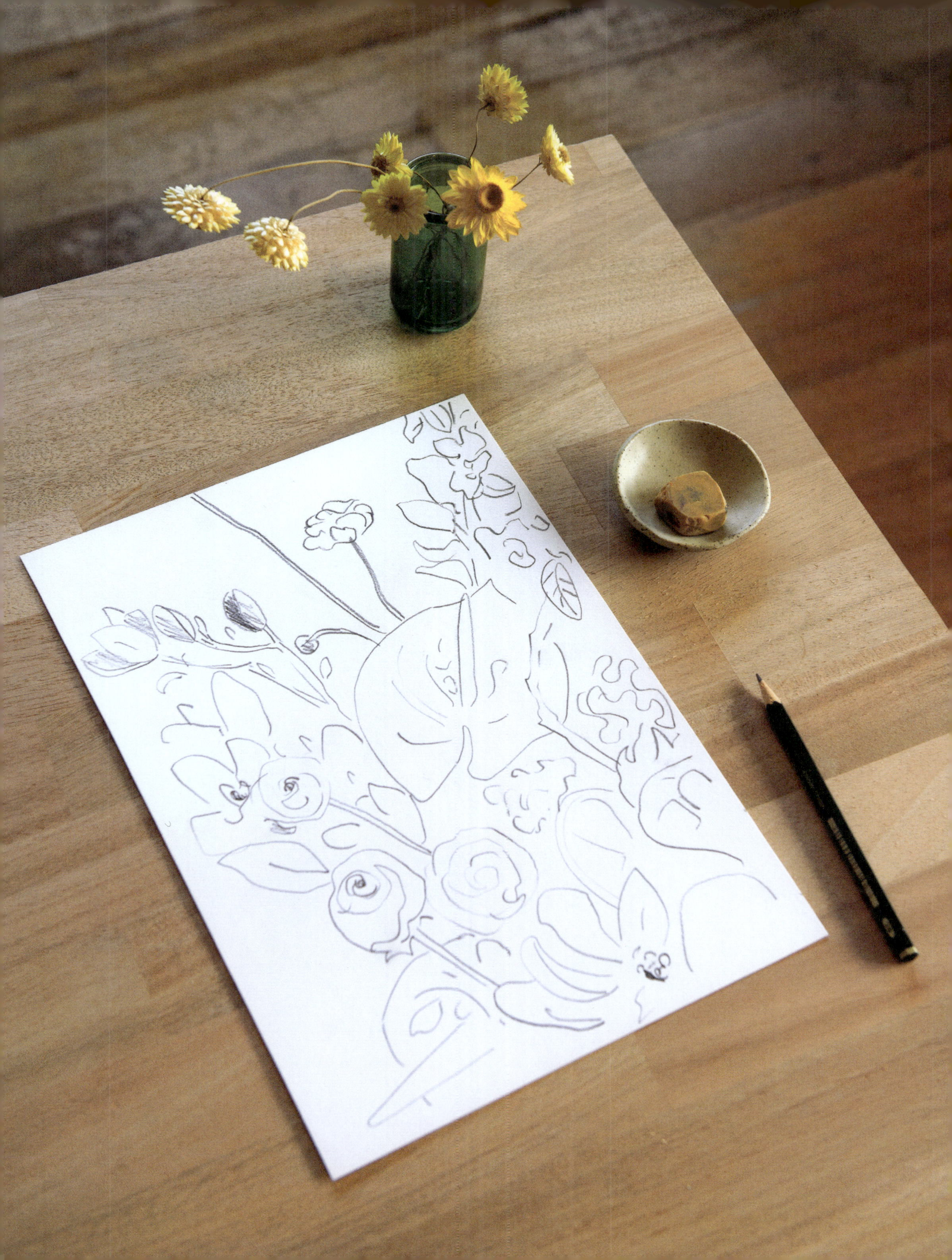

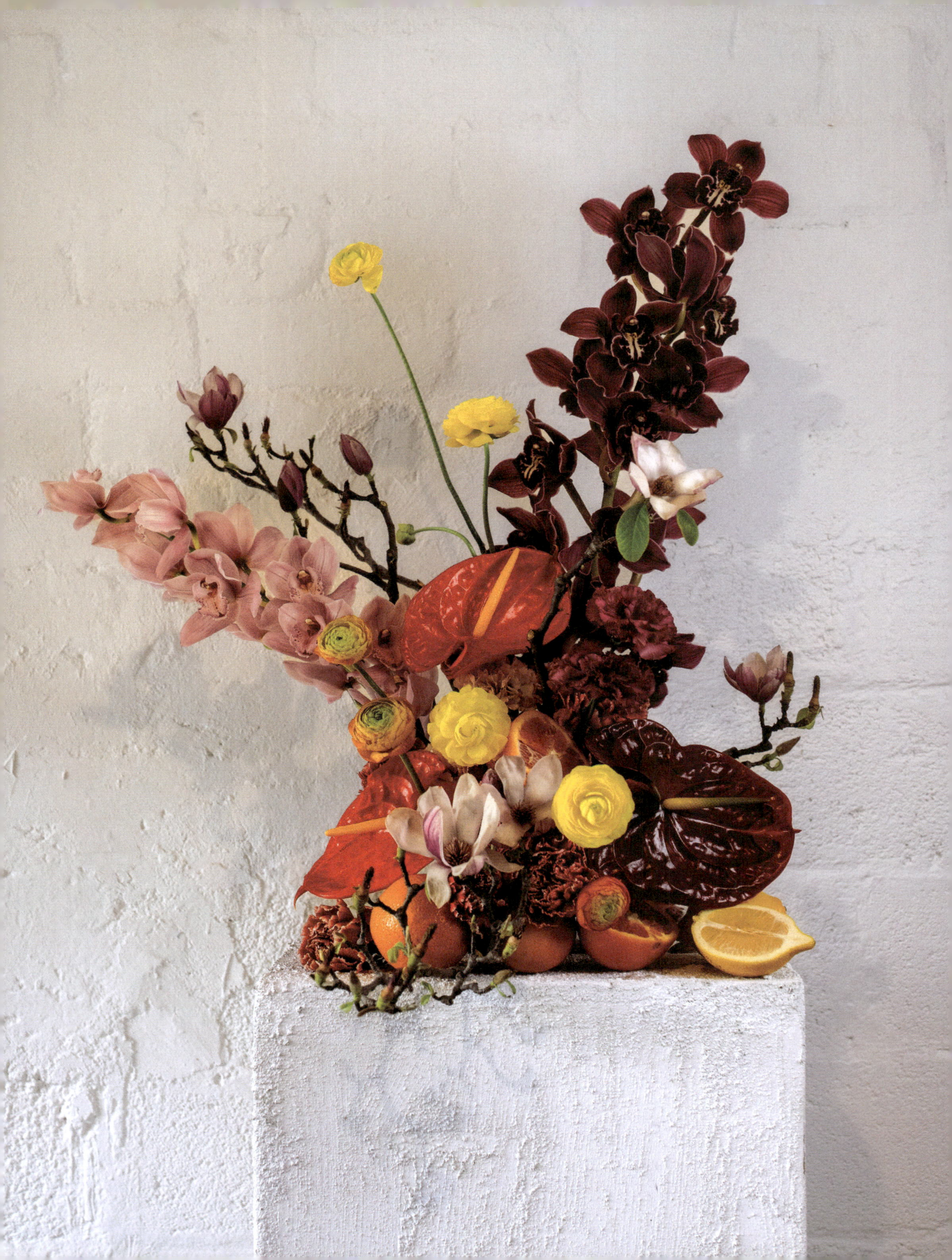

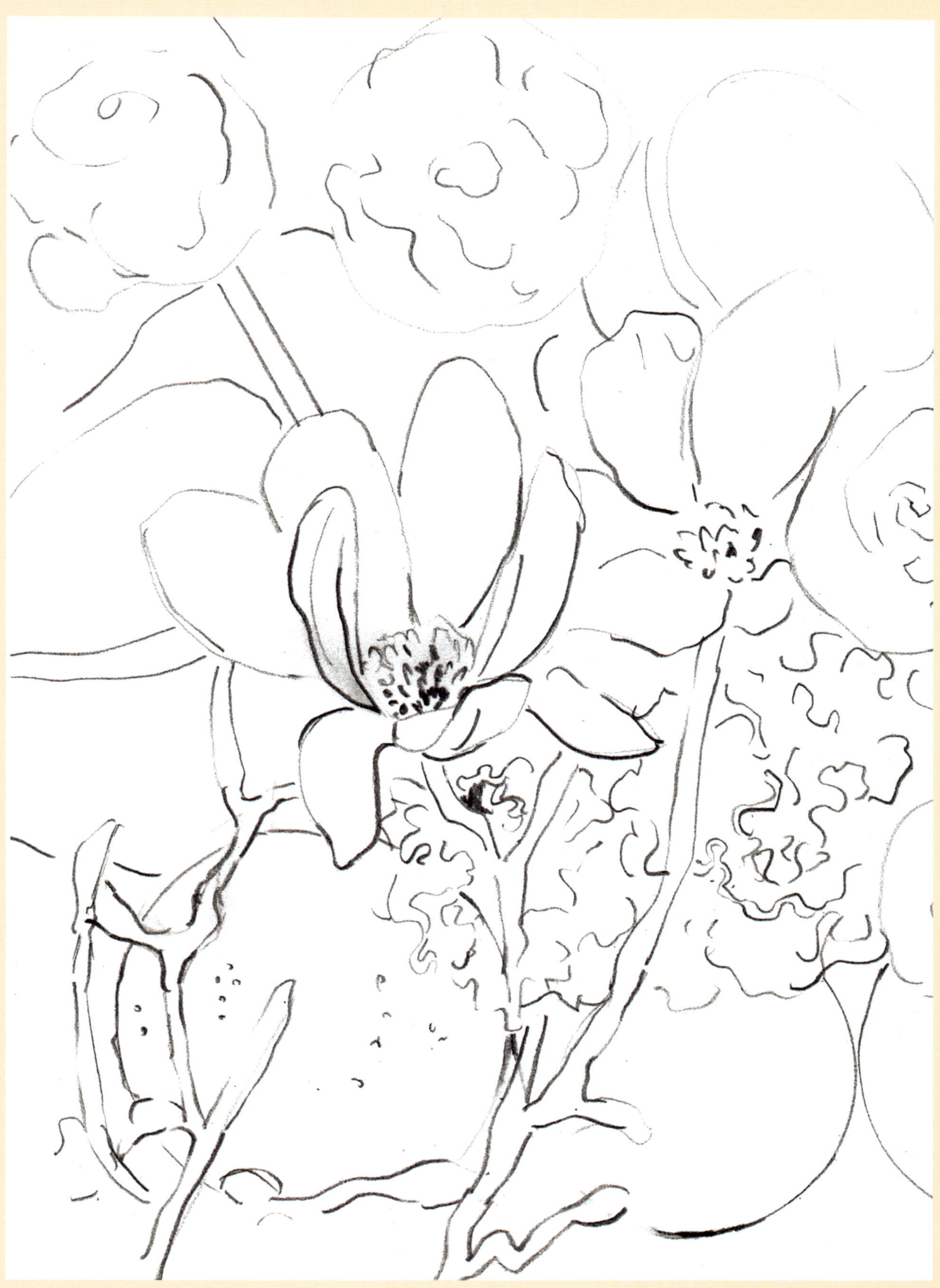

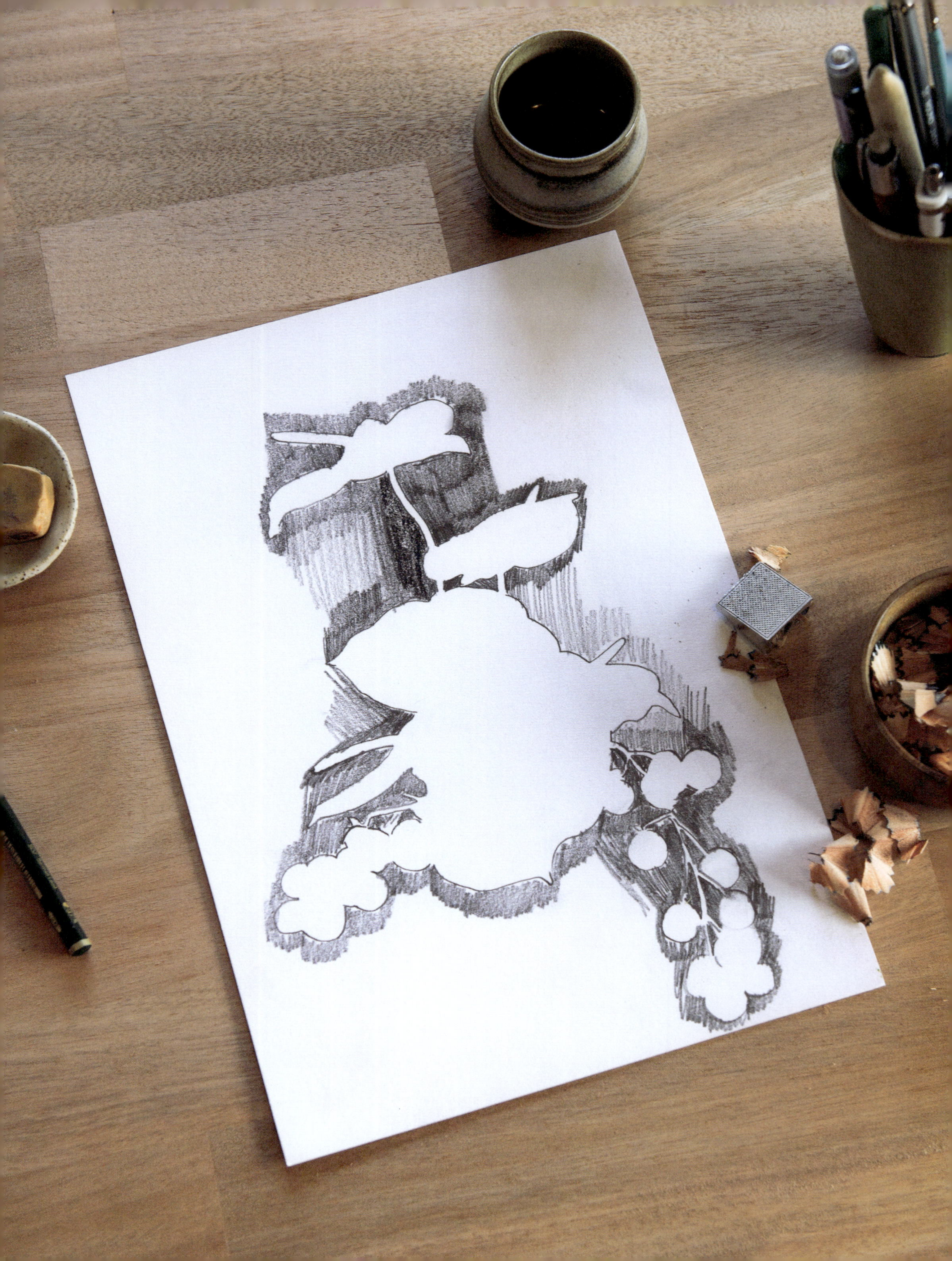

Negative space

**Sketch the negative space in the reference
image, leaving the botanicals blank.**

Negative space, also known as 'air space', is the
empty areas surrounding and between the main
subject matter within a composition. Analysing
the negative space around your subject can help
you to observe the spatial relations between
objects and the space they occupy. Breaking
the scene down to a series of shapes both
positive and negative makes it easier to view
the big picture and determine proportions and
positioning more accurately. Identifying the outer
edges, or outline, of an object or group of objects,
by noticing where the positive and negative
spaces meet, can simplify a complex scene.
It is great practice for initial sketching stages
when you may be mapping out the whole
shapes in a botanical arrangement.

1

Observe the reference image, focusing on
the negative space surrounding the anthuriums
and cherry tomatoes.

2

Using your pencil, sketch just the lines within the
image that demarcate the edges of the subjects.

3

Use your pencil to shade the negative space
surrounding and between the anthuriums and
cherry tomatoes, leaving them blank.

•

MATERIALS

Graphite pencil, 6B–9B
Paper, A4 or A3

TIP

*Think of this exercise as seeing the hole
in the doughnut. Practise by looking at
objects around you, observe their edges
and focus your gaze on the negative space
that surrounds them. This will aid you in
more accurately depicting an object's
shape when drawing it.*

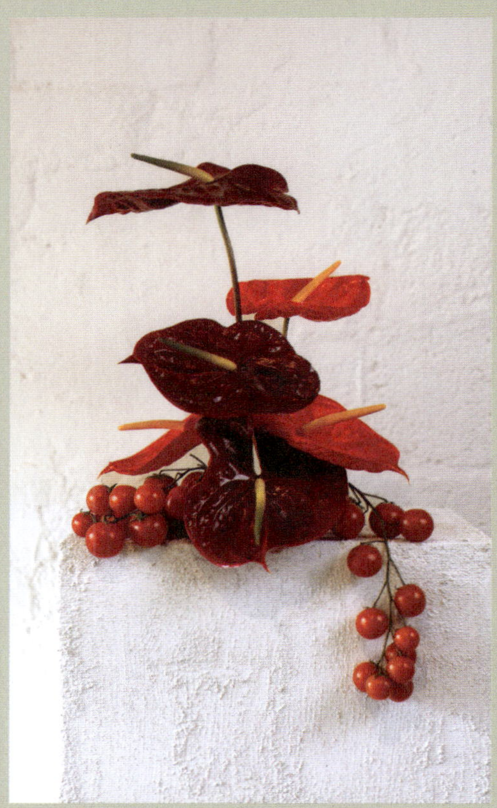

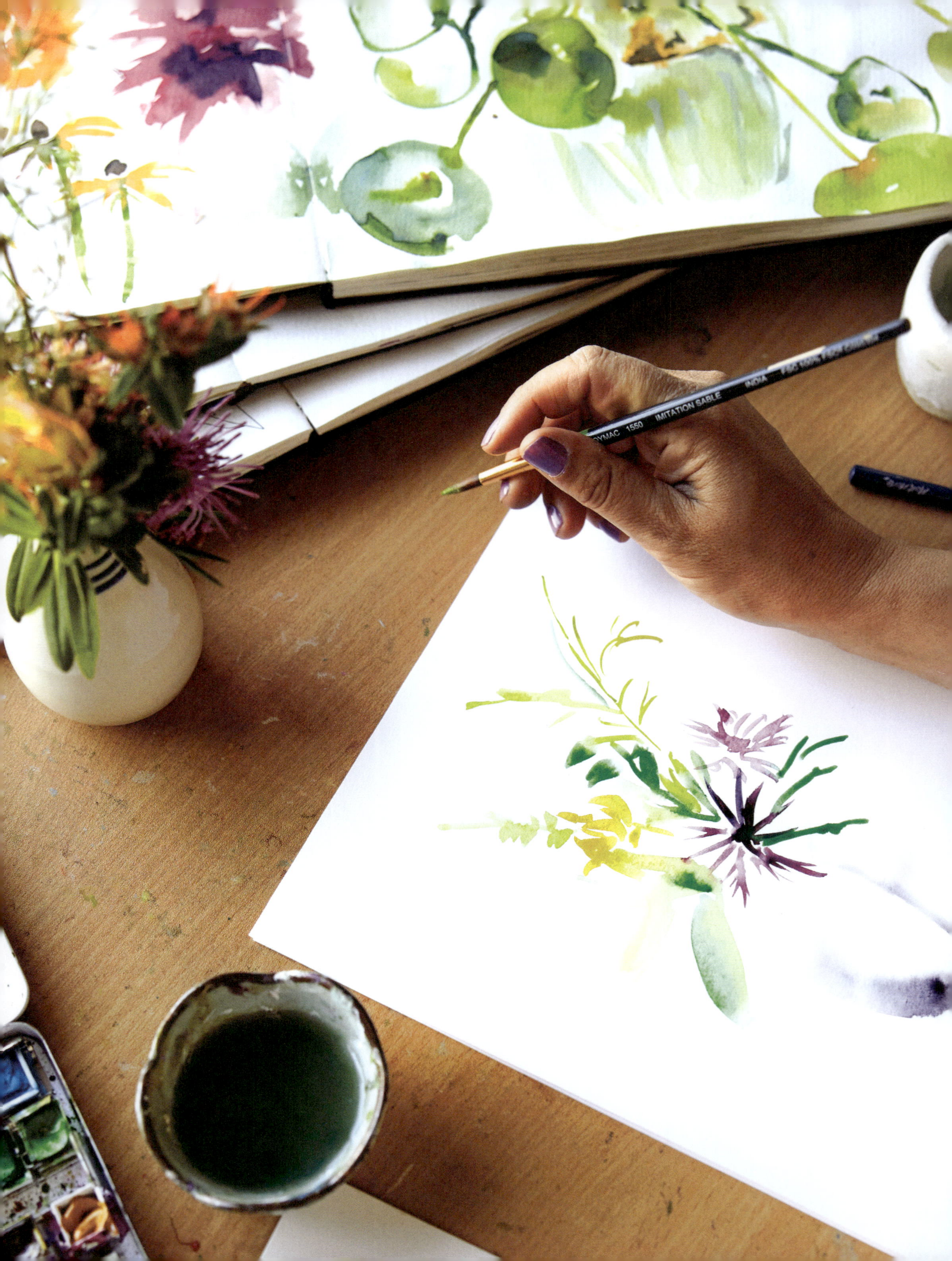

Watercolour and ink techniques

Watercolour and ink are fantastic mediums that can be used in a multitude of ways. In these exercises, you will be experimenting with methods of wet-on-wet, wet-on-dry, gradients and glazing. These techniques will give you a basic understanding of how the wet mediums of watercolour and ink work. The different approaches result in a variation of effects, and you may find there is one style that feels more comfortable and appealing for you. For more information about watercolour see page 111.

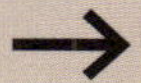

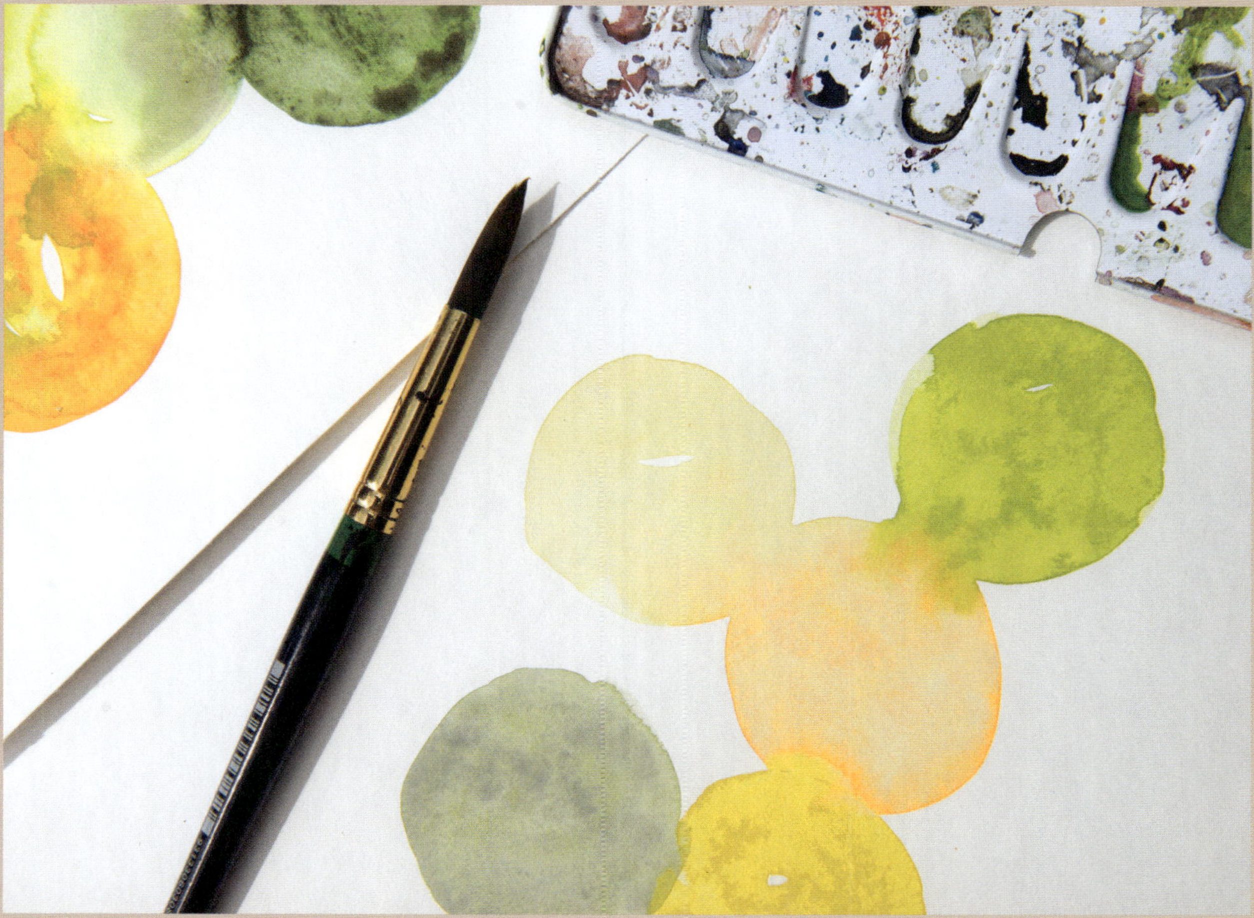

Wet-on-wet

Wet-on-wet is the process of applying wet paint on wet paper or on wet paint that has already been applied to the paper. It is great for creating effects like blends, bleeds, gradient washes and blooms.

1

Wet your paper with the mop brush.

2

While the paper is wet, add watercolour and watch it spread.

3

Continue to experiment, adding more watercolour to painted areas while they are still wet.

●

MATERIALS

Watercolour paper, A4 or A3
Watercolours and/or ink
Mop brush, large
Round brushes, sizes 8 and 12

TIP

Work quickly and gesturally before your paint or paper has the chance to dry.

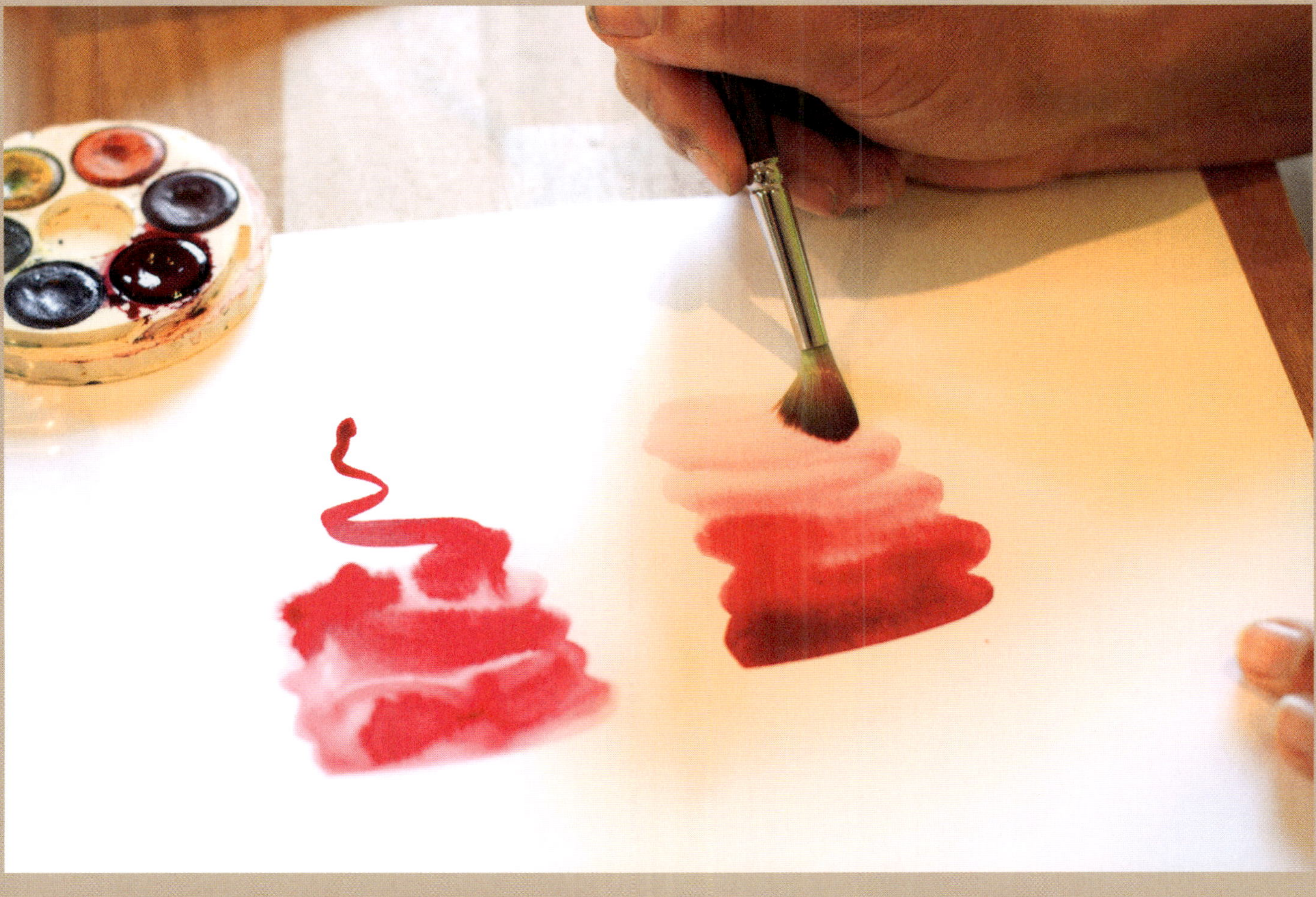

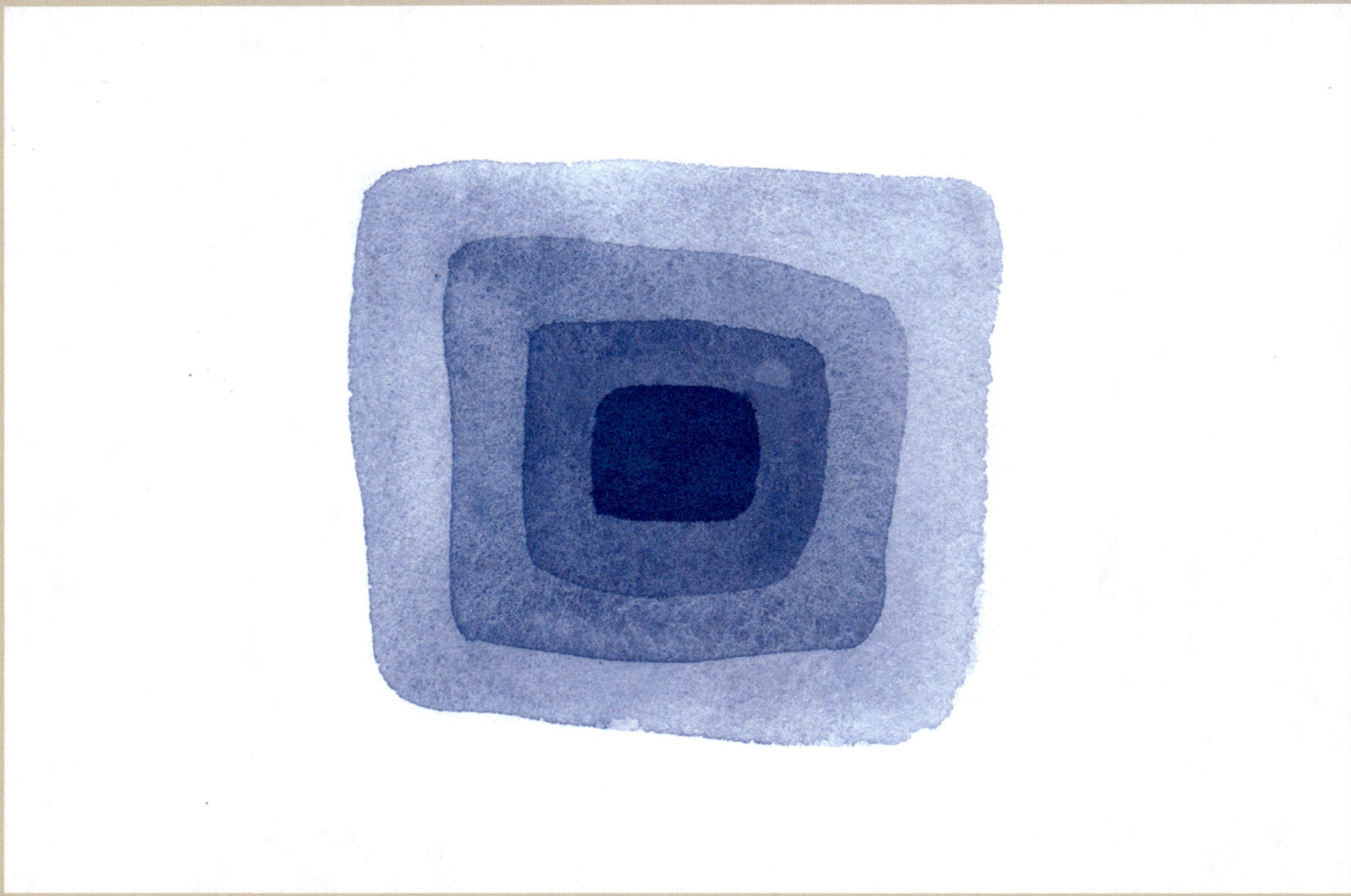

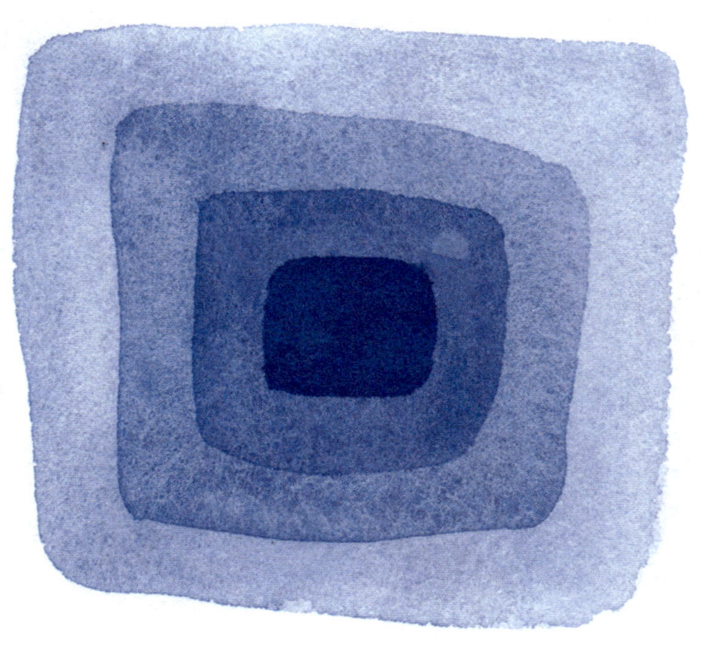

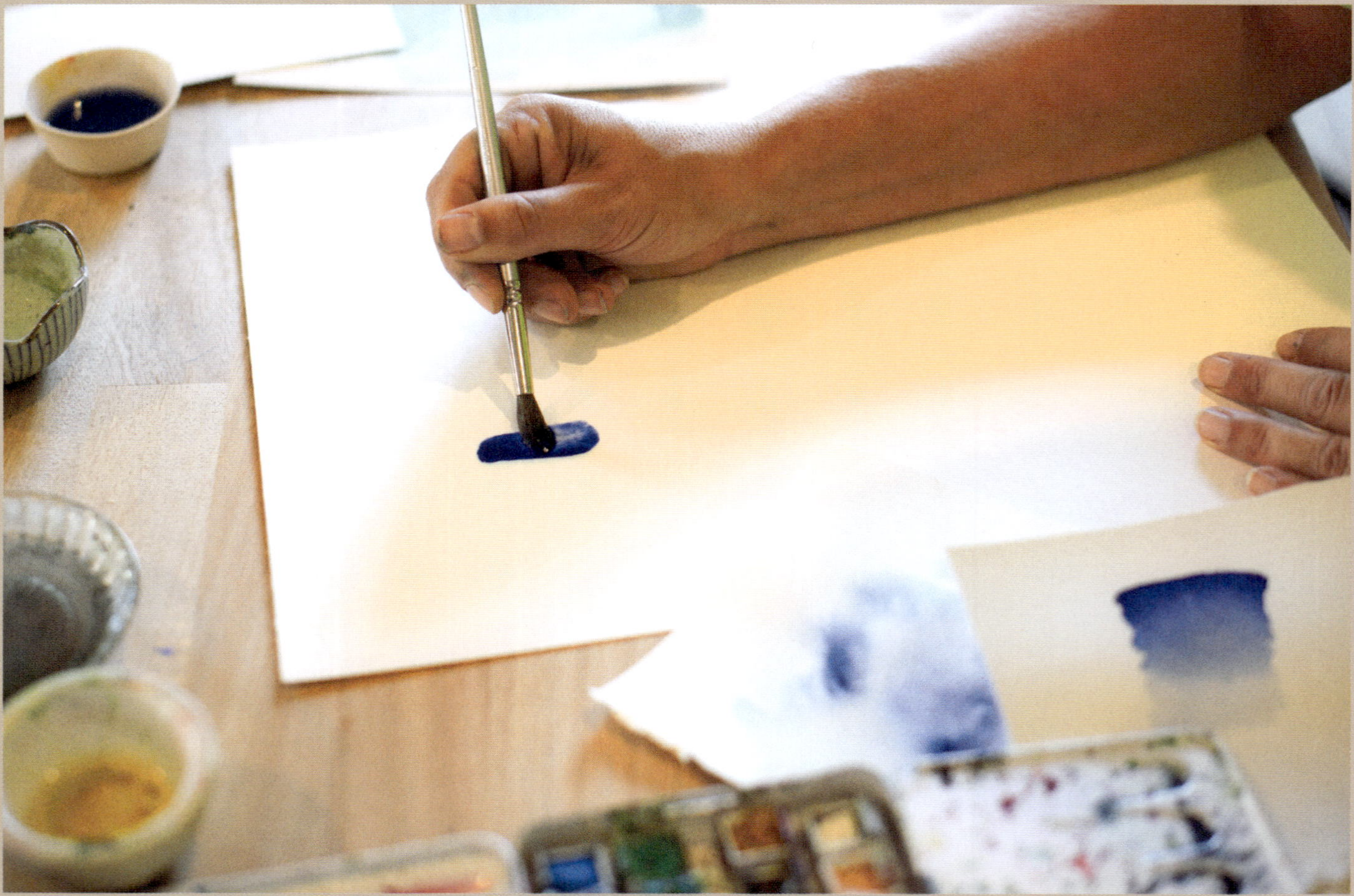

Wet-on-dry

Wet-on-dry is a method of working with wet paint on dry paper or over a layer of watercolour or ink that is already dry. It works well for adding detail and for more precise works.

1

Using the size-12 brush, paint using your lightest colour first.

2

When this is dry, use a darker colour over the top of it.

3

Wait until this layer is dry and experiment using your size-8 brush and an even darker colour to add fine lines and patterns.

●

MATERIALS

Watercolour paper, A4 or A3
Watercolours and/or ink
Mop brush, large
Round brushes, sizes 8 and 12

Glazing

Watercolours are a transparent medium, which means you can layer colours to change the base colour. Glazing, or layering, can create a luminous effect as the colours overlie each other. Imagine layered pieces of stained glass: you would get some beautiful colour nuances.

1

Use a thin wash of watered-down watercolour to paint a shape.

2

Wait until this layer is dry, then use another thin wash to overlap the first shape.

3

Continue layering to create multiple overlapping shapes of colour.

4

Use a yellow wash as a top layer to create a dreamy filtered-sun effect.

MATERIALS

Watercolour paper, A4 or A3
Watercolours and/or ink
Mop brush, large
Round brushes, sizes 8 and 12

TIP

Keep your paint transparent (watered down) to let the base colours and lightness of the paper surface shine through.

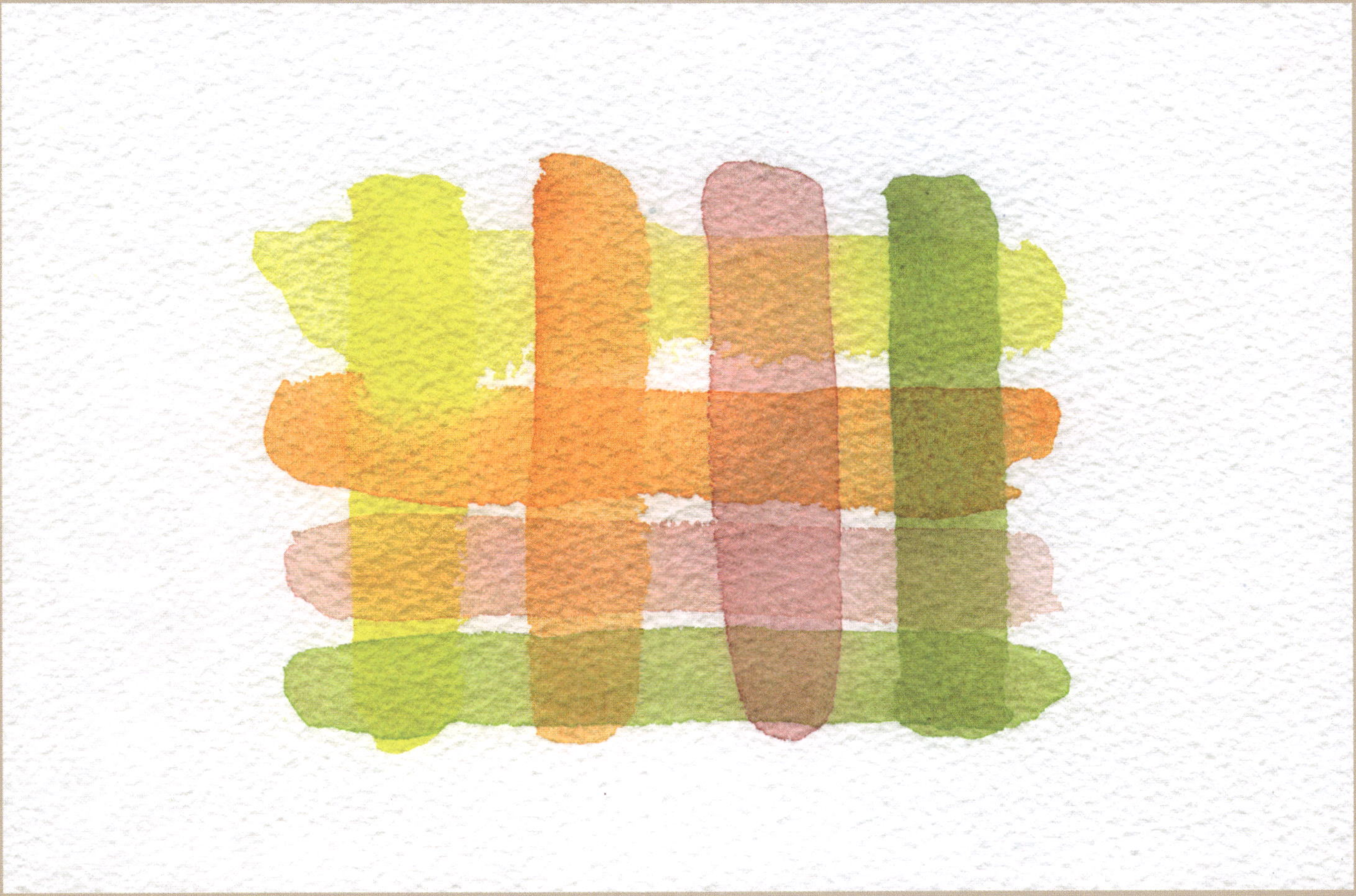

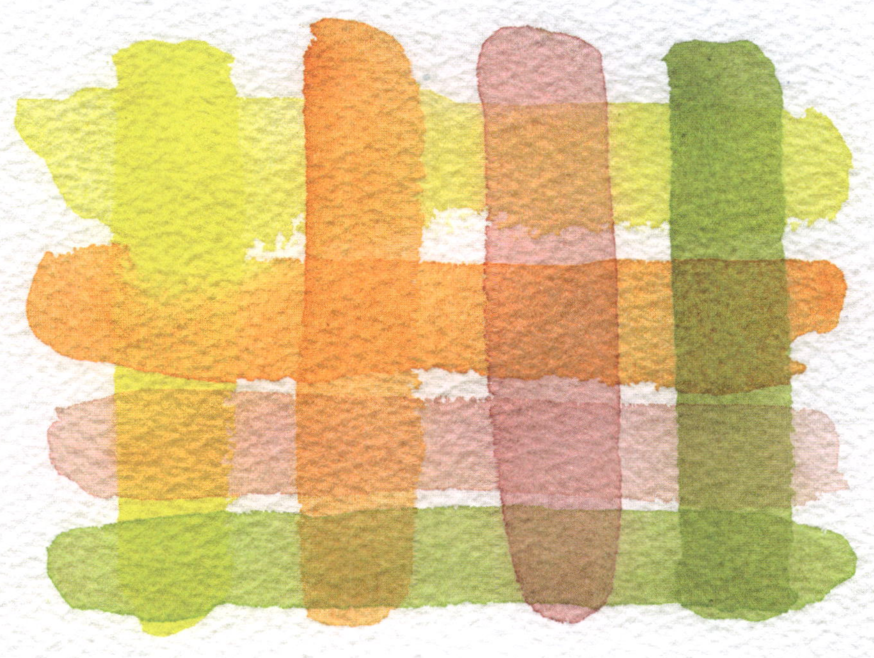

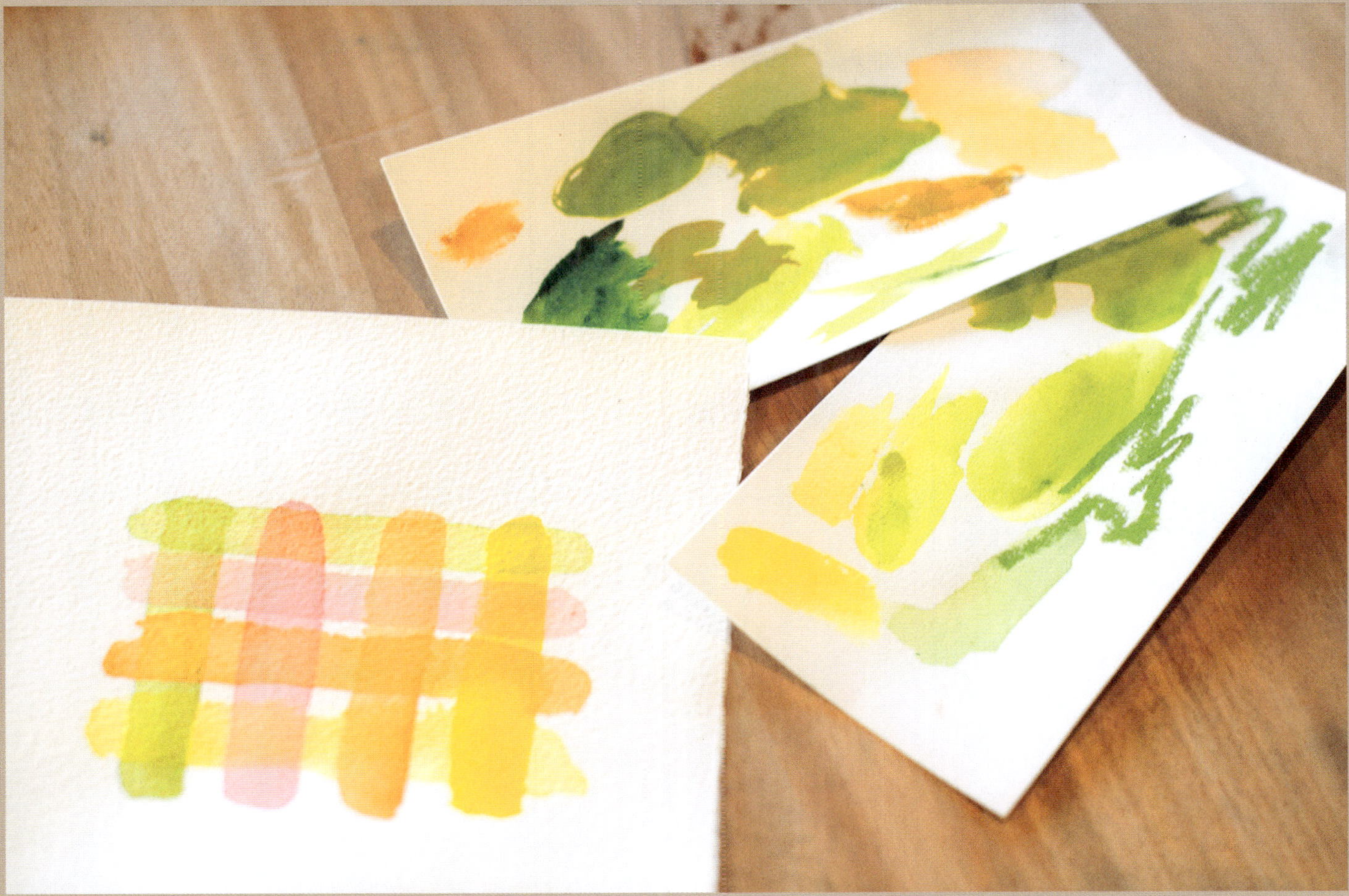

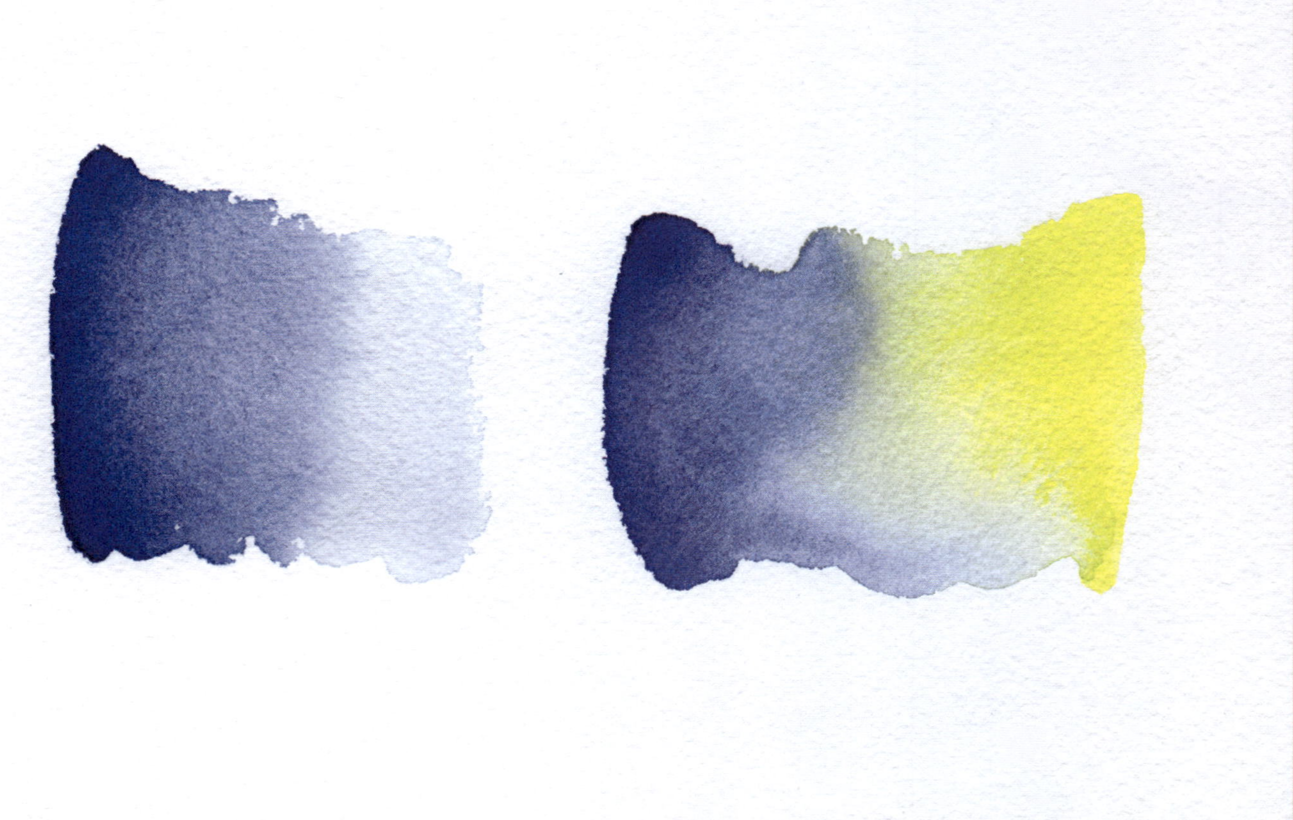

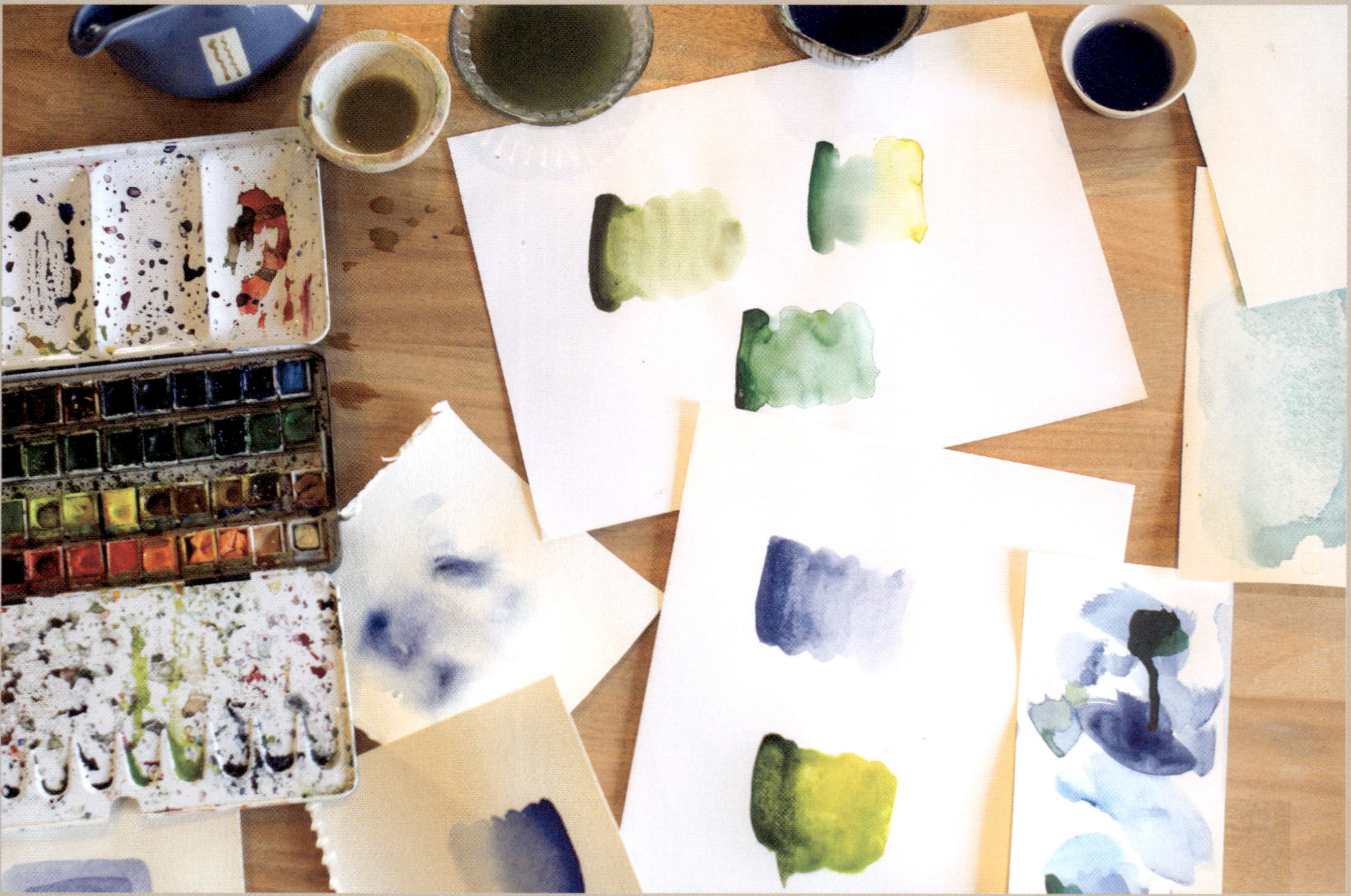

Gradient

Making gradients in watercolour involves blending from opaque to transparent or blending from one colour to another. It is also a useful technique for working in ink.

1

Pick up a lot of paint on your brush, using pressure on the brush as you swirl it in the pigment.

2

Paint a thick stroke on the paper.

3

Dip your brush in water and, moving the brush up and down, pull the paint out from the first stroke until the colour fades away.

4

Choose an alternative colour and repeat steps 1–3, painting the second stroke about 5 centimetres from the first.

5

Use water to join the two strokes together. You can pick up and tilt your paper to help the wet paint run and merge.

●

MATERIALS

Watercolour paper, A4 or A3
Watercolours and/or ink
Mop brush, large
Round brushes, sizes 8 and 12

TIP

Don't be afraid to use lots of water to make the most of the magical qualities of watercolour.

Watercolour circles

Using contrasting colours, create a harmonious combination of light and dark circles.

The beauty of botanical art is that nature has already done the hard work of creating wonderful colour combinations. This quick exercise will improve your brush control and allow you to explore water-to-paint ratios, practise blending wet shapes and create beautiful gradients of colour.

1

Choose a reference image in this book that shows an arrangement of various types of flowers and observe the colours within it. Select four or five of the colours to use in your artwork.

2

Wet your brush and swirl it in the pigment of one of your chosen colours to pick up lots of paint. This exercise is executed with the wet-on-wet technique (see p. 52), so work energetically with spontaneous movements.

3

Hold the brush at a 45-degree angle to the page and twirl it around to paint a circle shape anywhere on your paper in one fluid motion. Paint several more circles, experimenting with the amount of water and paint you use and exploring the colour's full tonal range from light to dark.

4

Continue the exercise using each of your chosen colours in turn, creating circles to fill the page in a balanced and harmonious blend of colours and tones.

MATERIALS

Watercolour paper, A3, your choice of texture

Watercolours

Round brush, size 12

TIPS

Use scrap paper to test out each colour before you apply it.

Play around with how much water each circle has. Notice that if two circles have roughly the same water content, the darker circle will blend into the lighter. Adding a circle with much more water to a circle that is starting to dry will result in water pushing into the first circle and creating a cauliflower-like bloom.

Experiment with having the circles barely touching and watch as the colour or water floods from one circle to another.

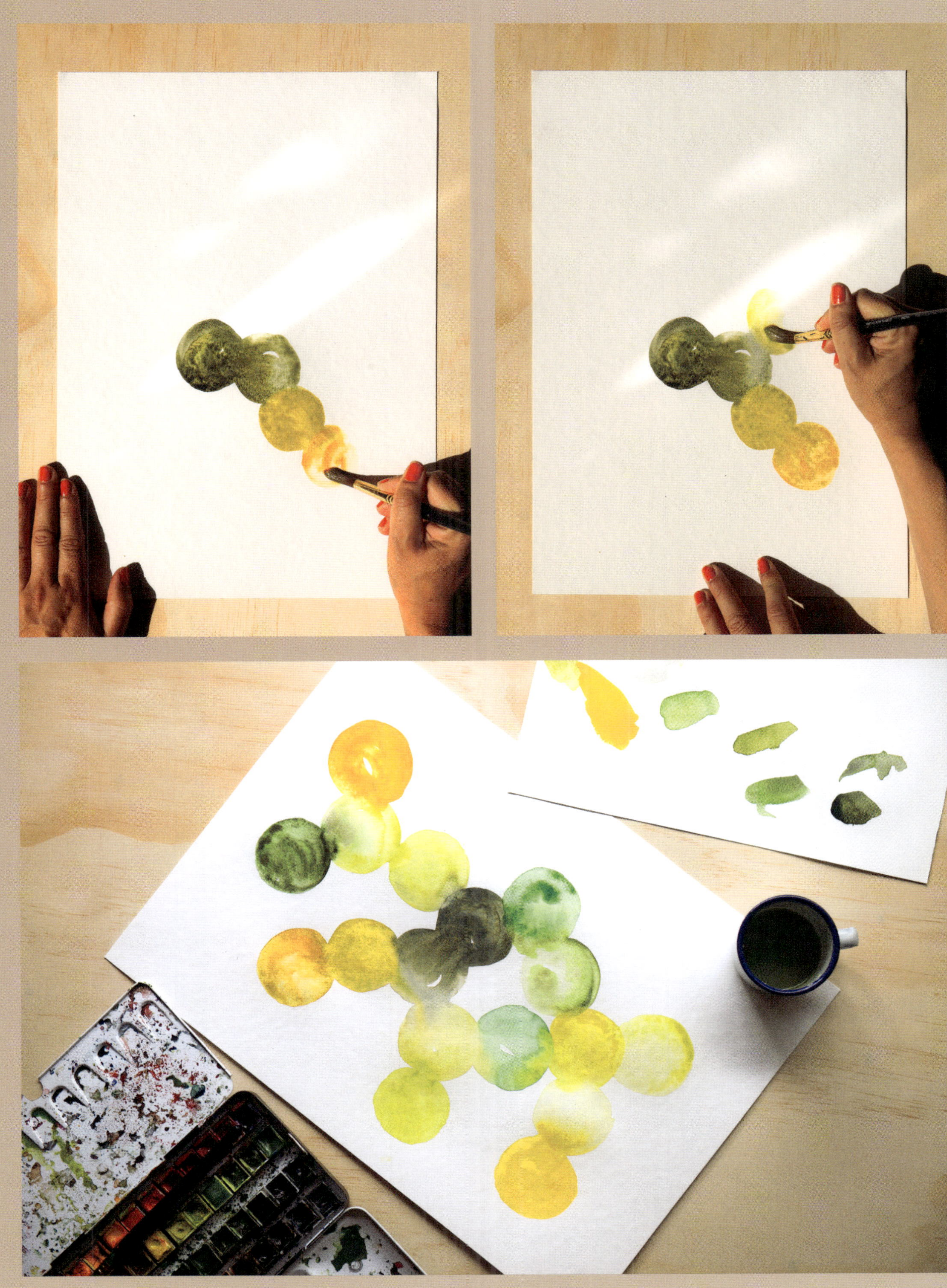

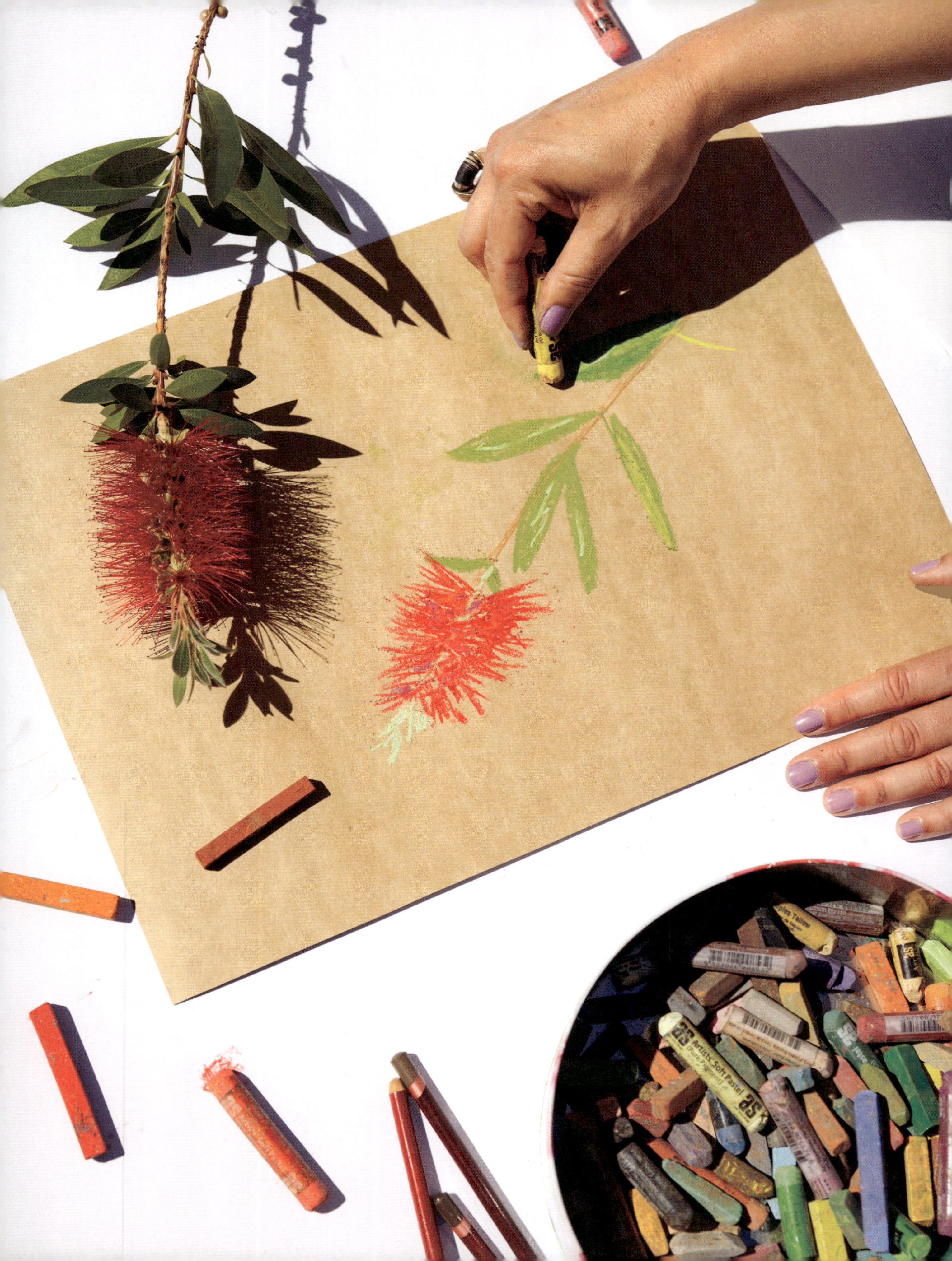

· PROJECTS ·

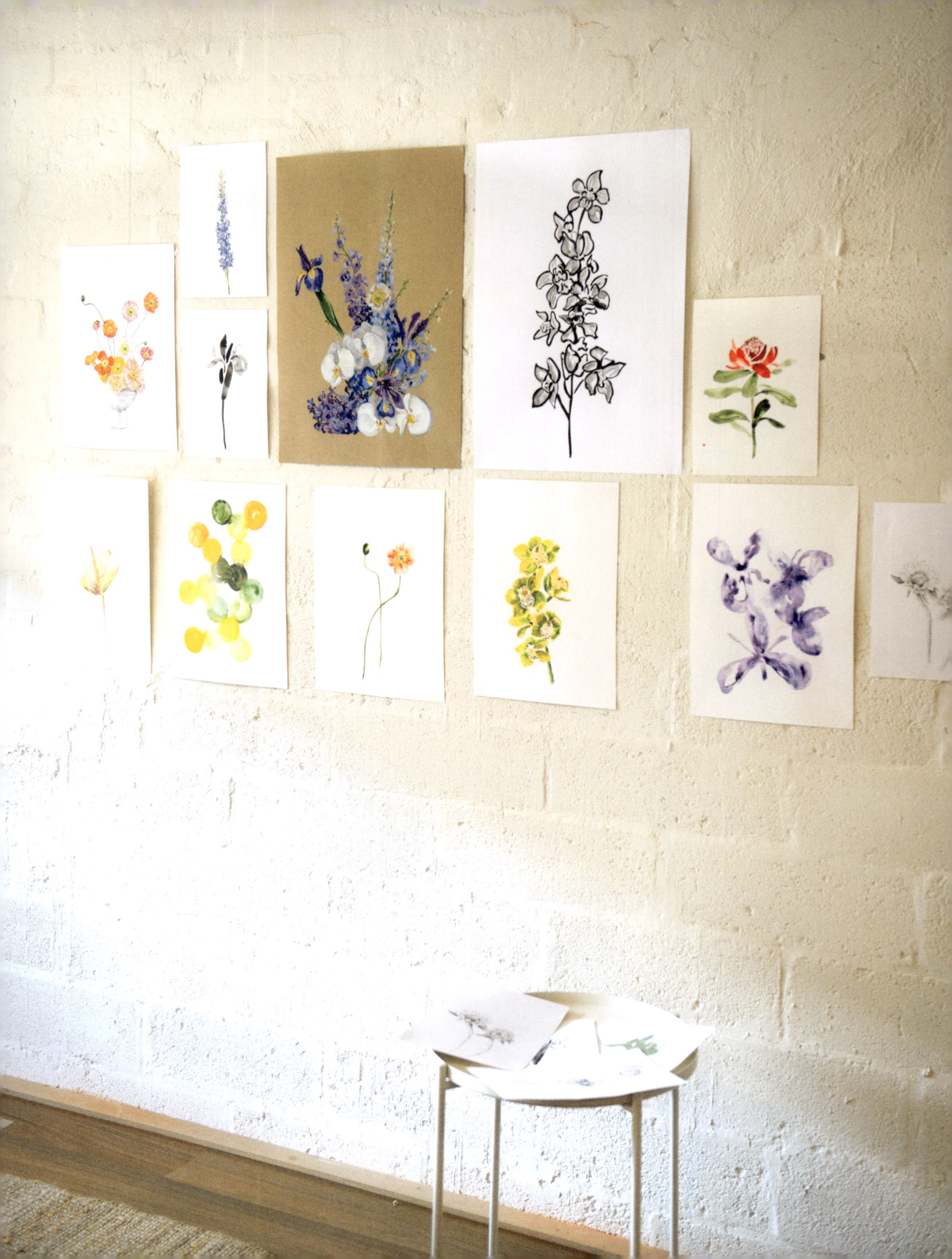

**Using skills practised in the exercises, the following projects include
step-by-step instructions to create botanical artworks. By this stage
you will be familiar with observing your subject, noticing textures,
colours and values, and utilising negative space. You have played
with some different mediums and will have a feel for how they work.**

The projects use graphite pencil, charcoal, coloured pencil, pastels,
watercolour and ink. Material diversity enables you to experiment with
textures, colours and form, and by trialling different mediums and techniques,
you will get a sense of what works best for you while you hone your technical
skills and build a dynamic and expressive artistic practice. This journey will
result in a collection of works that reflect both personal expression and
increasing mastery of materials.

In many of the projects, you will be working from the whole, to details and
complexities, and then back to the whole, switching your gaze and attention.
In others, such as the ink and watercolour artworks, you will be more
spontaneous and gestural.

For extra practice and experimentation, you can mix and match the reference
images throughout the projects with the mediums and techniques described
in the text.

The projects include step-by-step instructions for depicting the specific
reference images with the suggested mediums. There are some general
steps that apply to all the projects and will help you to improve your practice;
these are listed below.

BEFORE YOU START

1 Observe the shapes of the flowers: the curves and angles
   of the stems, leaves and petals.

2 Observe negative space and how objects relate to each other.
   Notice the edges or contours of the elements.

3 Look at the textures of the botanicals.

4 Notice colours and areas of light and dark.

WHEN YOU'RE NEARLY DONE

1 Take a break, stretch, rest your eyes and then have another look at the
   reference and your artwork. It will appear quite different to fresh eyes,
   and there may be areas you would like to change or build up.

2 Add anything you have missed that could improve balance or definition.

3 Congratulate yourself for mindfully enjoying the process and allowing
   yourself the time for creating art.

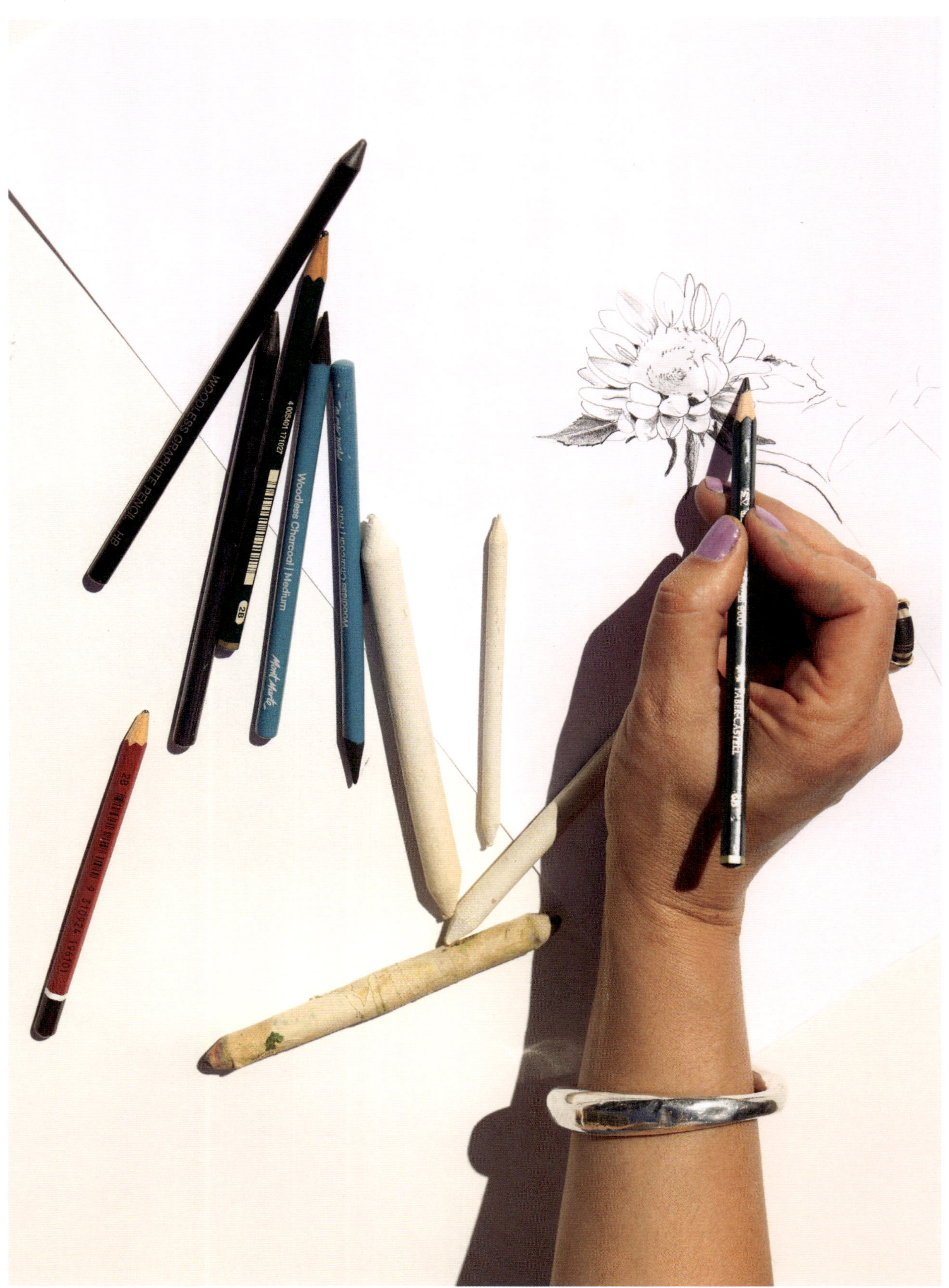

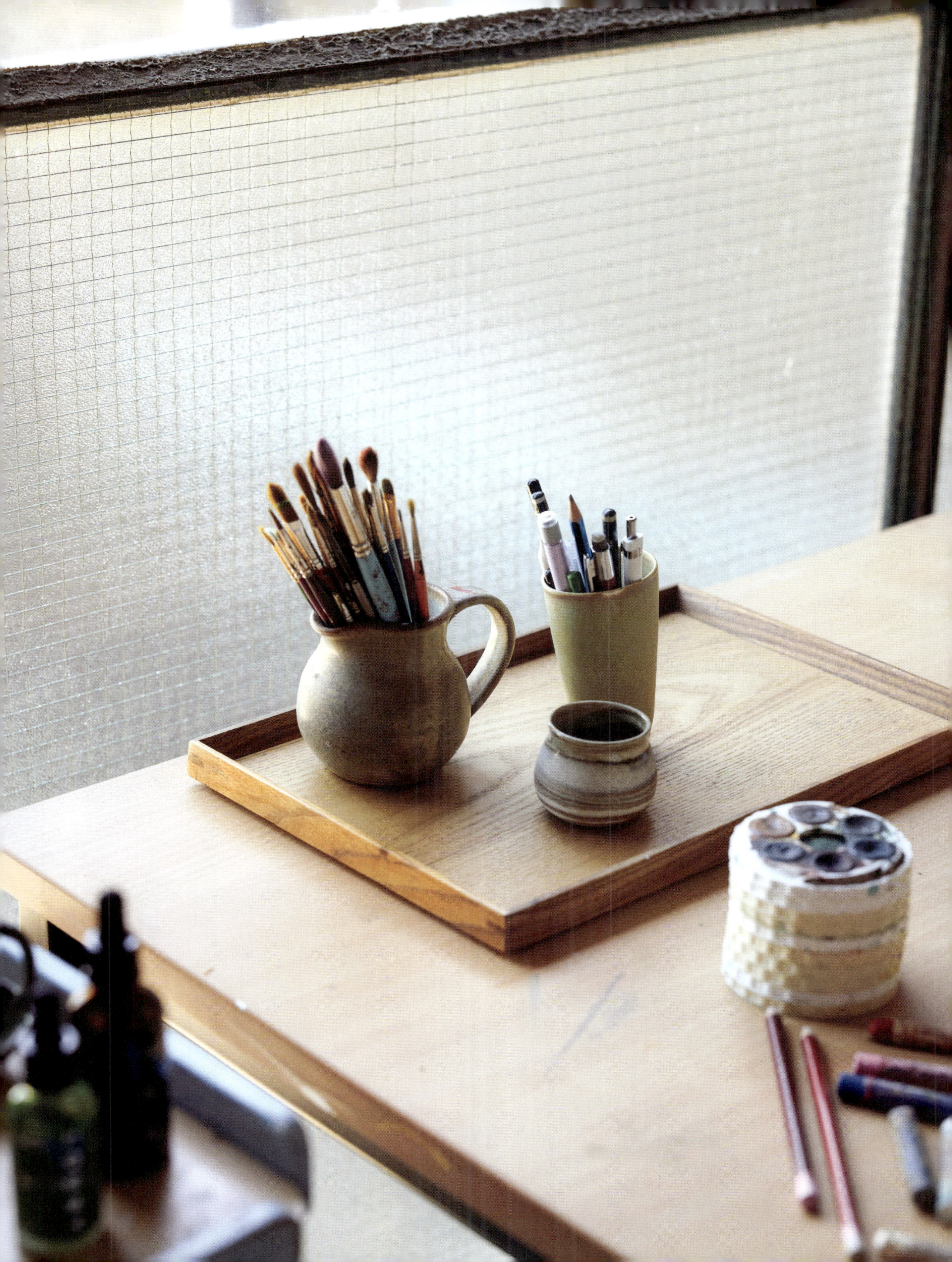

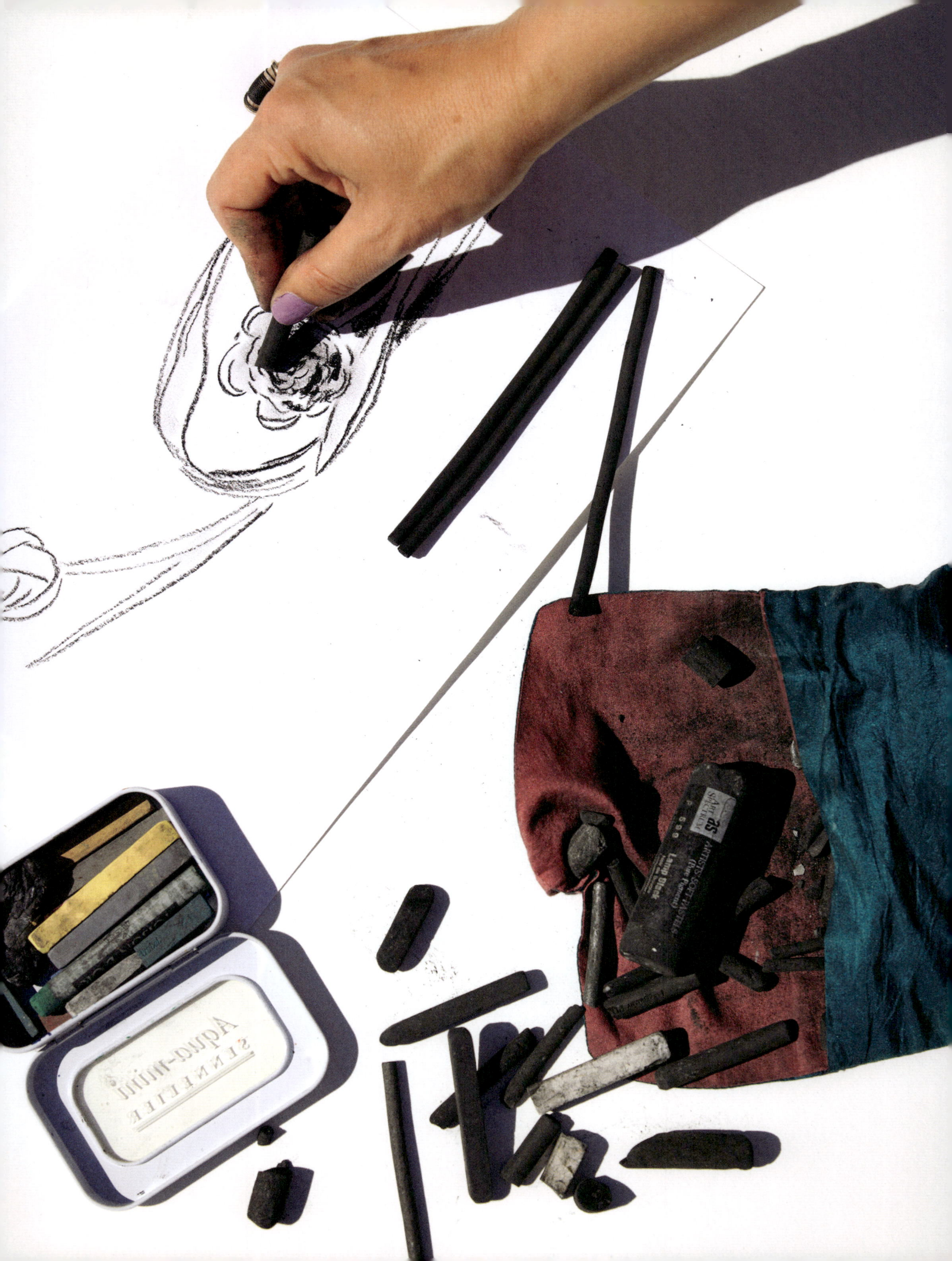

Graphite pencil and charcoal

It is said that drawing is the foundation of art. Graphite and charcoal are the perfect place to start.

Graphite pencils allow for both control and energy. They have sixteen degrees of variation, ranging from softer and darker to harder and lighter. I primarily use a 2B or 4B pencil; they are soft enough to get a solid line but hard enough to be sharpened to a precise point. I love having a strong contrast in my pencil drawings, so it is really important for me to be able to build up the tone. Contrast helps create visual interest in artworks and can enhance focal points as well as demonstrating areas of depth. I keep my pencils very sharp for defined lines, so I always have a sharpener on hand.

Charcoal allows you to start light, recorrect easily and build up when you are happy with the layout. You can use it or its side for blending and use a finger to smudge and shade the pigment. There are two main types of charcoal: willow charcoal and vine charcoal are soft and light, while compressed charcoal is much denser and darker. I recommend starting with willow or vine, and as your confidence grows, move on to compressed. You can also use willow or vine for an underdrawing, which is a very rough sketch to map out the composition. When you are happy with your sketch, move on to compressed charcoal to build up the artwork. Compressed charcoal is less forgiving but can add beautiful contrast and depth. I sometimes use charcoal pencil, which is an expressive medium and produces a stronger black than graphite.

When working with any soft or chalky medium, such as charcoal or soft pastel, I use a fixative spray to prevent smudging and help preserve the medium on the paper. Lightly spray your work when complete to secure particles in place.

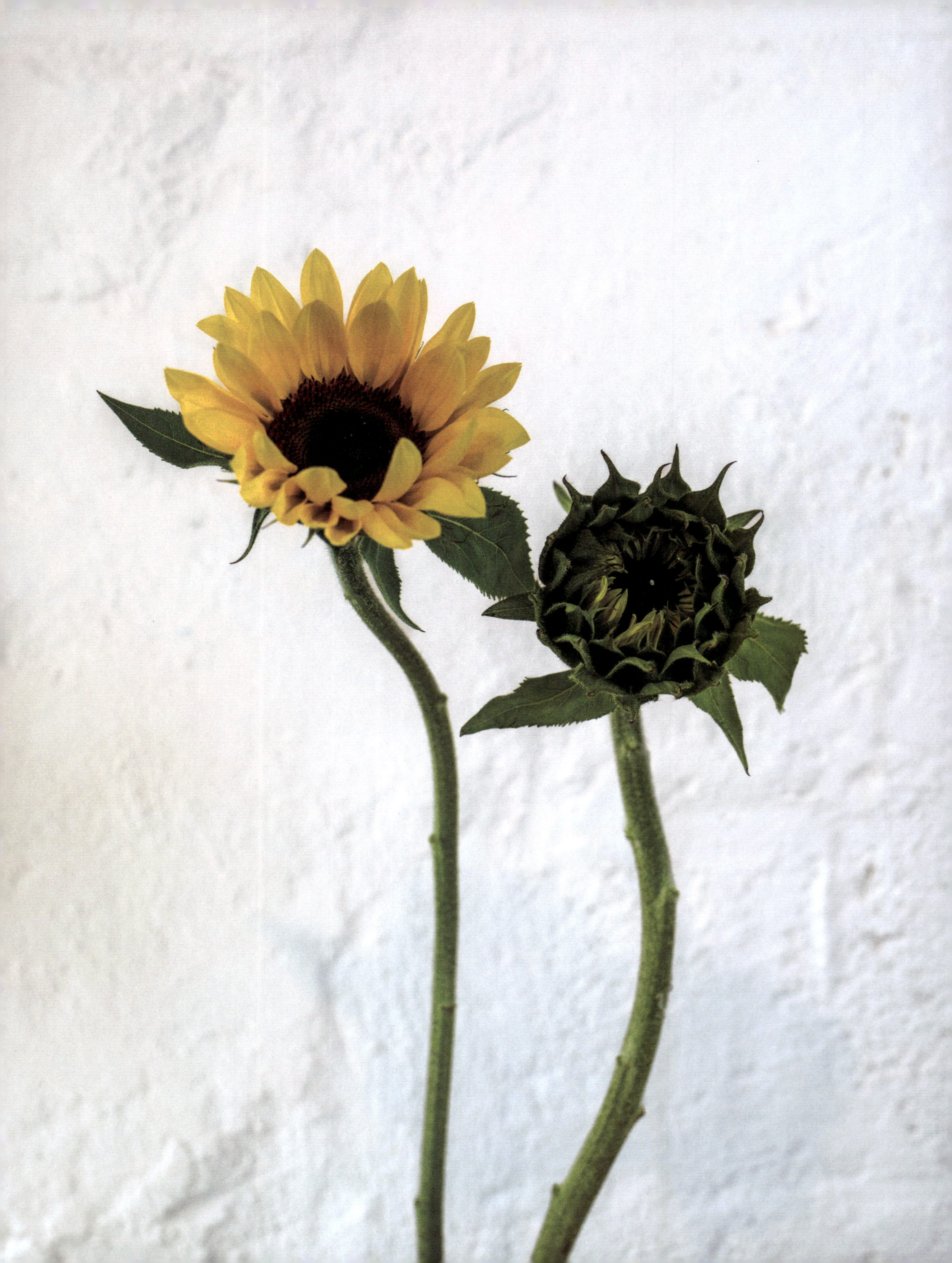

Sunflower

Sunflowers are bright, cheerful flowers that exude joy with their golden, geometric petals. They are natives of North America, and the flower buds follow the sun through the day, a behaviour known as 'heliotropism'. In art, sunflowers are a popular subject matter, perhaps depicted most famously in Vincent van Gogh's series of *Sunflower* paintings.

While sunflowers appear simple to draw, there is a remarkable amount of detail in each flower, and pencil is the perfect medium to capture this.

The reference image shows sunflowers in various stages of blooming. Use your observation skills to define the relationships between elements, such as petals and leaves, and remember to draw as you see, rather than drawing what you assume objects look like. Continue to observe the reference as you draw and be guided by your intuition to make some areas more detailed and others less. Keep your pencil sharp and vary the pressure when drawing your lines to create an appealing mix of bolder strokes and more delicate, softer areas.

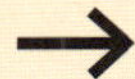

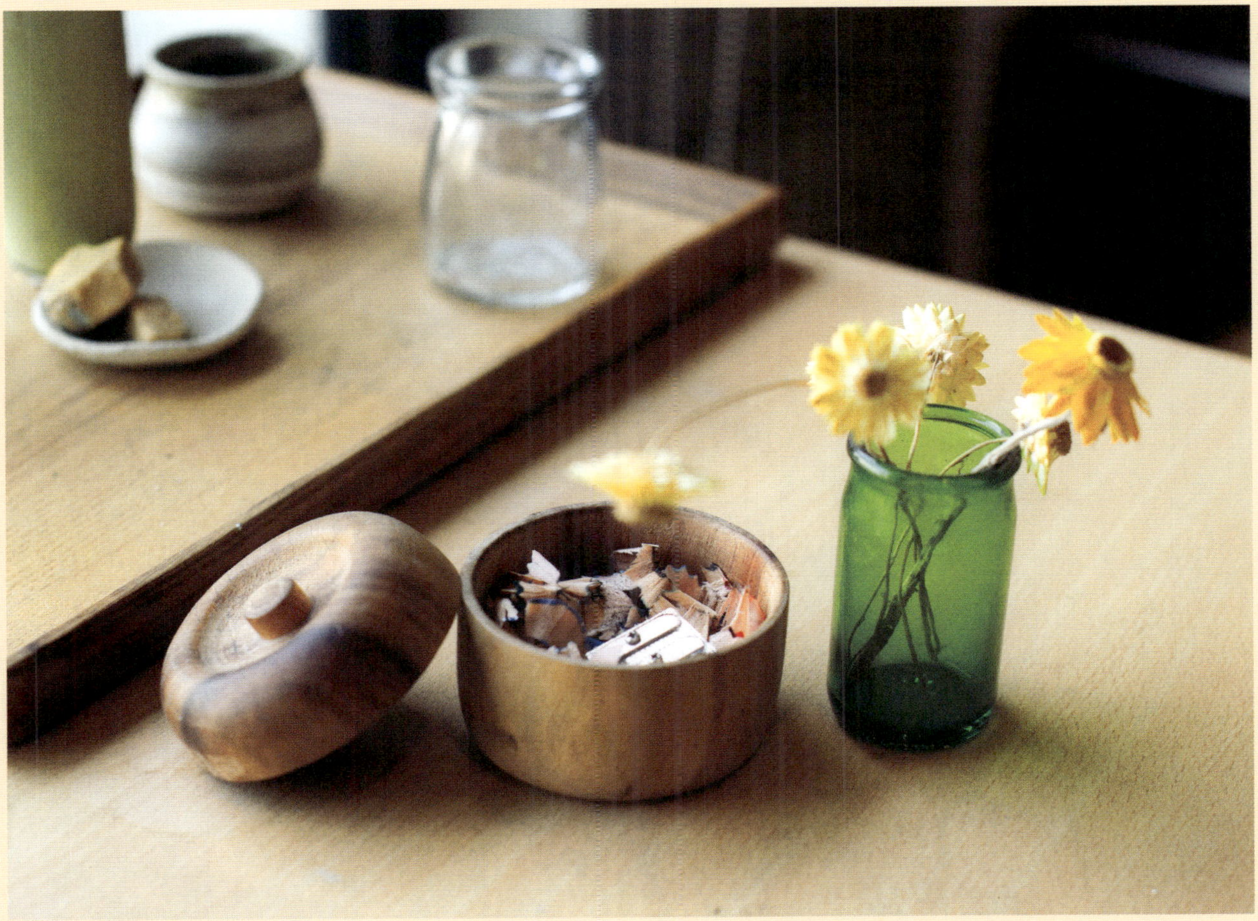

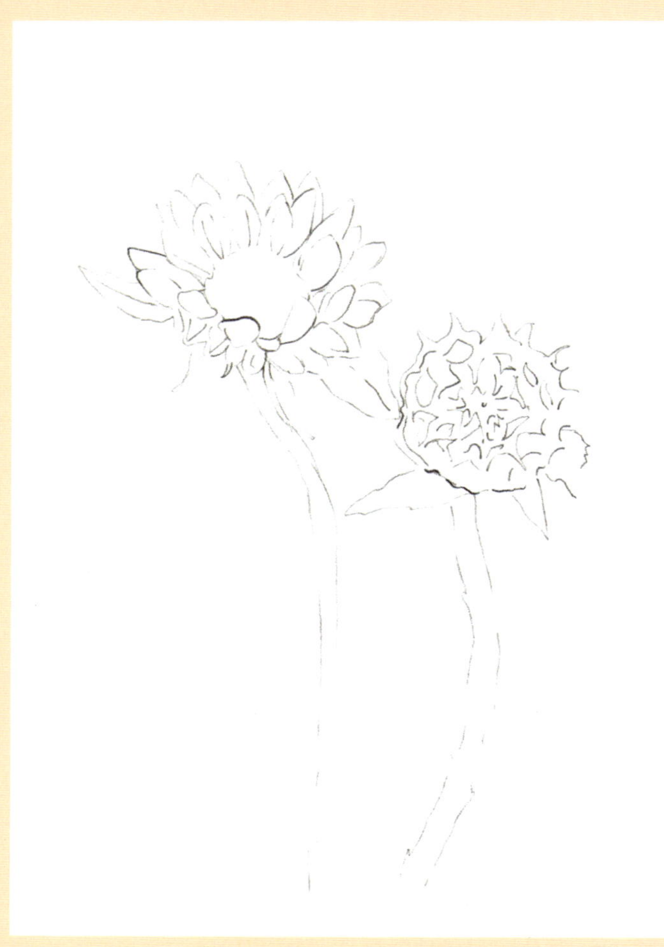

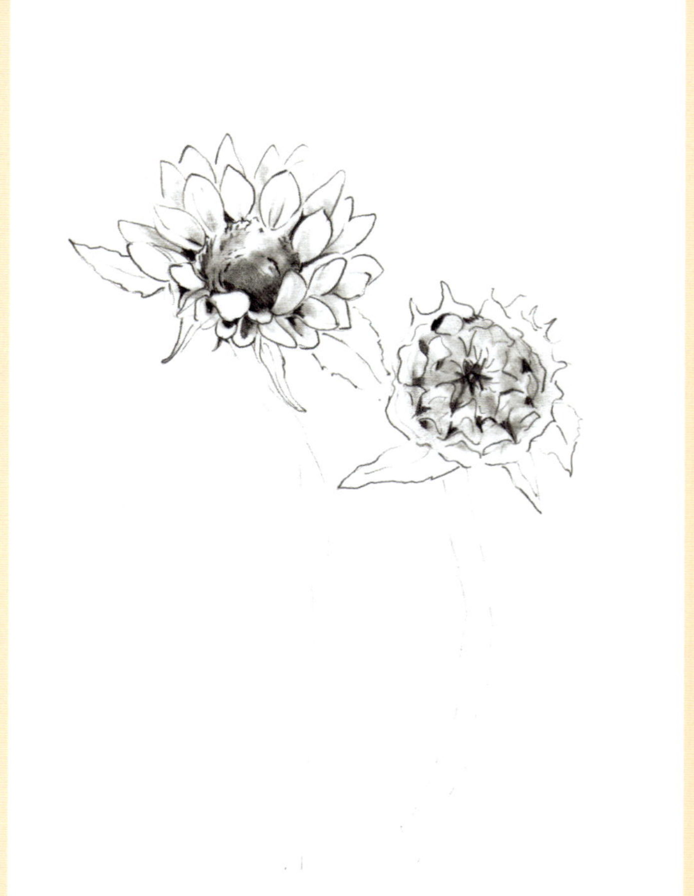

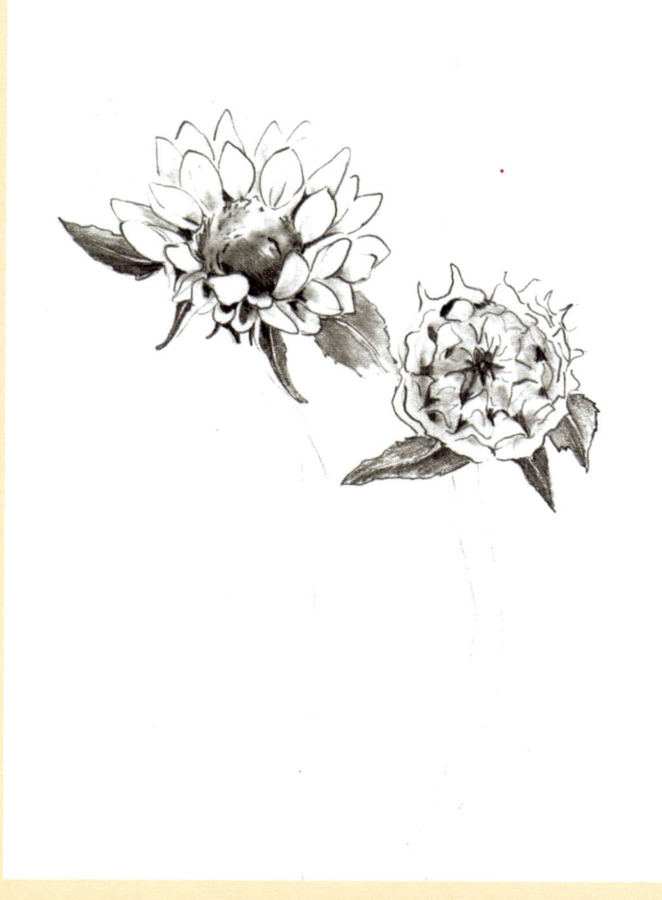

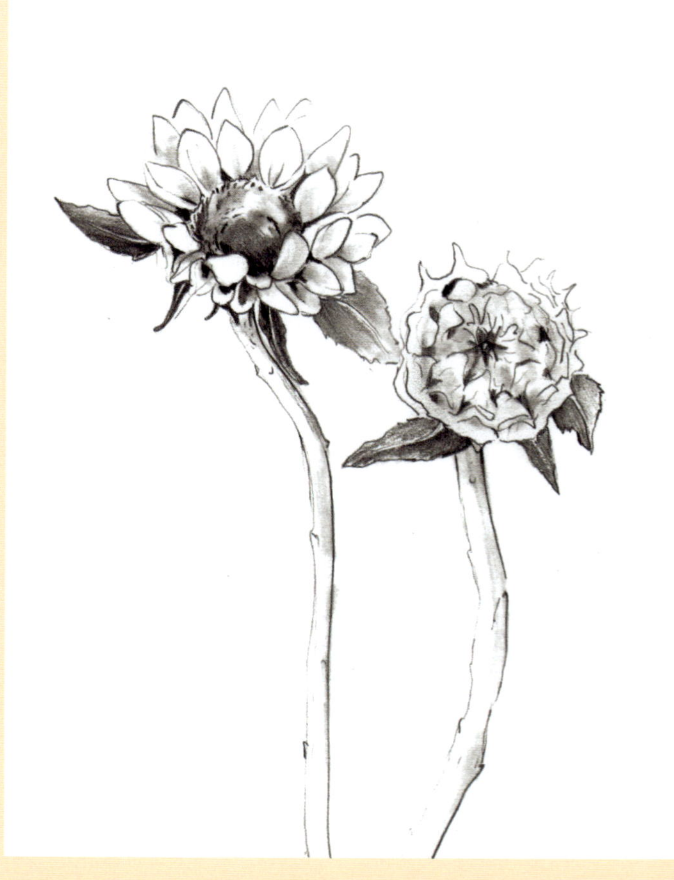

1

Lightly sketch the flowers to map out the shapes, starting with the large circle core of seeds and then moving on to the petals, stems and leaves. Keep your lines light and loose, so they can be erased if required. Take care to note where the petals overlie and are unruly. Don't be afraid to correct, rework or try again.

2

Once you are happy with your guide lines, observe the textures and patterns of the seeded cores and build up a darker tone in those areas, using more pressure on your pencil.

3

Softly shade the creases within the petals and the shadows where the petals curl in on themselves. Notice that the darkest areas of the petals are where they connect with the core and use your finger or a smudge stick to shade these areas. For the sunflower that is less fully open, darken the sections between the leaves and the core to create the illusion of depth.

4

Build up a darker tone on the leaves. Demonstrate the inner vein by keeping this blank to bring contrast to the leaves. Don't feel the need to shade the leaves entirely; instead, observe the darkest and lightest points and using your finger or a smudge stick, lightly smudge out the graphite to create a gradient of tone.

5

Define the stems by using more pressure when drawing the right-hand side to indicate shadow and enhance their form. Note the nodes on the stems and draw these in.

6

Sharpen your pencil and define any further details you see, such as patterns in the leaves or shadows in the petals.

MATERIALS

Smooth watercolour paper, A3

Graphite pencil, 2B

Sharpener

Eraser

Smudge stick (or finger)

____

TIP

Use an eraser to selectively lift graphite and create highlights where the light hits the petals, core and leaves.

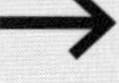

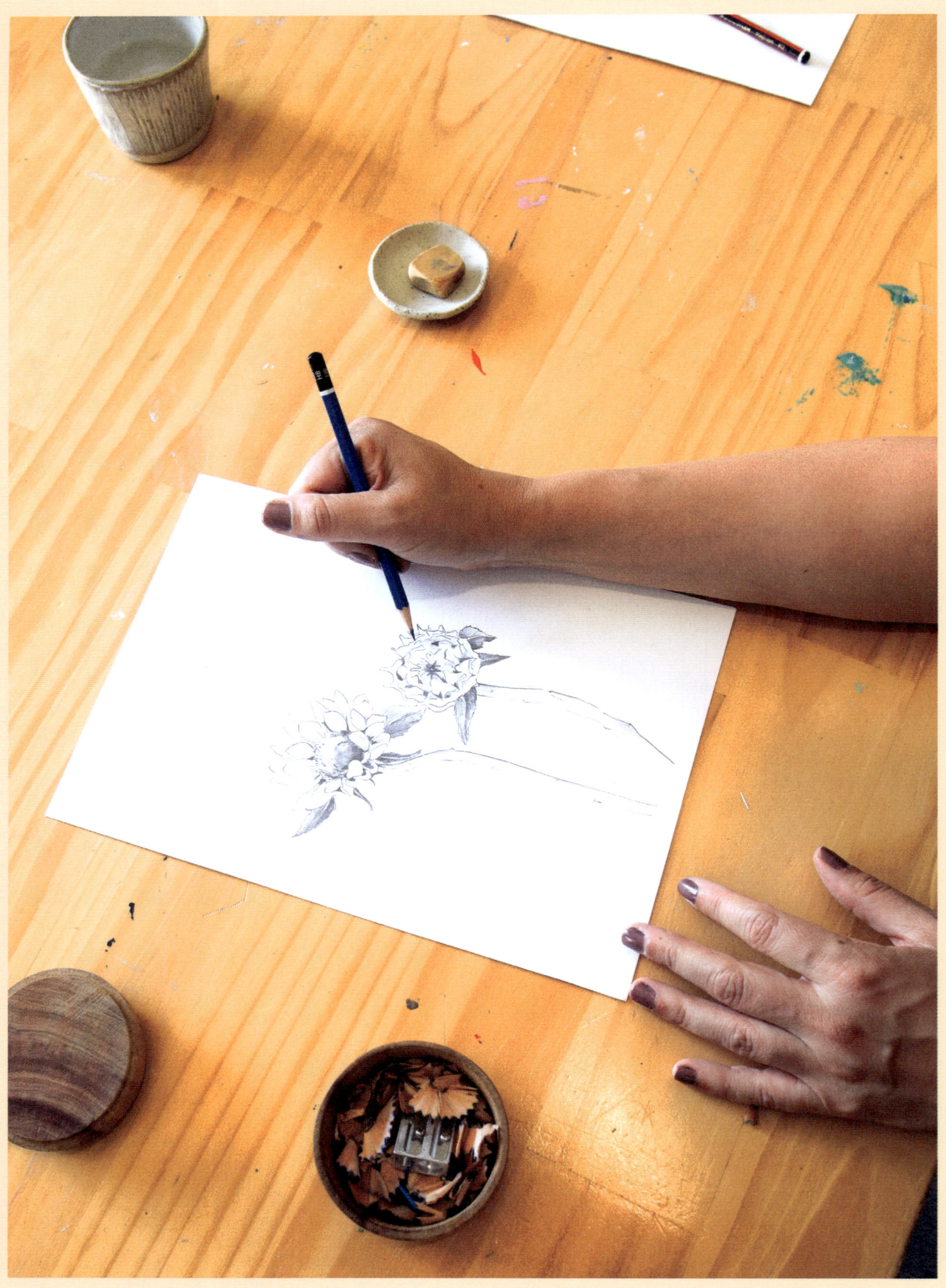

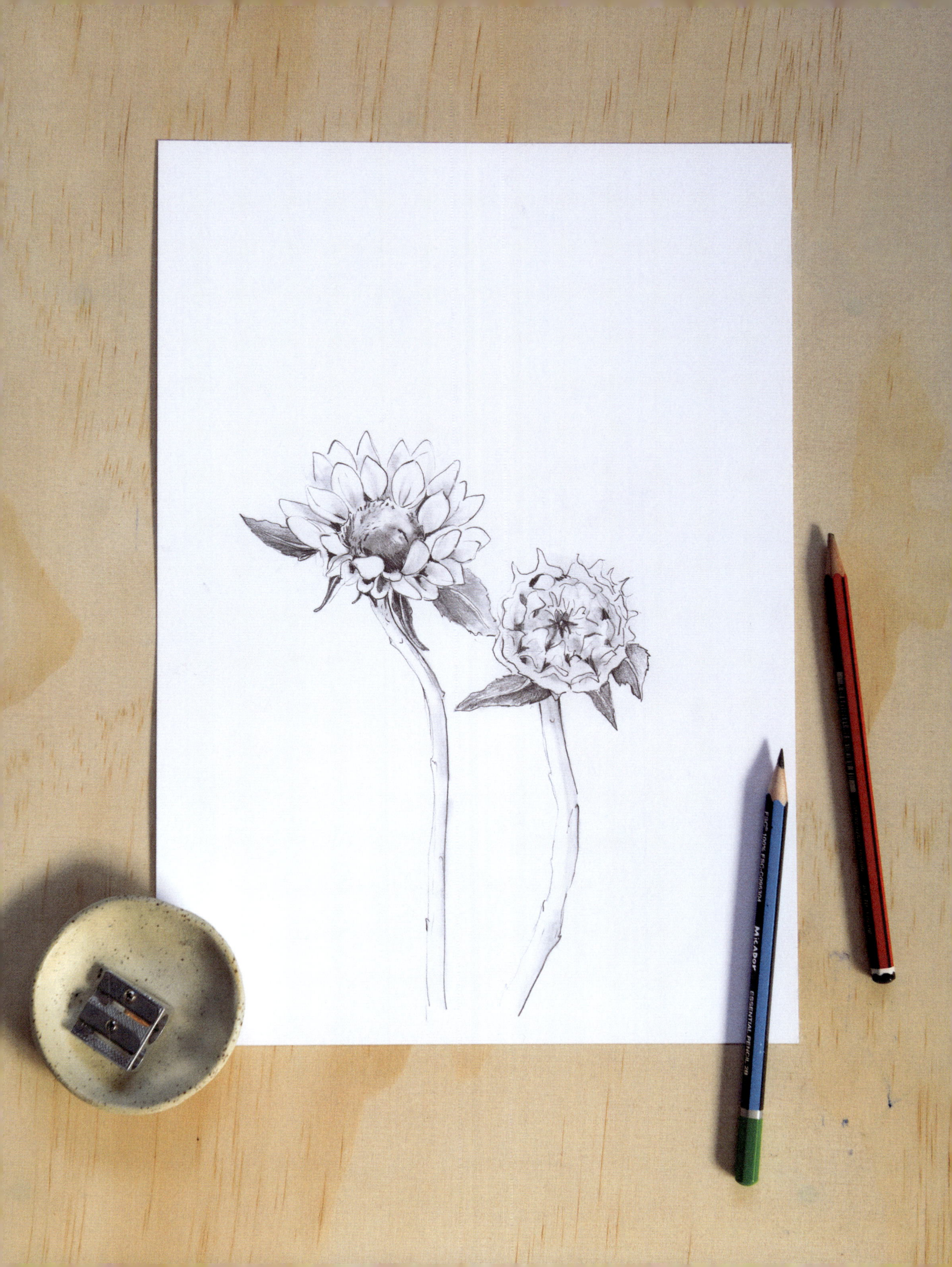

Tulip

Tulips are known for their distinctive cup-shaped, brightly coloured flowers. They are native to Central Asia and gained prominence in the Ottoman Empire, where they became a symbol of opulence and power. In the 17th century, exotic tulips became wildly popular in the Netherlands, with the rarest tulip bulbs costing almost six times the average person's annual salary. These days, they are much more affordable.

In this artwork you will be drawing two overlapping tulips. Vary the pressure on the charcoal to create dark and light lines. I used compressed charcoal for this piece, but you could experiment with willow in a trial run to build your confidence.

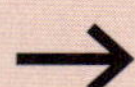

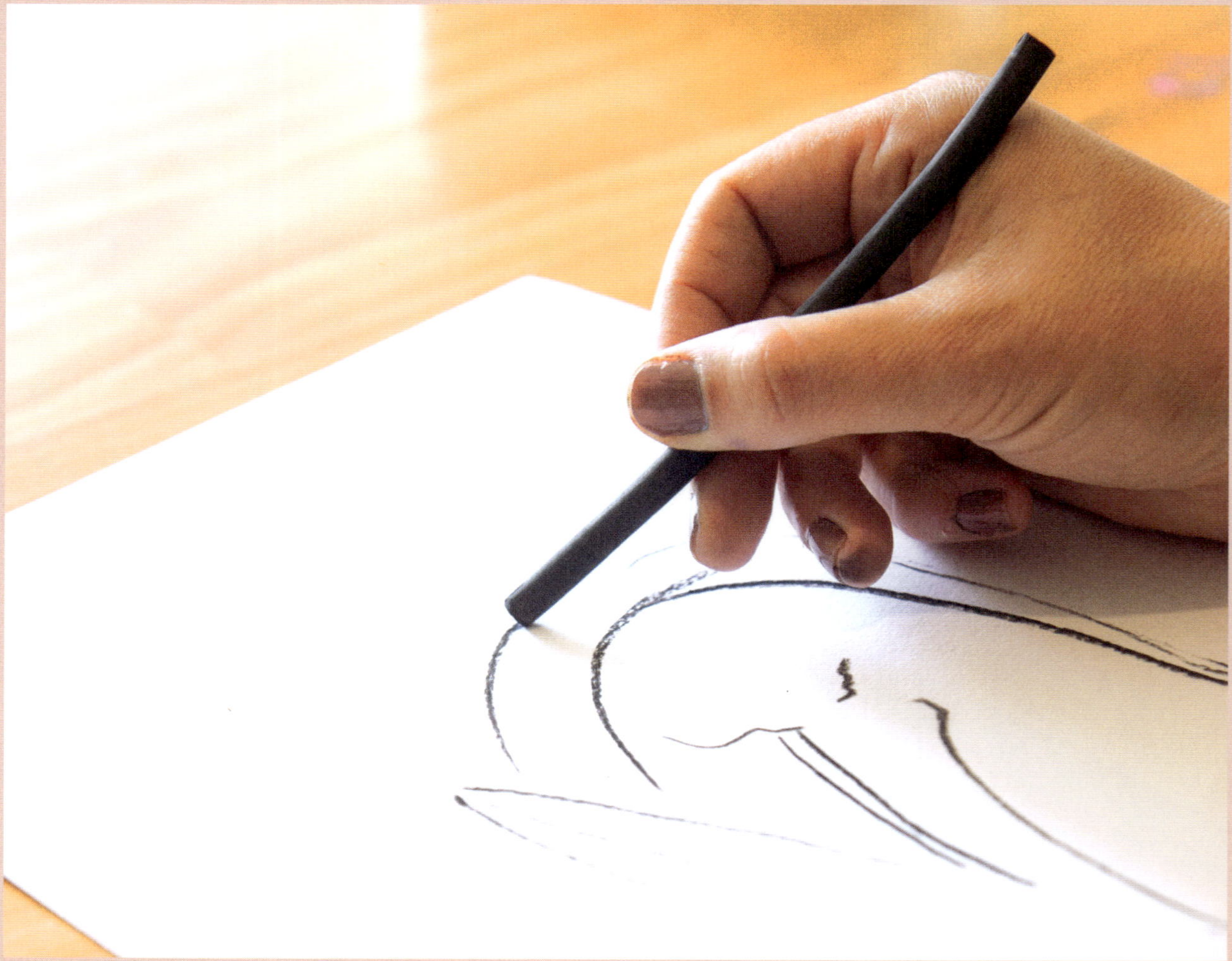

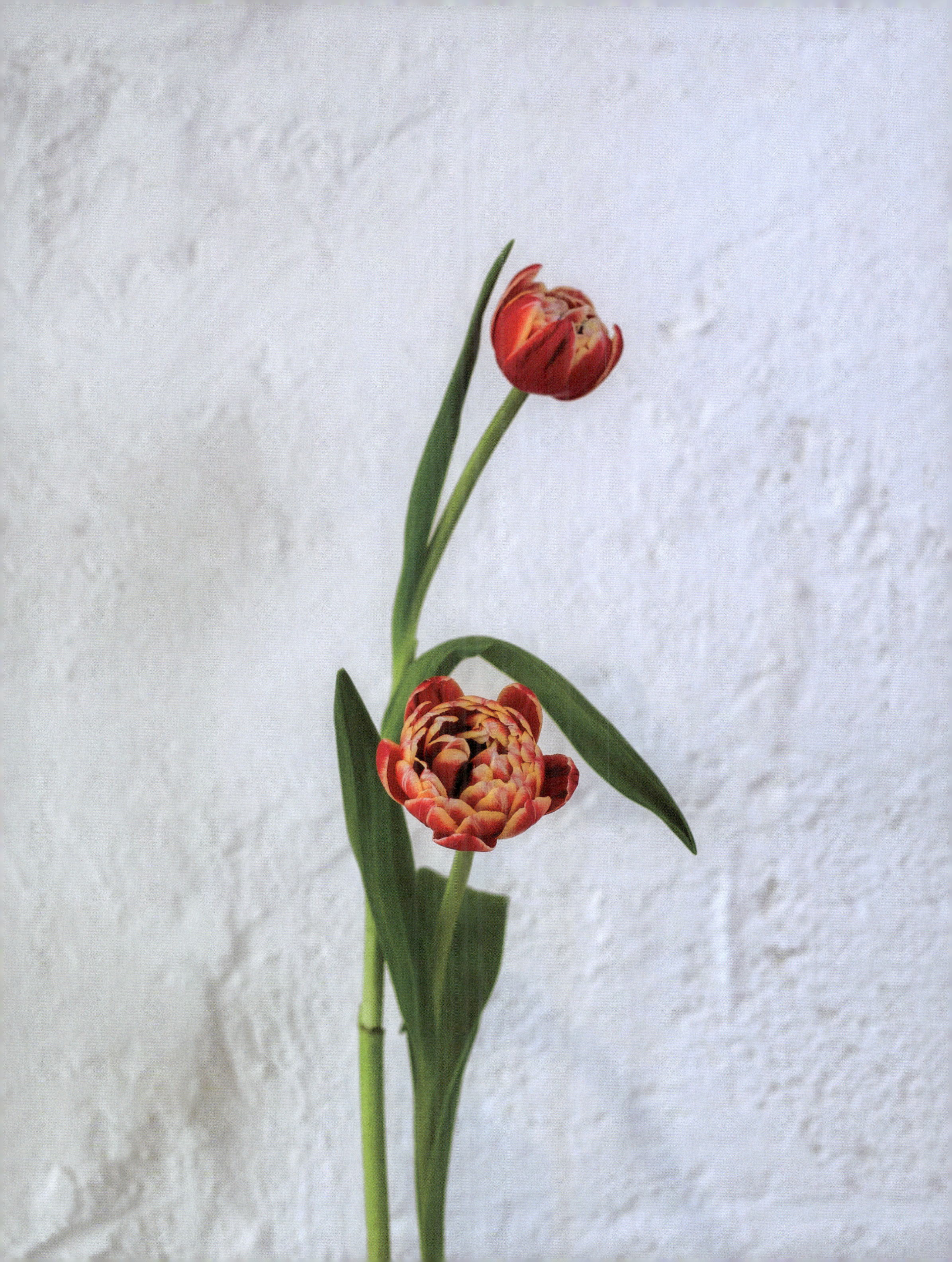

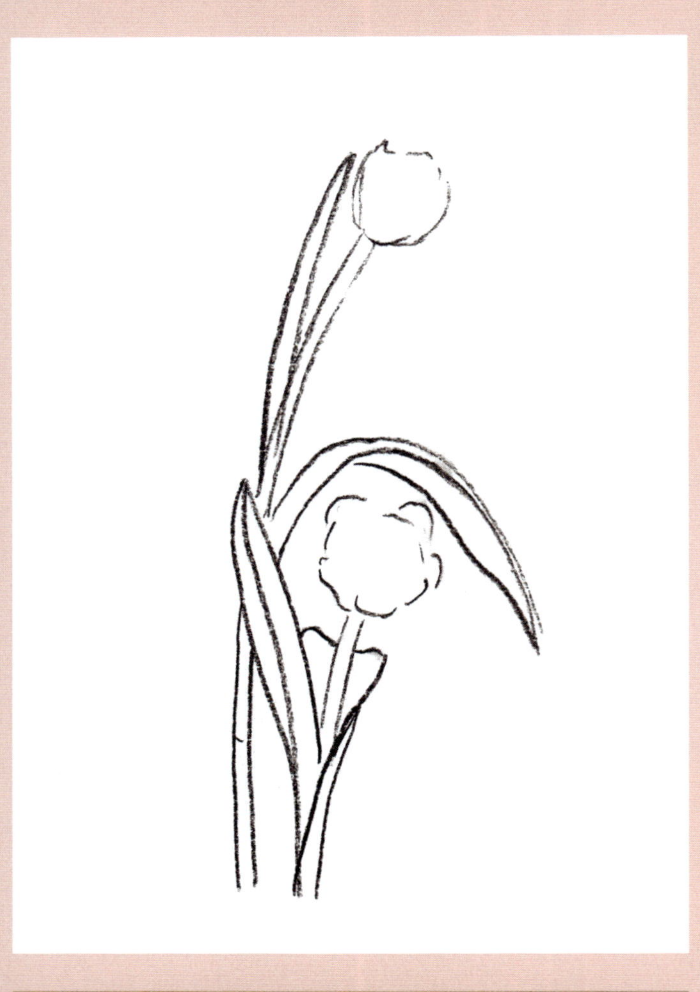
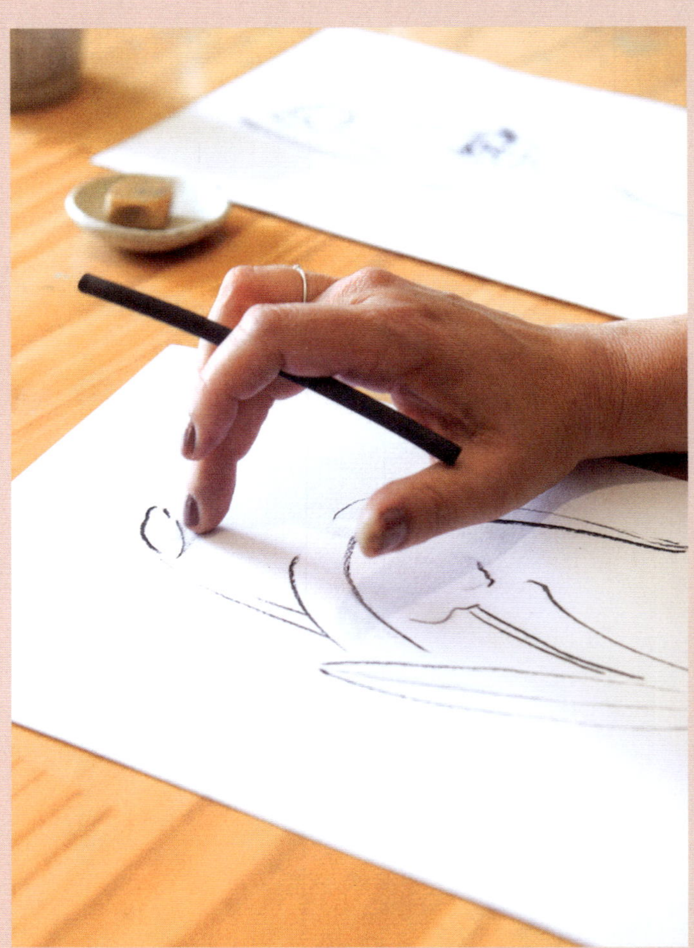
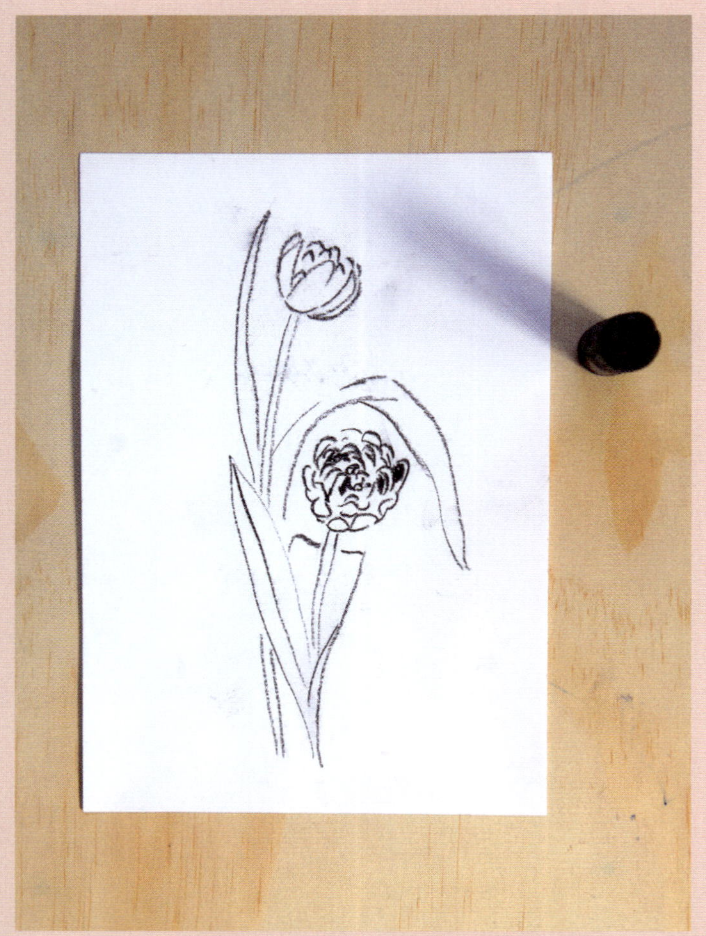
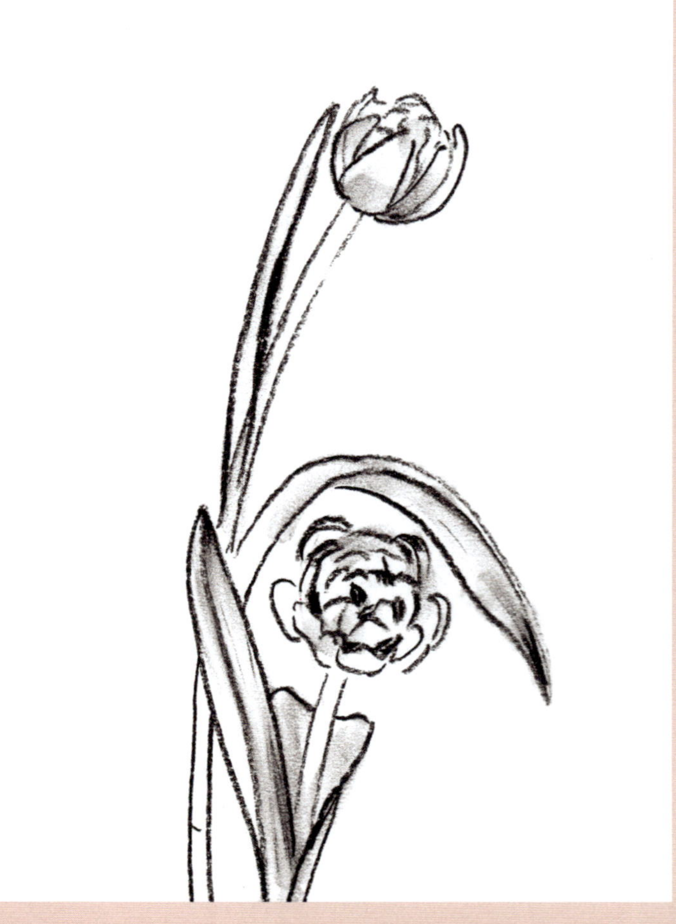

1

Beginning with the lower tulip, draw the outline of the leaves, stem and outer edges of the petals in a solid line, noticing where the leaves fold and curl in. Then do the same for the upper tulip.

2

Work on the lower tulip and sketch curved lines inside the petal shape to give an indication of density within the petal cluster. Block out the dark, shaded areas in the centre of the flower. Use your finger to smudge the charcoal to add the illusion of depth.

3

Move on to the upper tulip's petals, noting the gesture of their curves. Shade with your finger.

4

Gently smudge the charcoal along the leaves, adding shading to the edges. Use the charcoal lightly, to replicate the soft lines visible in the leaves. Blur your eyes as you look at the reference and note the darkest points on the leaves, then use more pressure on the charcoal to darken these lines.

5

When you are satisfied that the piece is finished, lightly spray it with fixative.

●

MATERIALS

Smooth watercolour paper, A4
Charcoal
Fixative

TIP

Don't worry about capturing an accurate depiction of the reference so much as making confident lines and dynamic shapes.

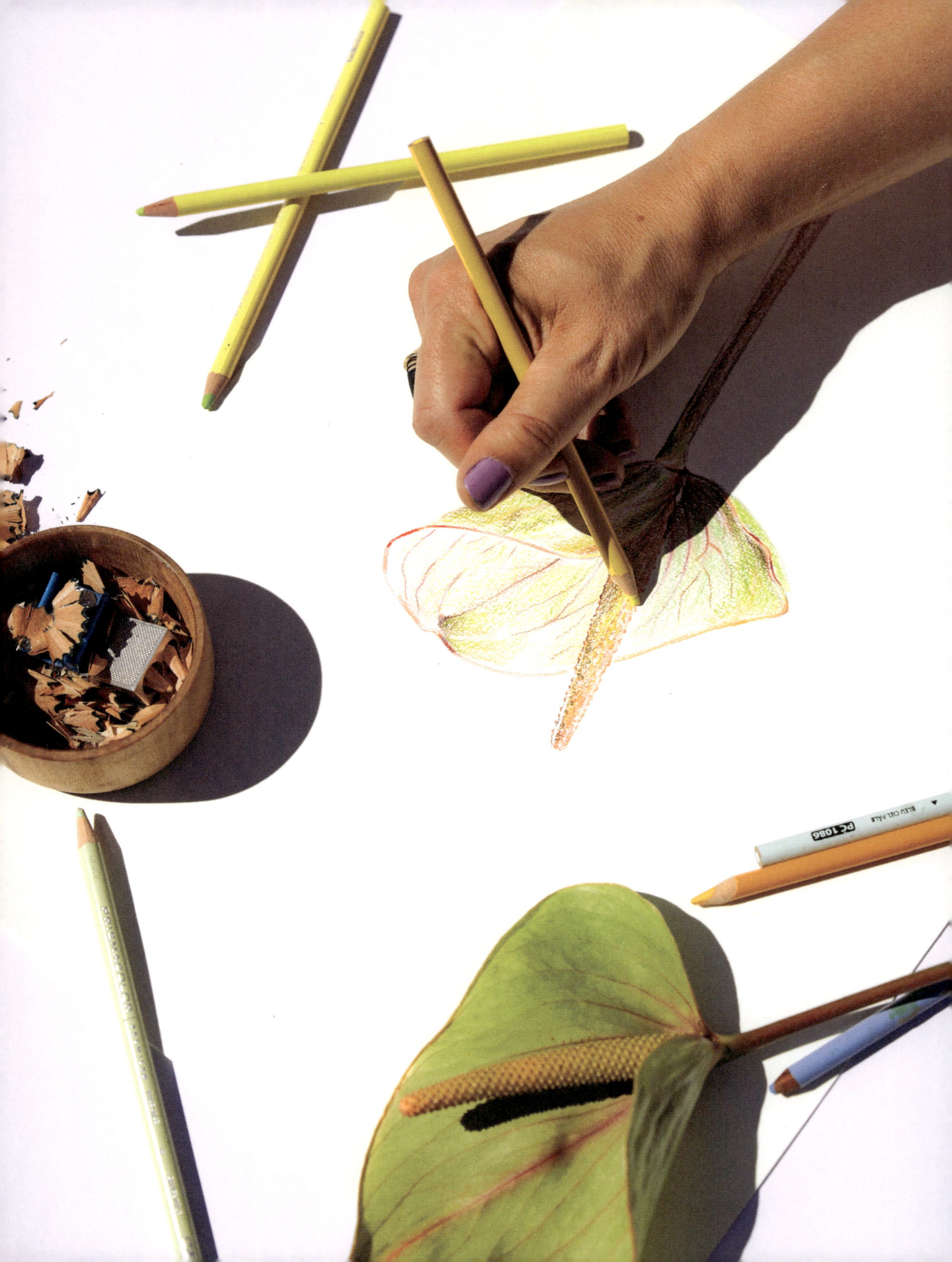

Coloured pencil

Coloured pencils are creamy and highly pigmented, come in extensive colour ranges and layer beautifully. They can be used lightly and whimsically or with more control and precision. I use them when I want to capture the intricacies and details of a flower or arrangement.

Tones can be easily built up by using the pencils lightly, so keep your use soft and don't overwork them. Try to have a wide colour range so you can blend colours together in gradients and create tonal variations and colour blends.

If you are purchasing coloured pencils for this project, choose artist-grade pencils that are lightfast, which means they have a high level of permanence and won't fade over time.

Experiment with different paper varieties, as the appearance of coloured pencil changes according to the texture of the paper. I prefer the look of smooth paper, which provides a fluid application, meaning pencils can blend well and result in a soft finish.

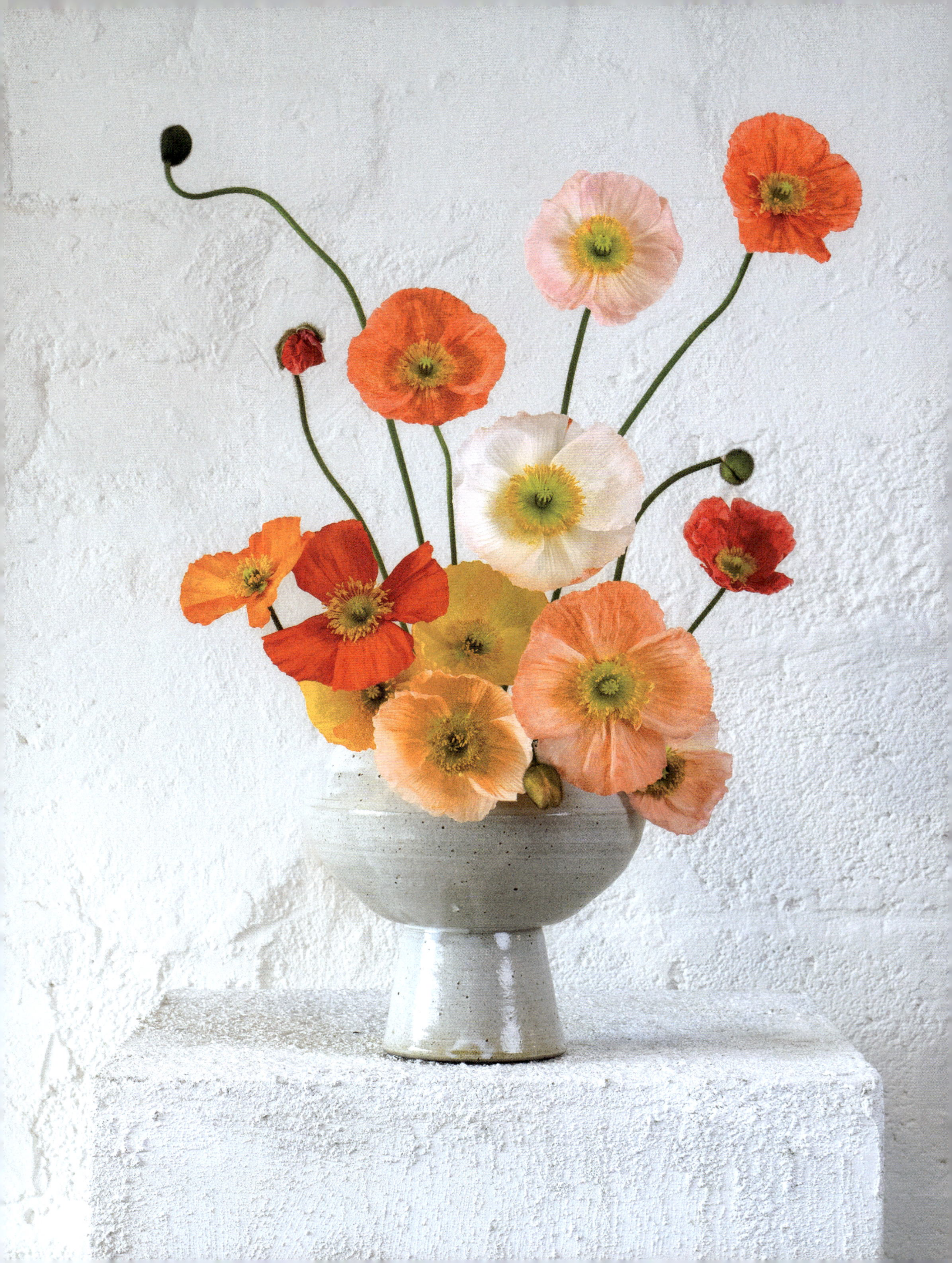

Poppy

Poppies are vibrant and showy, and their petals have a delicate and paper-like texture. Native poppies are found all over the world, but the earliest references to poppy use are from Mesapotamia, where the ancient Sumerians cultivated its use for medicinal and recreational purposes.

The arrangement features a collection of velvety, luminous Iceland poppies in warm tones. Have a play around with coloured pencils before you begin and experiment with getting more intense tones by applying pressure and getting lighter tones by using the pencils more softly. Depending on the consistency of your pencils, you may be able to layer colour over colour to blend or, using a softer touch, blend tones together lightly. Note how colour radiates from the centres of the flowers and apply your marks to achieve the same effect.

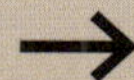

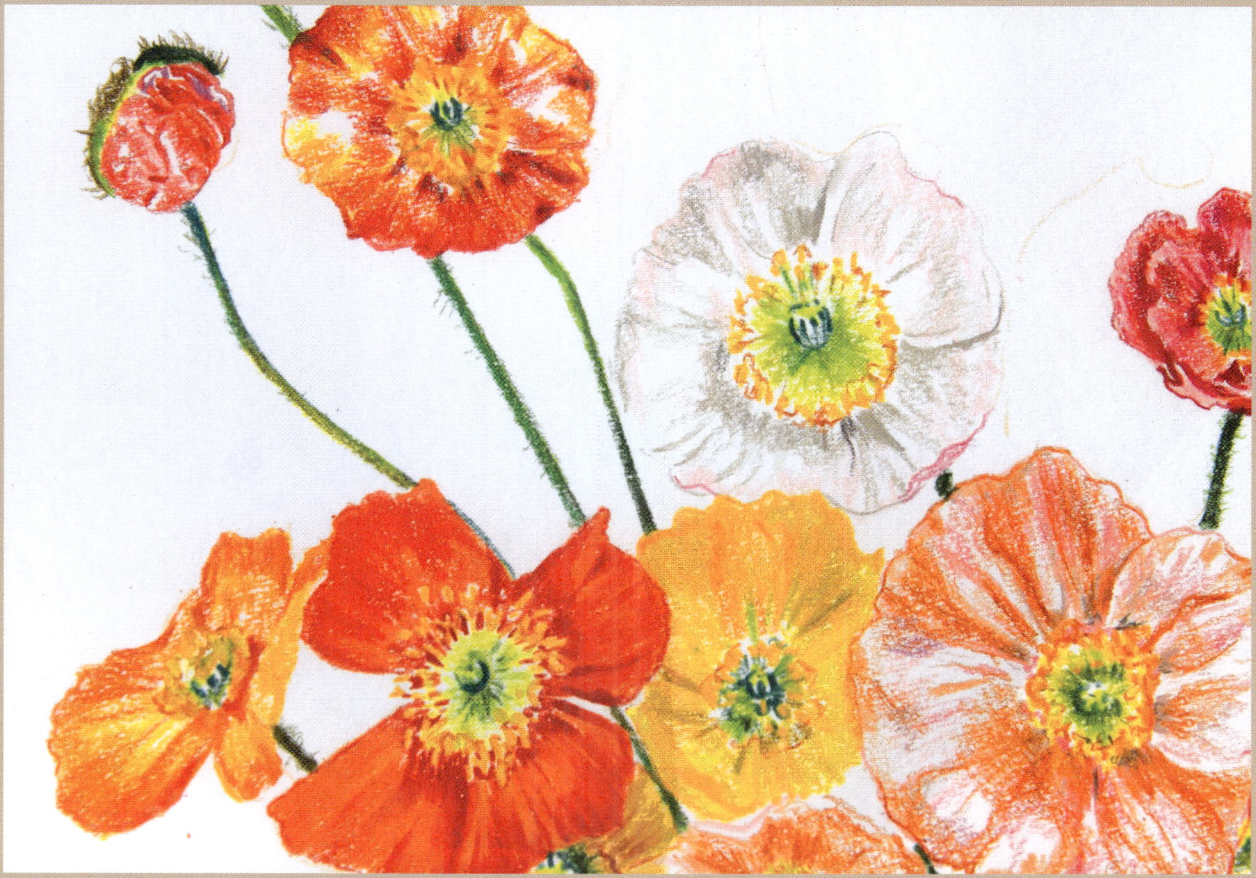

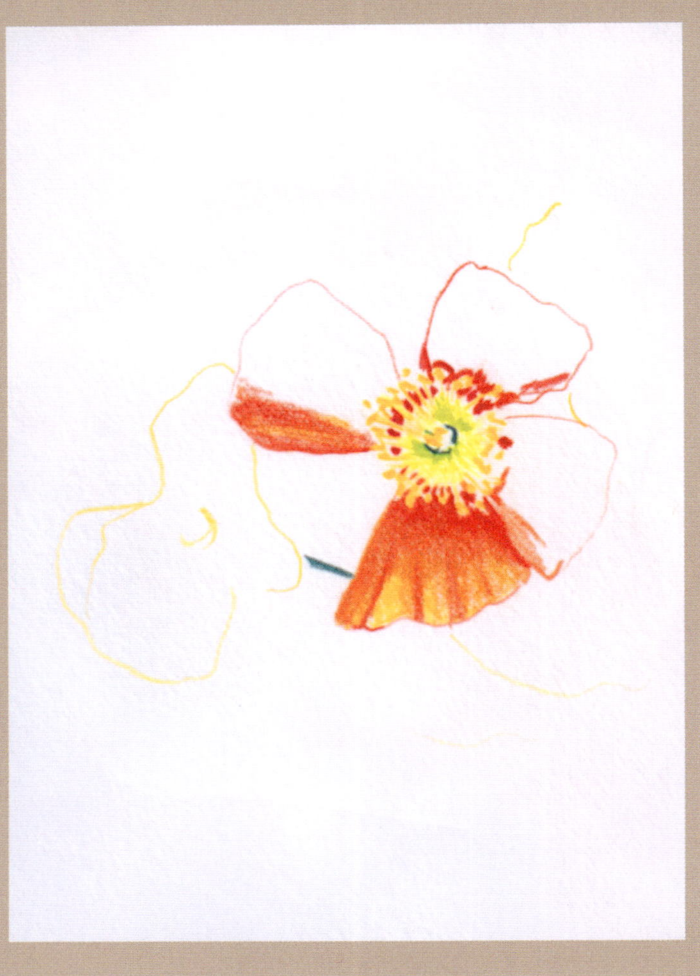
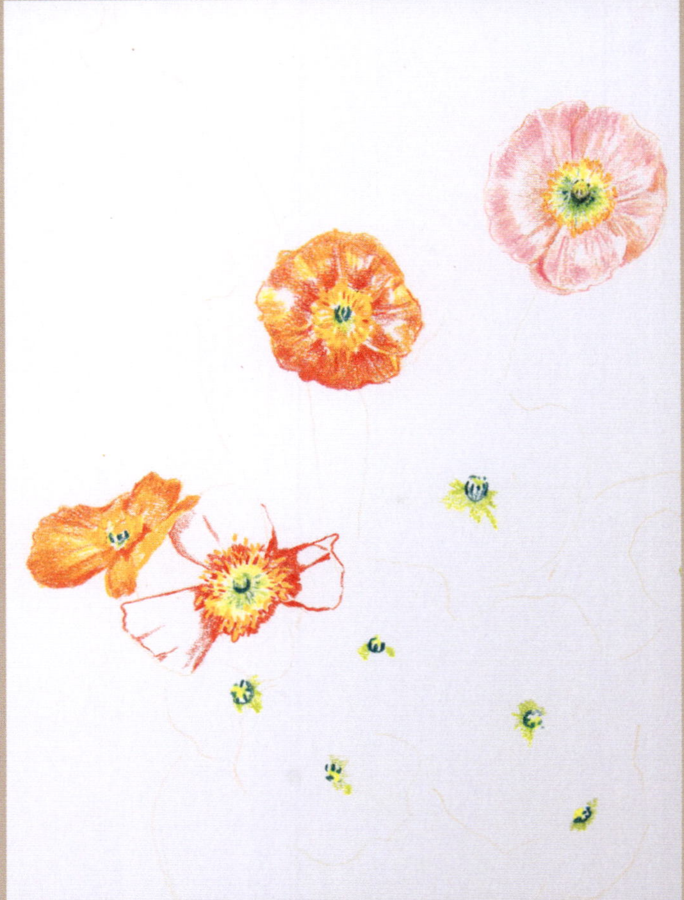
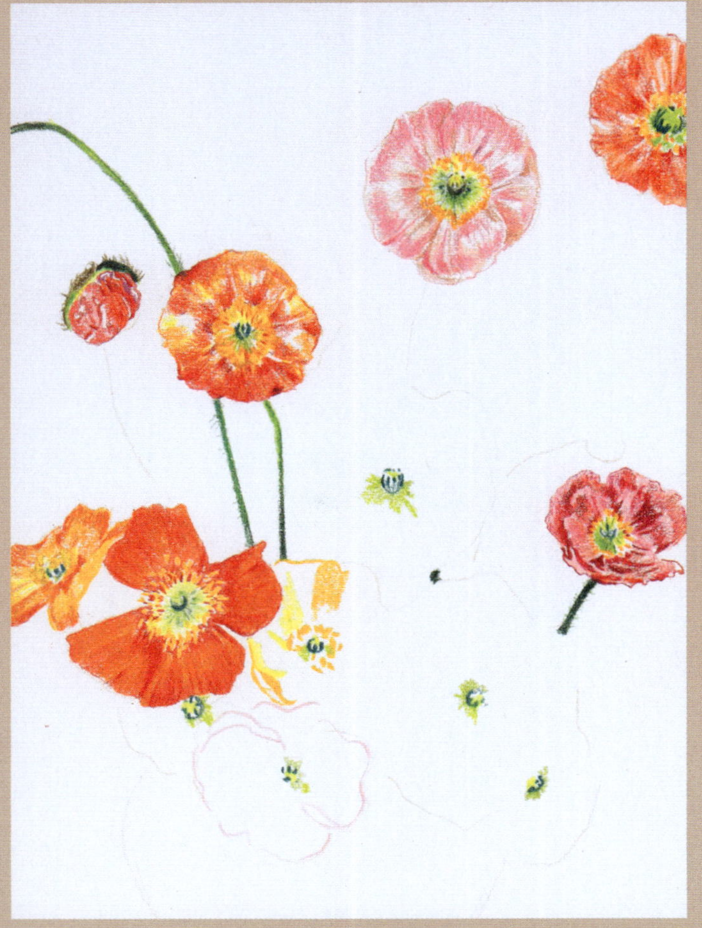
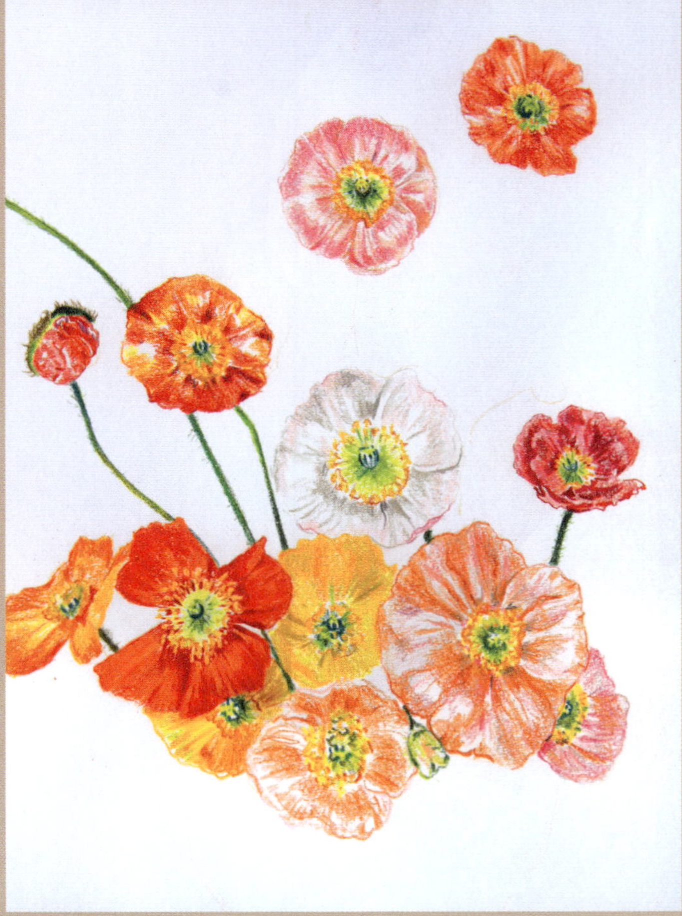

1

Use a light-toned pencil to softly draw outlines, mapping out the arrangement. Concentrate on proportions and the skills you practised in the exercises, such as drawing negative space. Look at the overall shape and form, and how the poppies' shapes interact with each other.

2

Focusing on one poppy at a time, first work on the centre of the flowerhead, which has a prominent cluster of stamens surrounding the round seed pod. Observe the intricate details on the pod and draw the base in a dark green with a yellow, star-shaped tip. Shade the stamens using green softly blending through to yellow, and then add darker orange-based yellow to represent the tips of the stamens. Softly colour the petals, leaving areas of highlights blank.

3

Observe the colour nuances and variations in the reference image and gradually build up depth by adding more pressure when shading. Observe the bowl-like shape of the poppy and note how the petals are generally darker in the centre and at the edges. Notice the subtle ruffled texture of the petals and add shading to replicate this distinct quality.

4

When you have finished all the open poppies, draw in the buds, using a fading of light to dark tone to create the idea of three-dimensional form.

5

Mark in the wobbly lines of the stems in an olive green, noting how they become darker where they meet the flowers. Add details to give the impression of the fine hairs on the stems.

6

Draw the vase, using more pressure on the right-hand side to indicate its form. Use various greys to fill the body of the vase loosely, observing the areas of shadow, and for an indication of the shadow of the vase on the table.

●

MATERIALS

Smooth watercolour paper, A3

Coloured pencils

Eraser

TIPS

Use an eraser to lighten any areas of highlights in the vase and petals.

This project takes time, so give yourself breaks throughout.

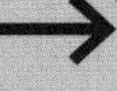

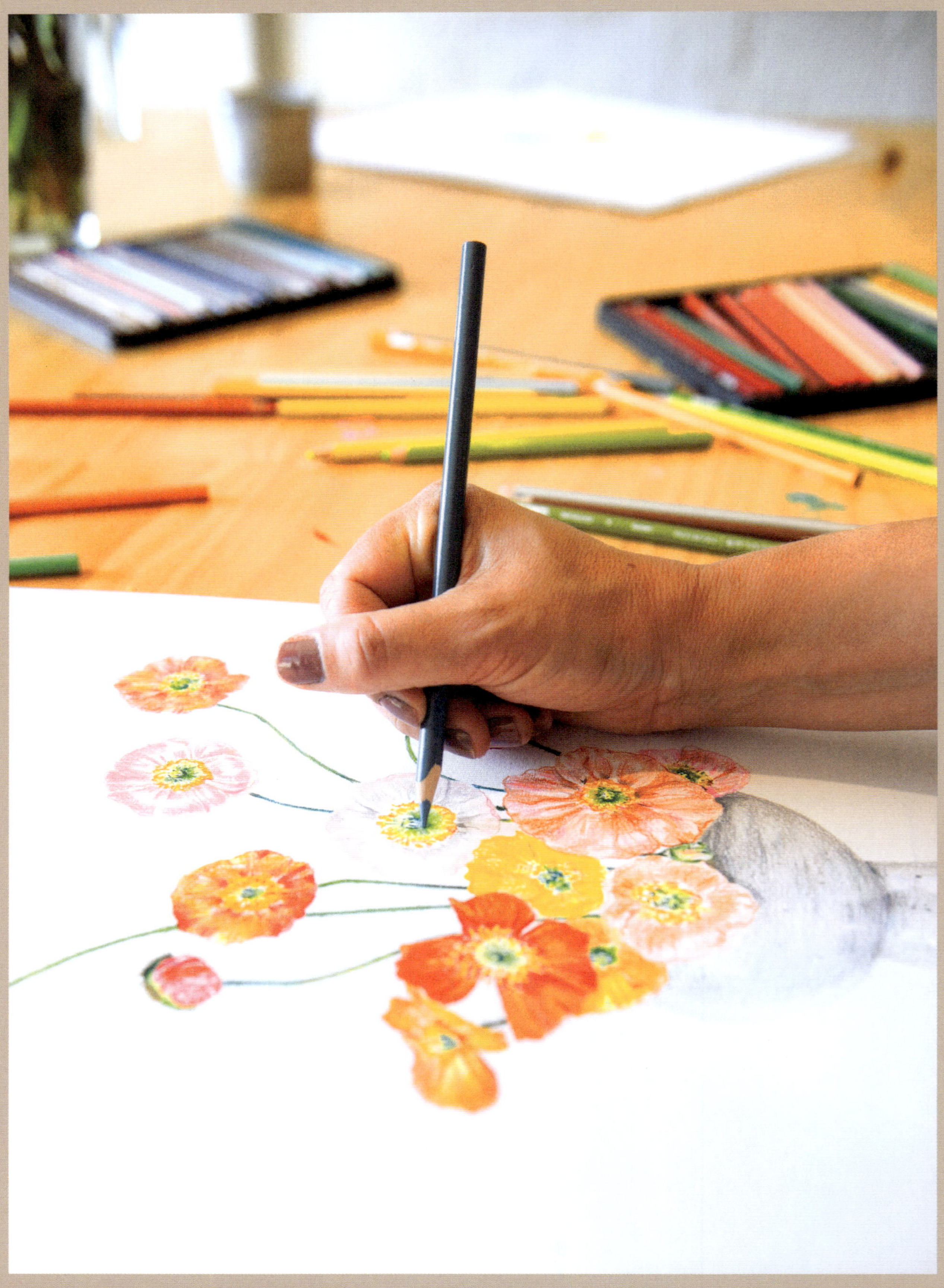

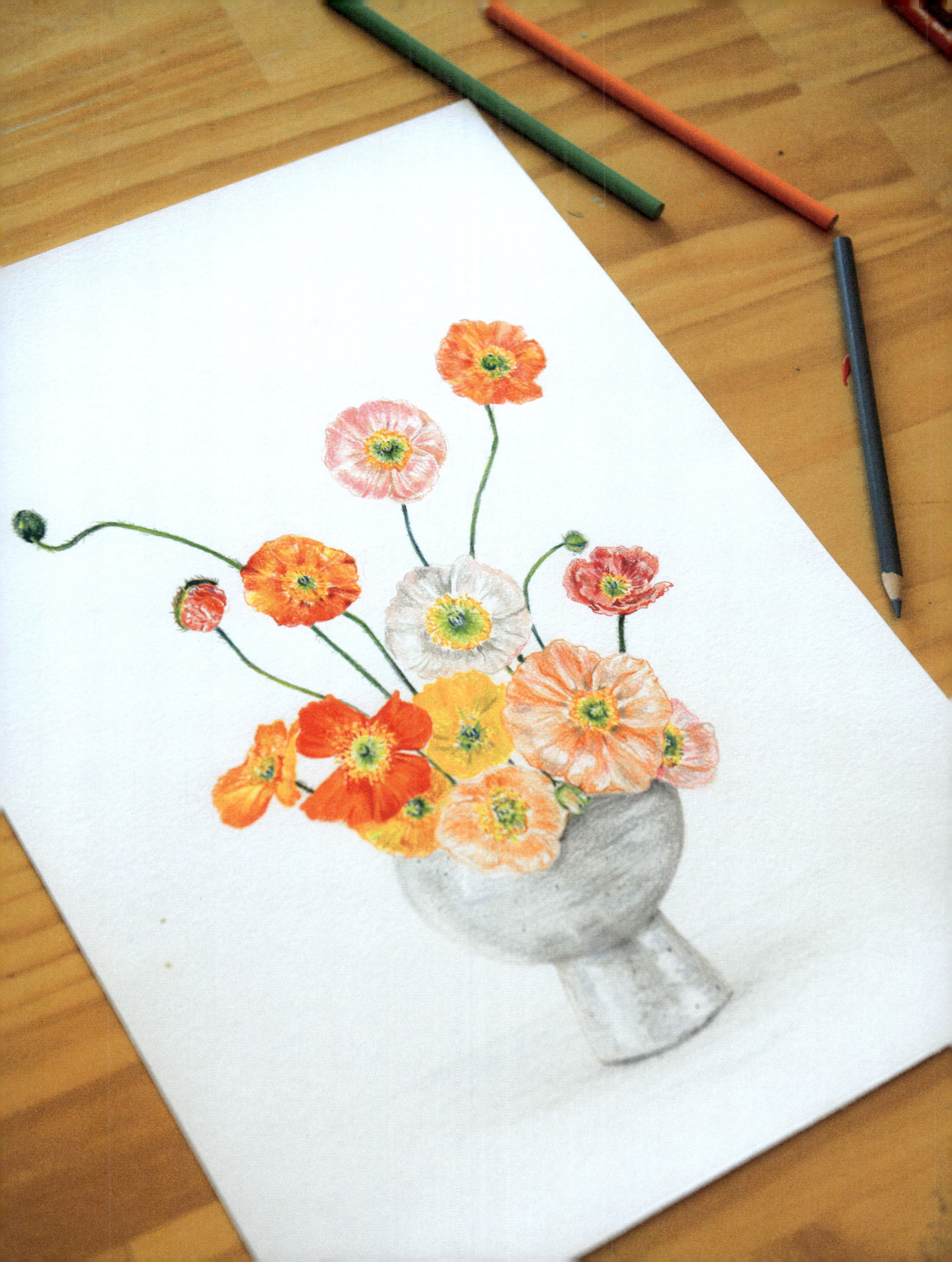

Anthurium

The anthurium, also called the flamingo flower, is bold and sculptural in form. Its leaves and stem are said to represent the arrows of Cupid, the Roman god of desire, love and attraction. Over time, the waxy, tropical bloom has been a popular subject for artists. It was a favourite of photographers Guy Bourdin and Robert Mapplethorpe, and the modernist artist Georgia O'Keeffe painted oversized anthuriums, transforming them into powerful symbols of femininity and nature.

MATERIALS

Smooth or medium paper, A3
Coloured pencils
Sharpener

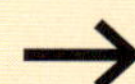

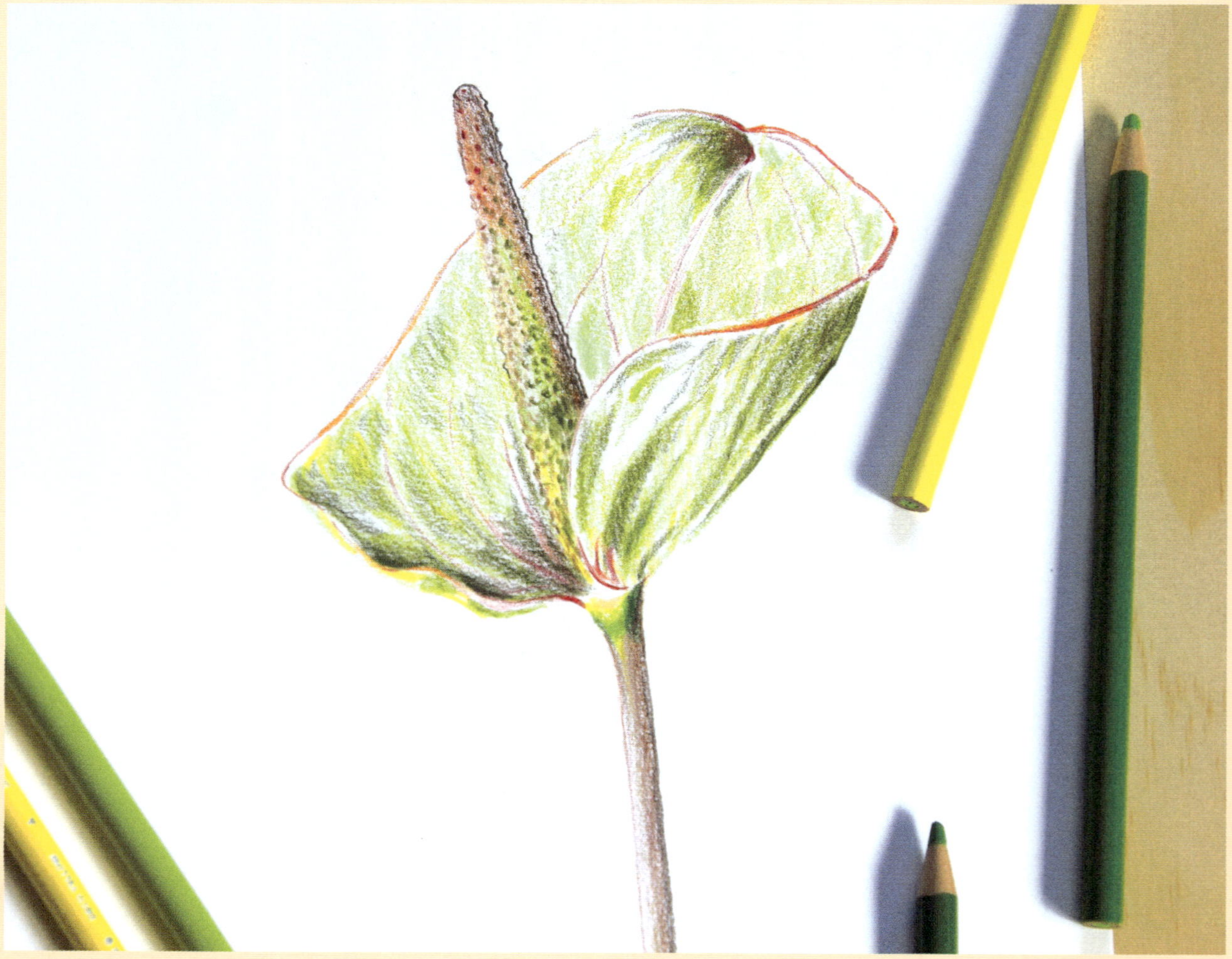

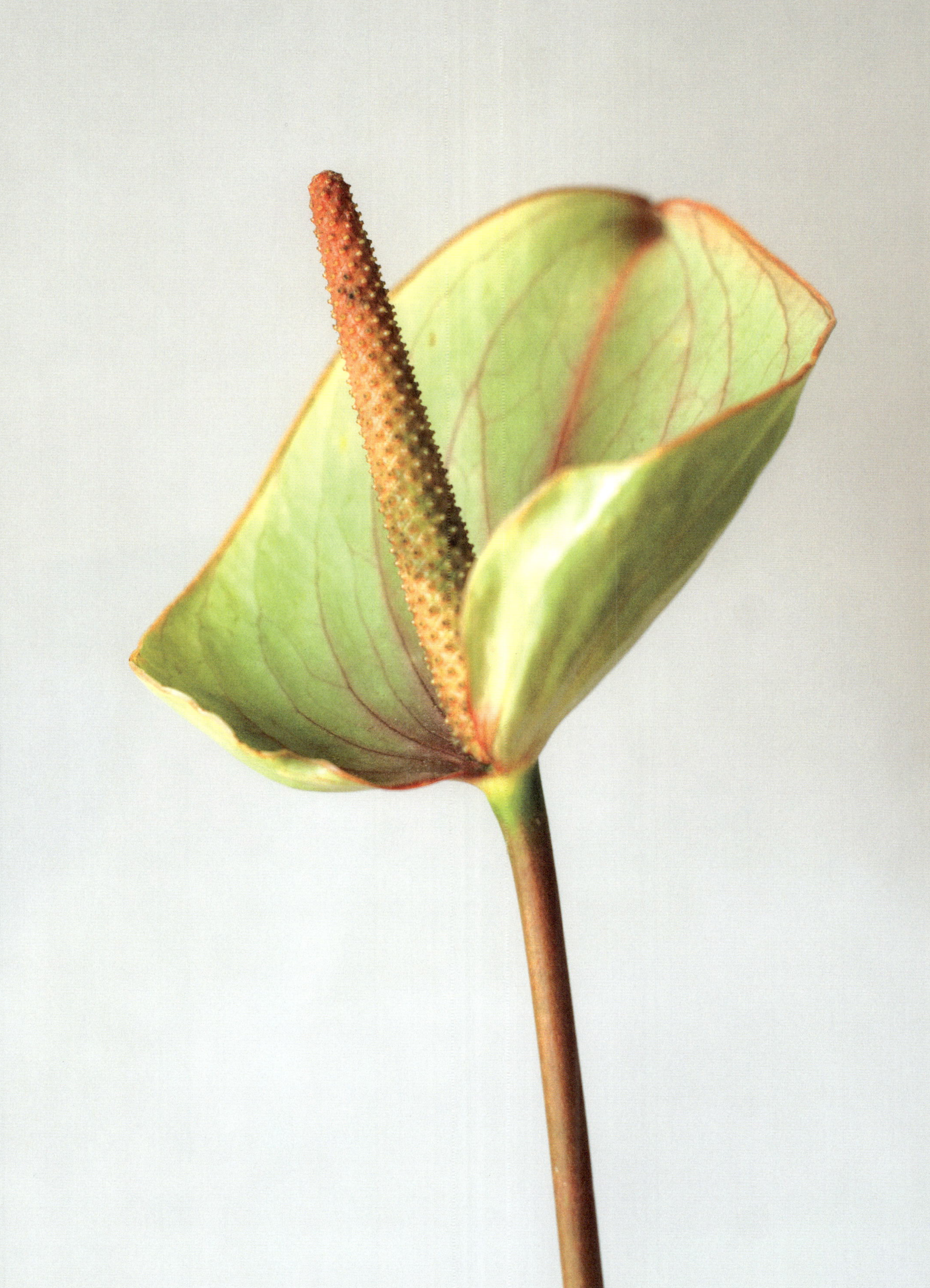

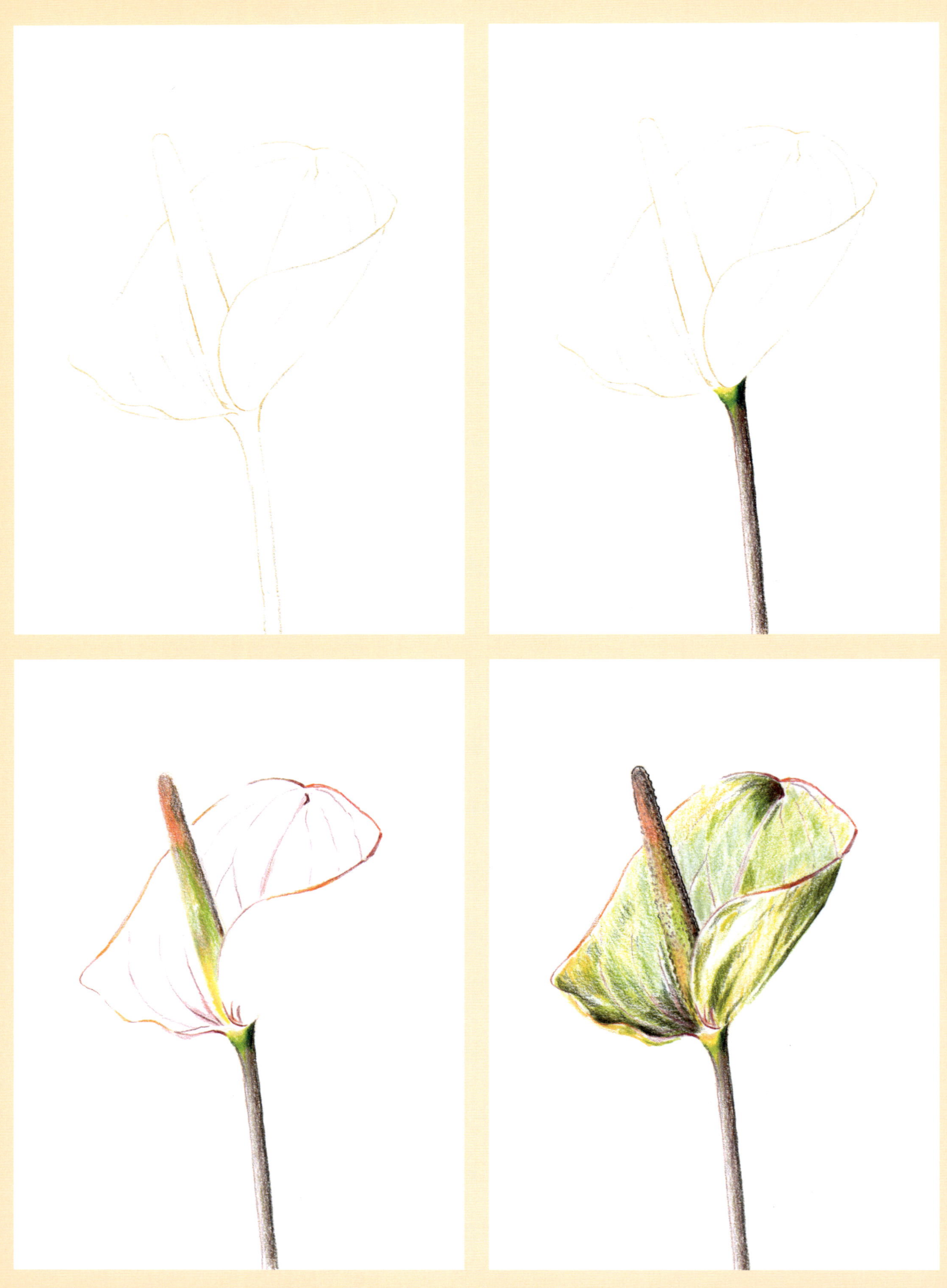

1

Map out the overall shape very softly in a light-shaded pencil. Note where the spathe curls over itself at the edges and point.

2

Build up colour in the stem, taking note of the green at the top, which blends into a sienna colour. Use a dark-brown pencil to shade the right-hand side and the very edge of the left-hand side of the stem.

3

Darken the outline of the spathe and draw its vein-like lines. Notice how the colour changes from burgundy to orange and then to sienna, grading from dark to light.

4

Shade the spadix, creating a gradient in tones ranging from pale lemon to green, coral and then brown.

5

Use a darker colour to mark in the miniature pebble-like flowers that make up the spadix. With a sharp, dark-brown pencil, create ridges along the right-hand edge of the spadix.

6

Observe the regions of light and dark within the spathe. Using light, medium and darker yellow-based greens, build up the green of the spathe, leaving empty areas for highlights.

7

Add some sharp outlines to bring more definition to the shape.

●

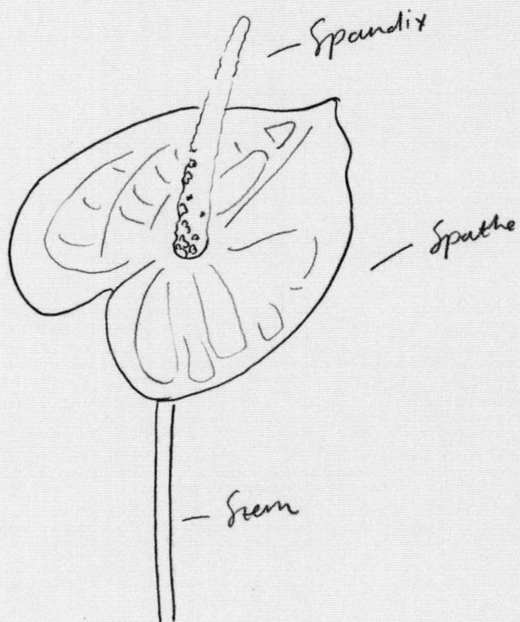

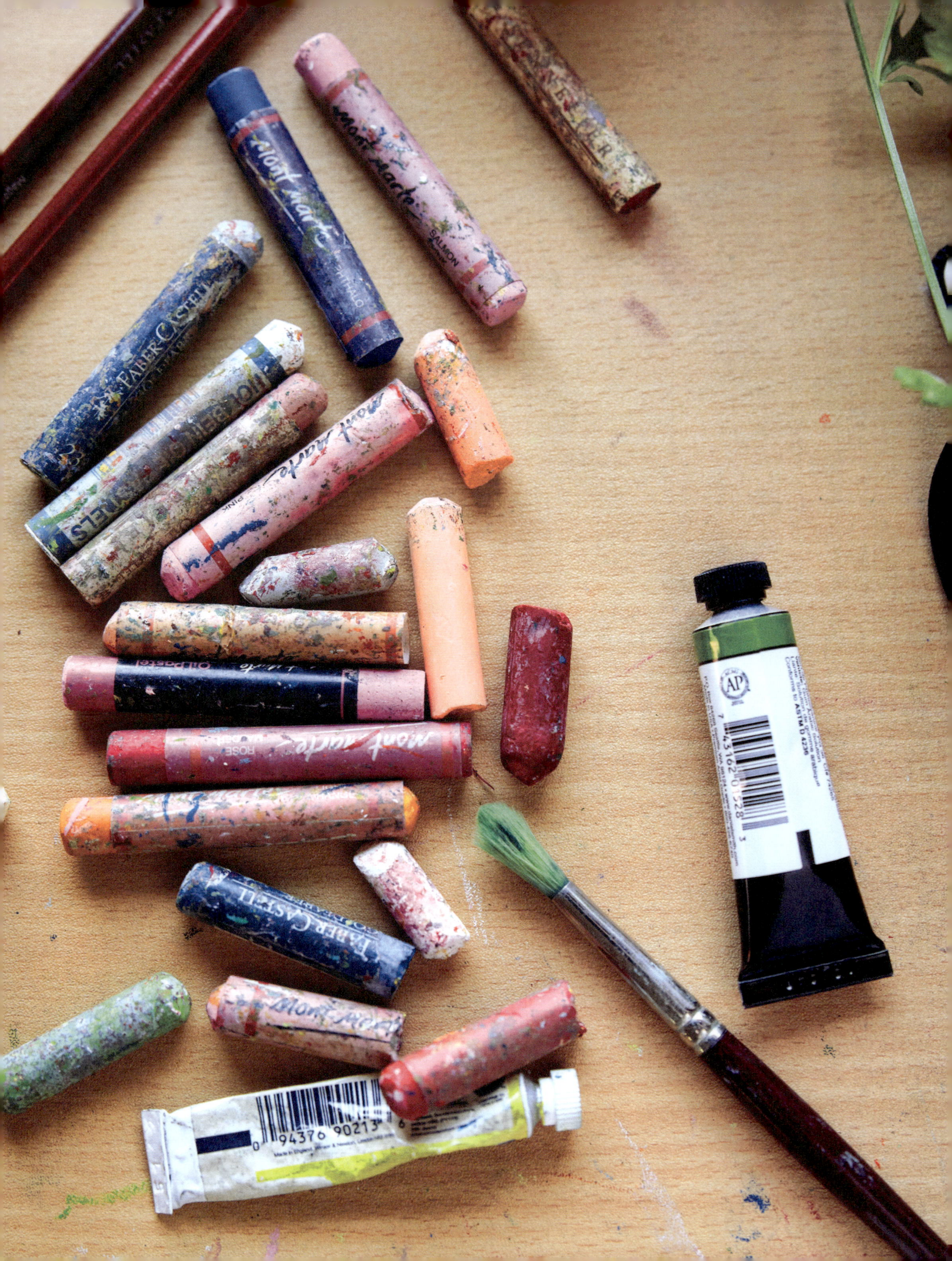

Pastel

Soft and oil pastels are rich, textural, bold mediums made from powdered pigments mixed with a binder. When I started experimenting with oil pastels, I quickly fell in love. Using them falls somewhere between drawing and painting. They have a beautiful immediacy: there's no need for brushes or palette, and they can be built up and layered like paint but without the drying times. They are more controllable than paint and brush.

Oil pastels are buttery, malleable and easy to manipulate, so tones can be easily created by mixing colours and overlaying shades on the page. They layer so effectively that it doesn't matter whether you work light to dark or dark to light. For each colour, I generally start with a midtone, which I overlay with darker tones for shadows and lighter tones for highlights. Pastels are also very forgiving, so if you're not happy with a colour or shape, you can keep working to amend it. With oil pastels, softer is best, as harder types don't blend as well.

Soft pastels also allow for multiple effects, ranging from delicate, subtle shading and blending to more bold, intense marks. Like oil pastels, they are velvety, but they have a softer, more chalk-like consistency.

Pastel pencils are another option for experimentation. They give the soft look of pastel but allow more control. And unlike regular pastels, they can be sharpened to fine tips. Use a craft knife to sharpen them, though, rather than a pencil sharpener, which can crack the pastel.

Each brand of soft and oil pastels has its own capabilities and ways of layering and blending. If you can, it's worth trying out a few brands to explore the available options.

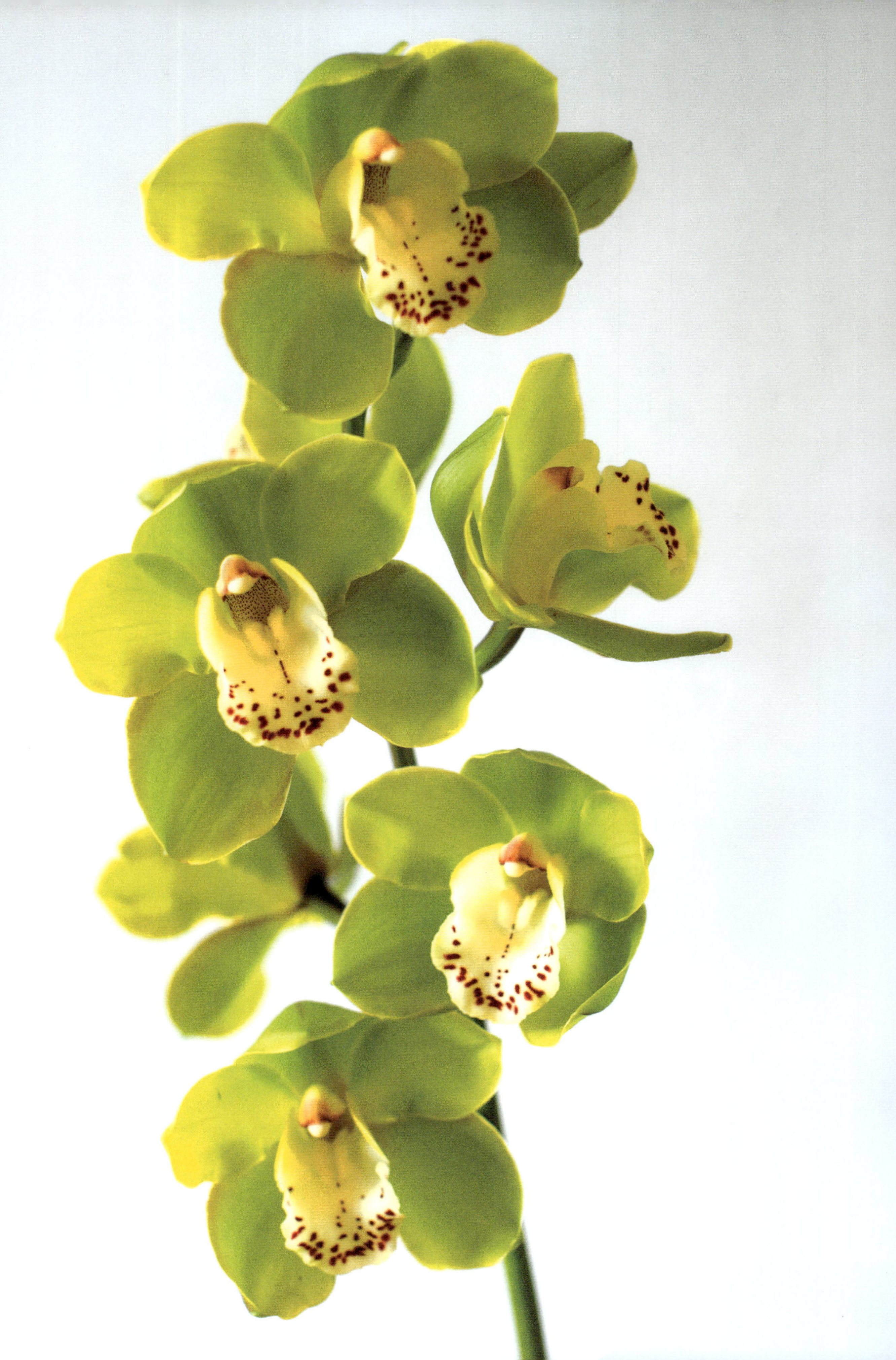

Orchid

In the 19th century, the orchid was so sought after in Europe that plant hunters were sent off to search the world for rare species. The ventures were often arduous and took the hunters through the jungles of Africa, hills of China and swamps of South America.

For this project you will be drawing the green cymbidium orchid on white watercolour paper. Using the skill practised in the exercise on page 49, look at the negative space in the image to help with mapping out the positions of the flowers. Also, notice their shapes and angles as you are viewing them.

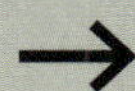

MATERIALS

Any type of watercolour paper, A3

Oil pastels

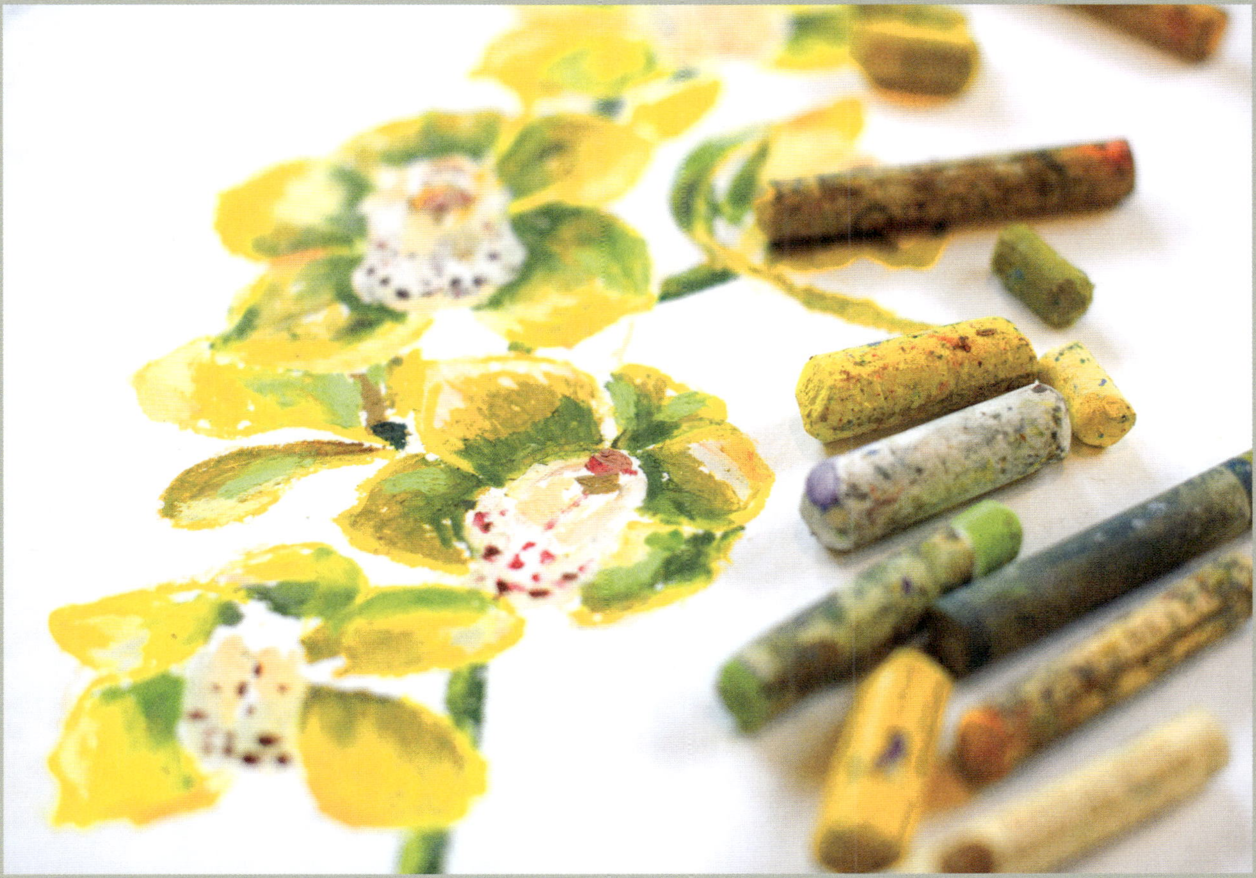

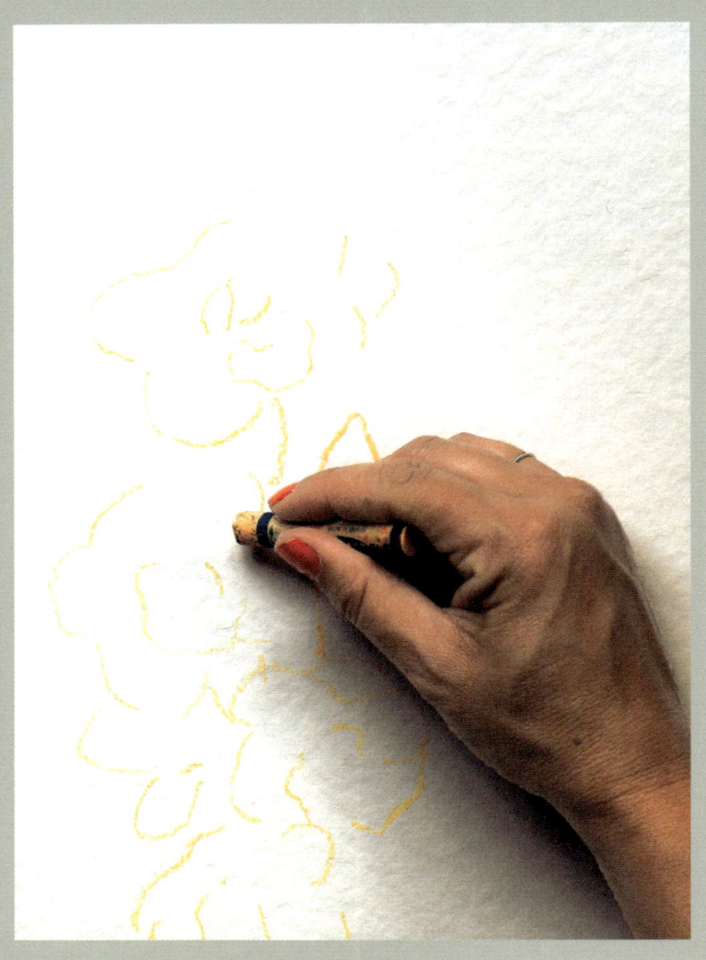
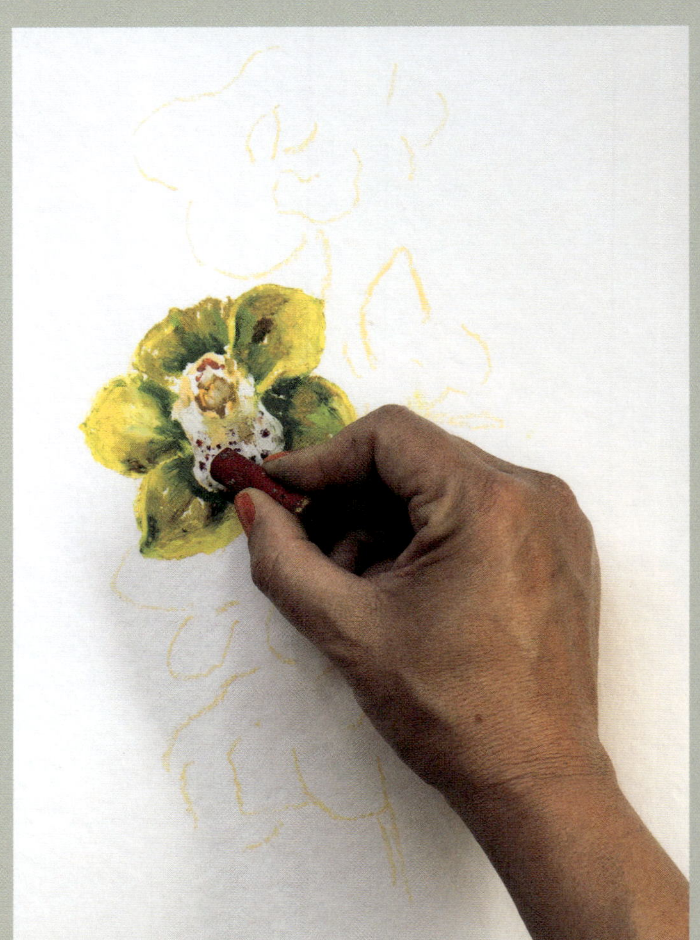
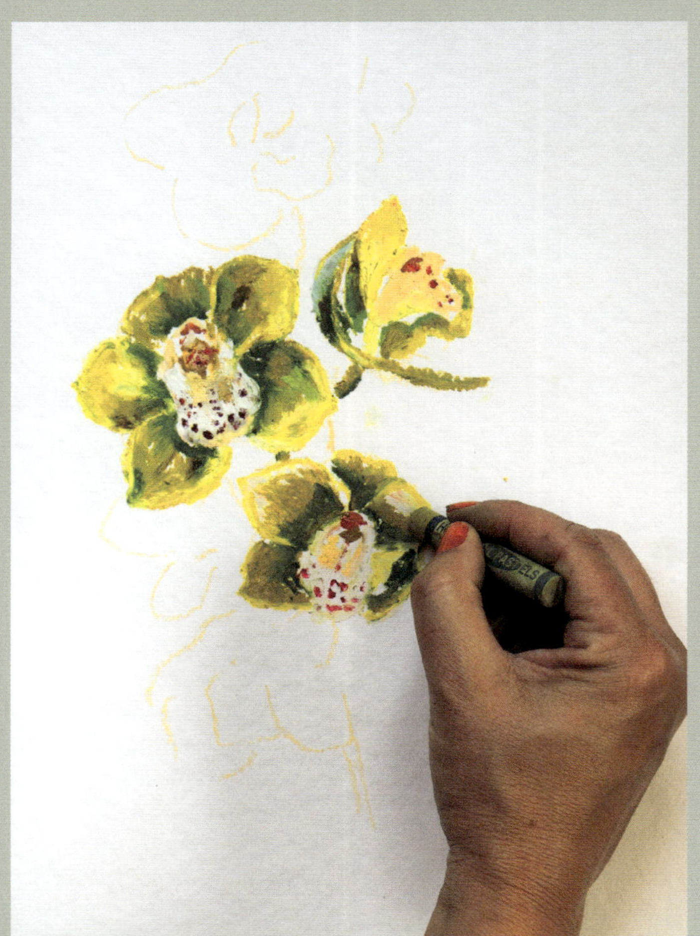
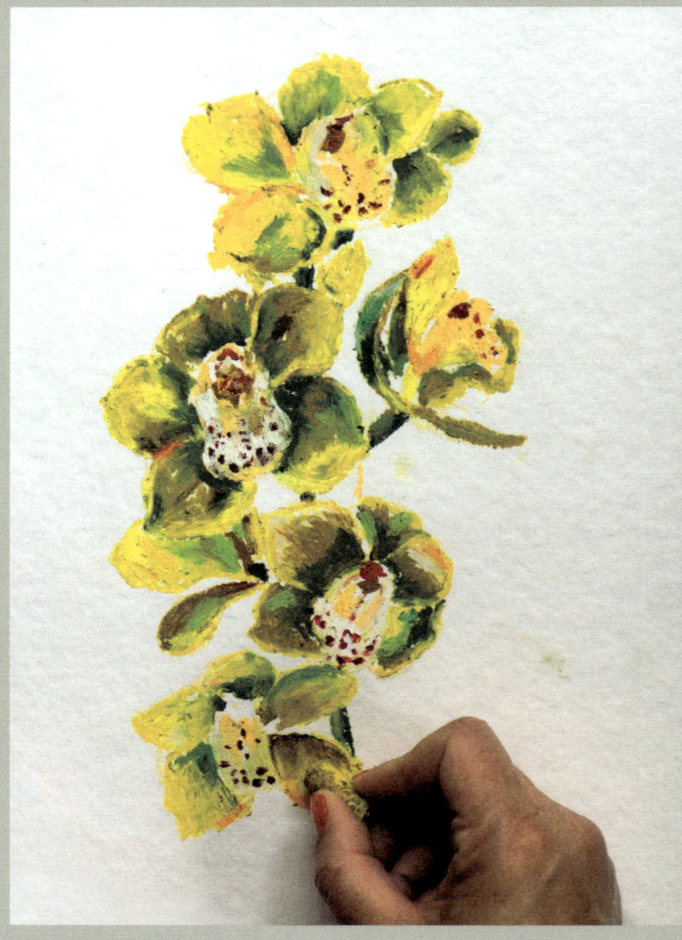

1

Loosely mark out the orchid flowers in a pale colour.

2

Focus on one orchid at a time. First, work on the flower's throat, lip and column in a cream-white tone. For the petals and sepals, blend the pastels to create light and dark areas. Use a darker tone to enhance shaded areas and a lighter tone to brighten highlights. Add the cluster of red patterned dots on the lip.

3

Draw the stem in a dark green, then use a light green to highlight the left-hand side. This represents where the light would naturally reflect and helps capture the rounded form of the stem.

●

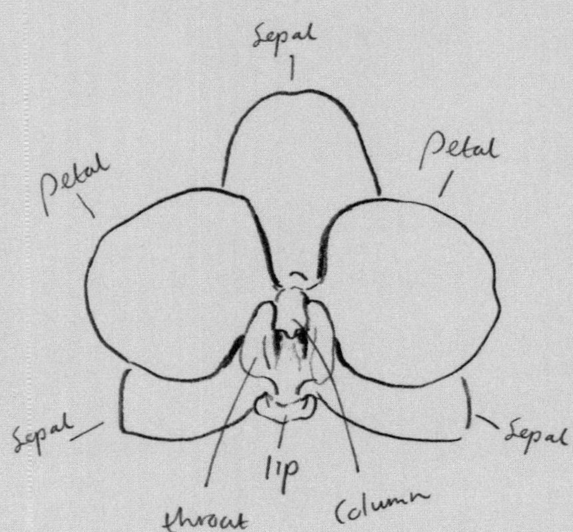

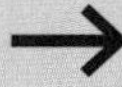

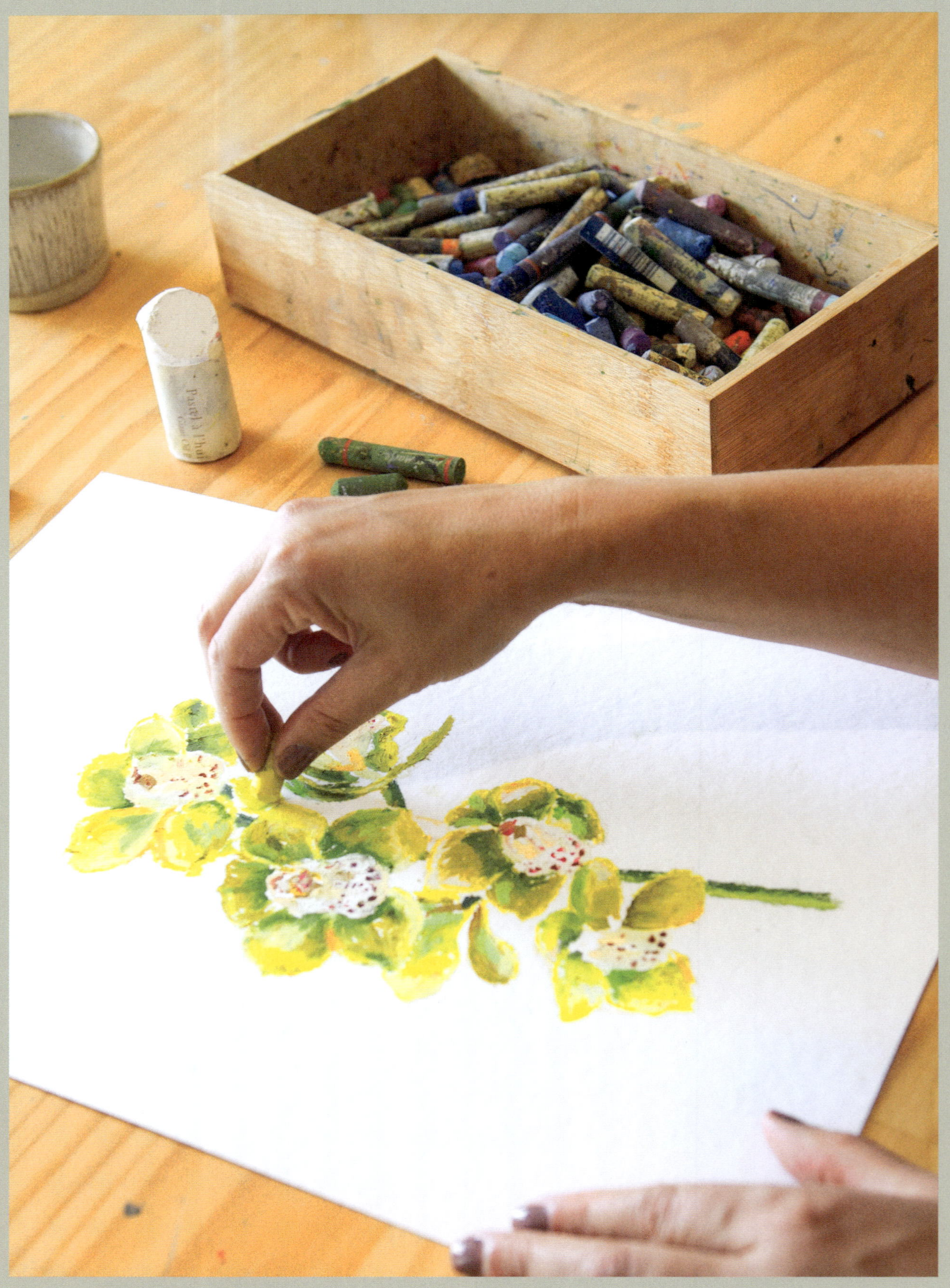

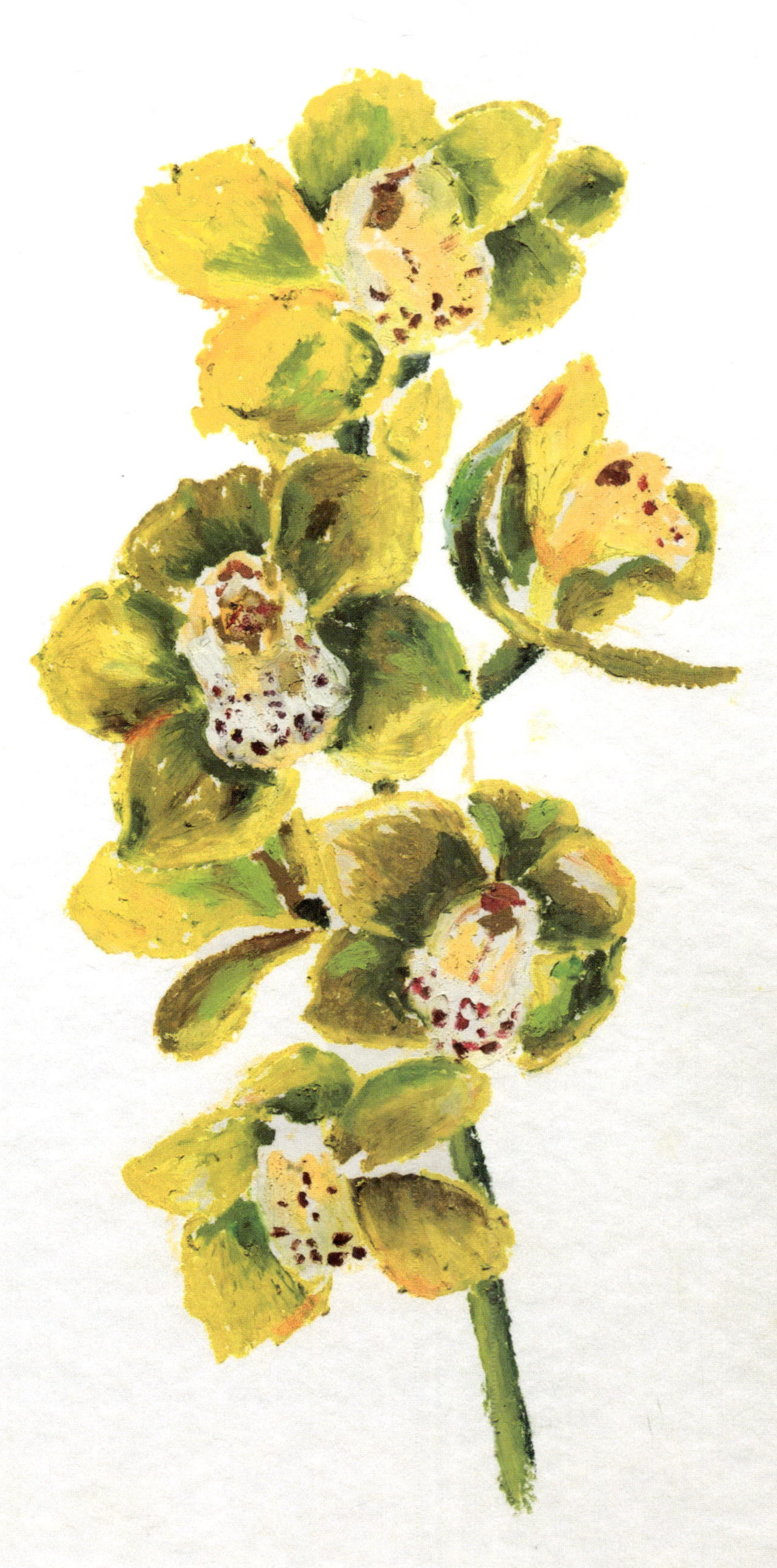

Moth orchid, iris, poppy and delphinium

This arrangement includes a heady mix of botanical delights. My favourite among them is the moth orchid, otherwise known as *Phalaenopsis*. It is believed that the common name moth orchids was originally bestowed by Swedish naturalist Pehr Osbeck in the mid-1750s. When he first sighted the rare blooms, he mistook them for a cluster of moths.

This is a bountiful, abundant arrangement, so take your time and appreciate the process. Kraft paper works beautifully with oil pastels. It's smooth, so the pastels sit on top of the surface and contrast against the light sheen of the paper. Once you have completed the layout, enjoy the buttery application of layering and blending the pastels.

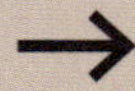

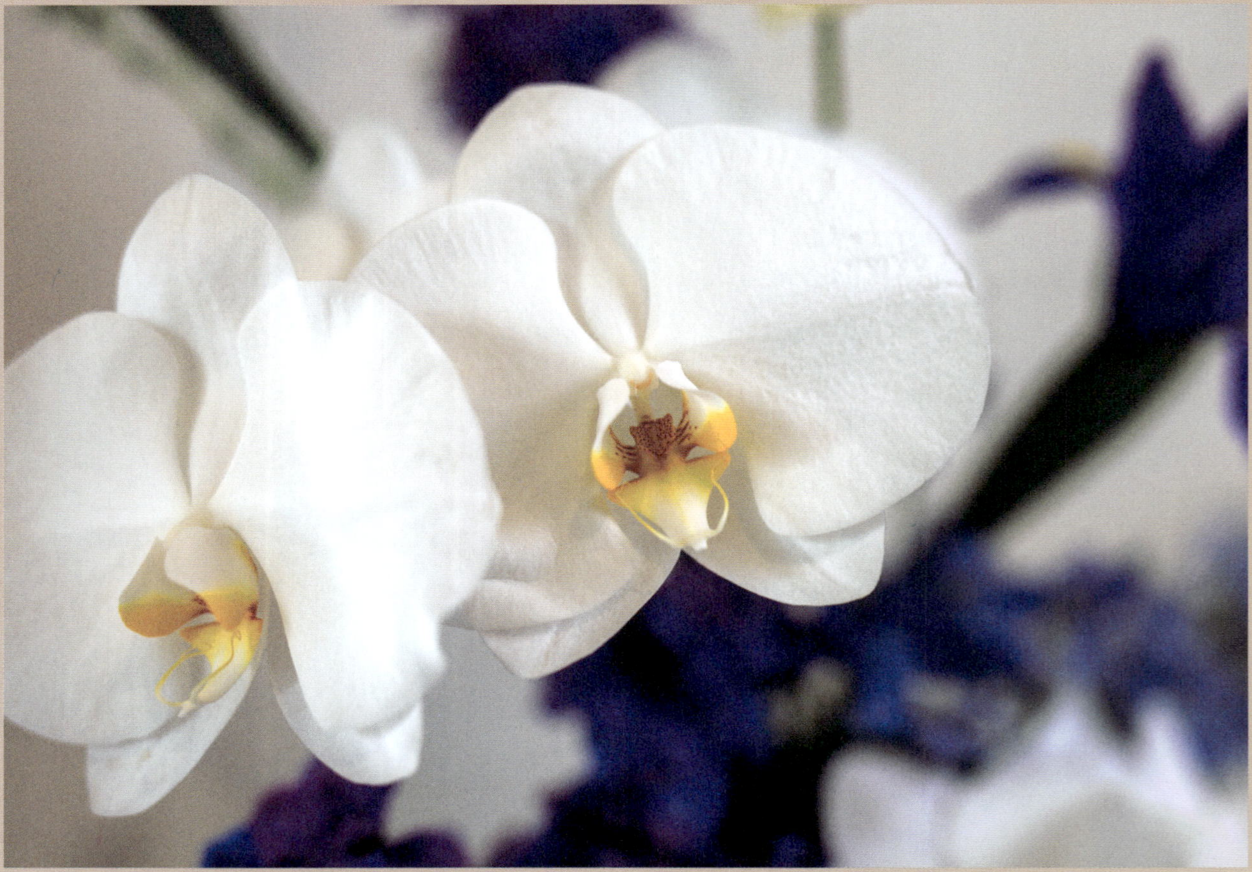

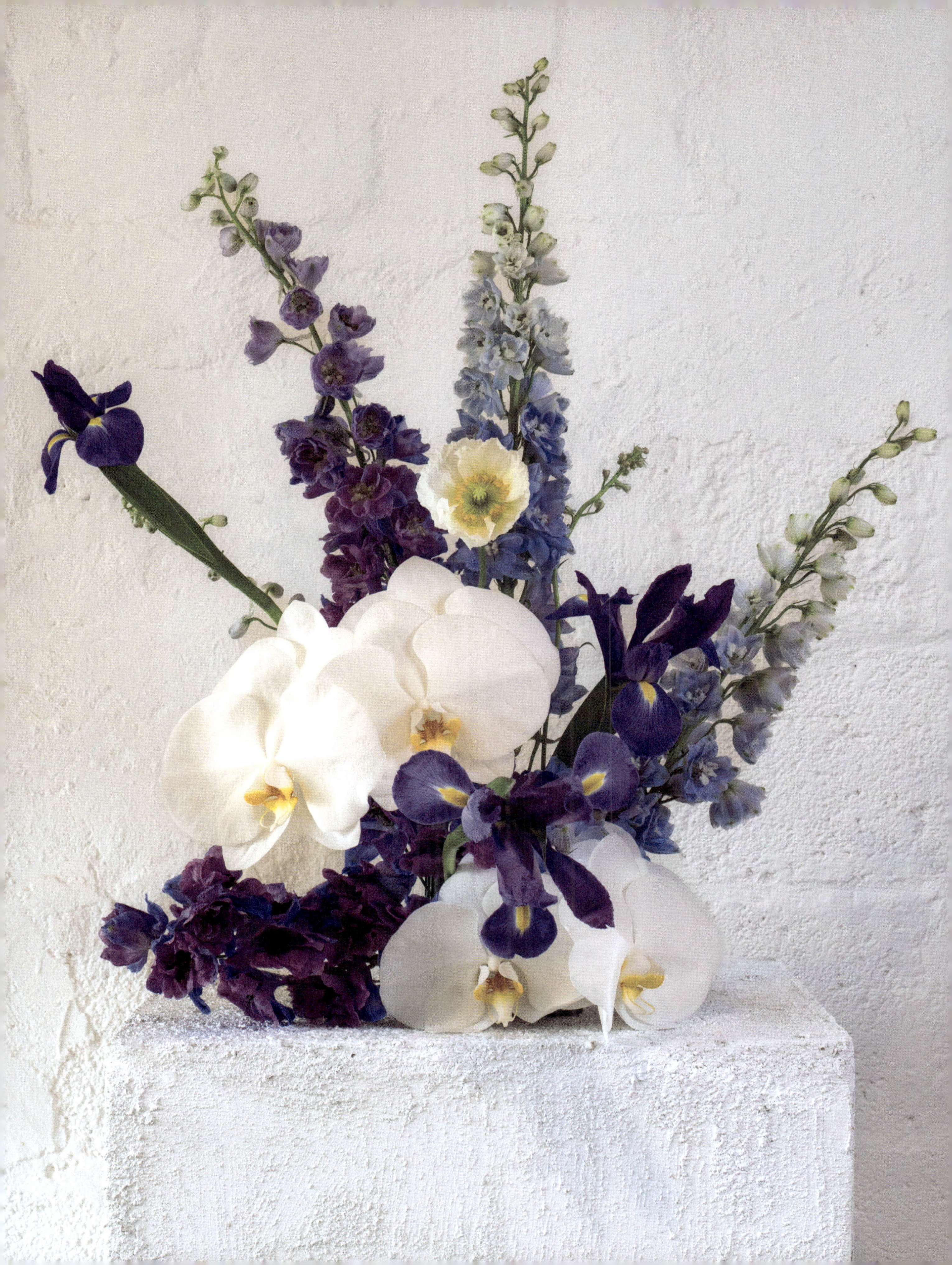

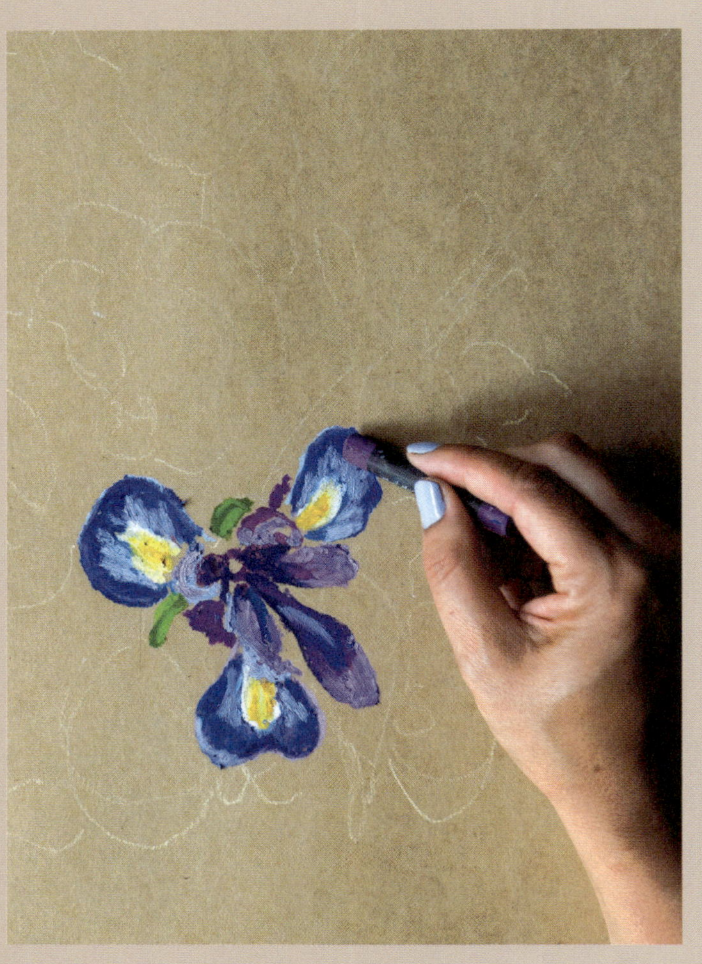
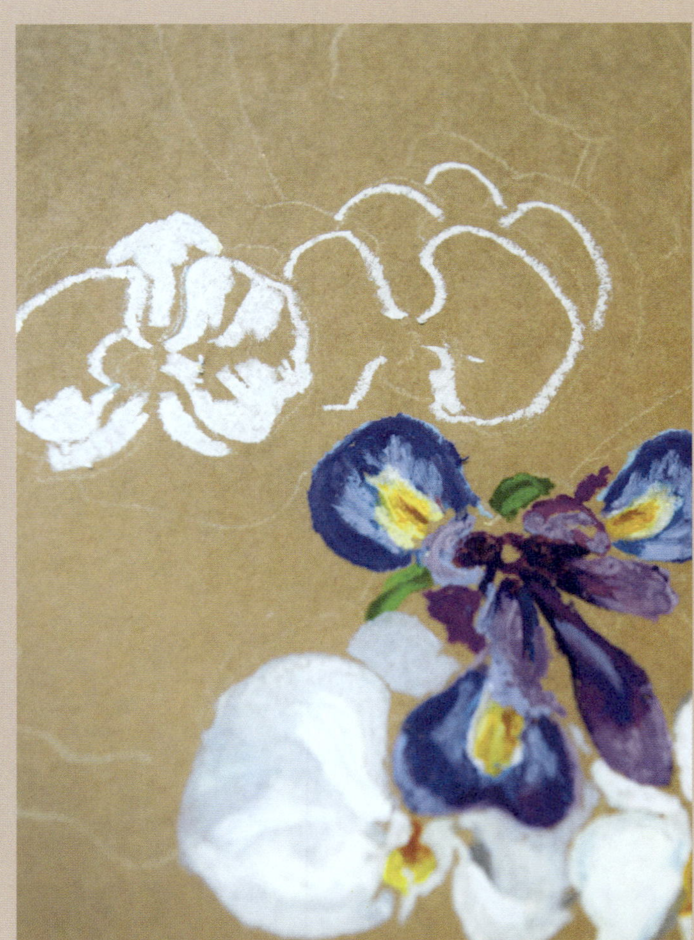
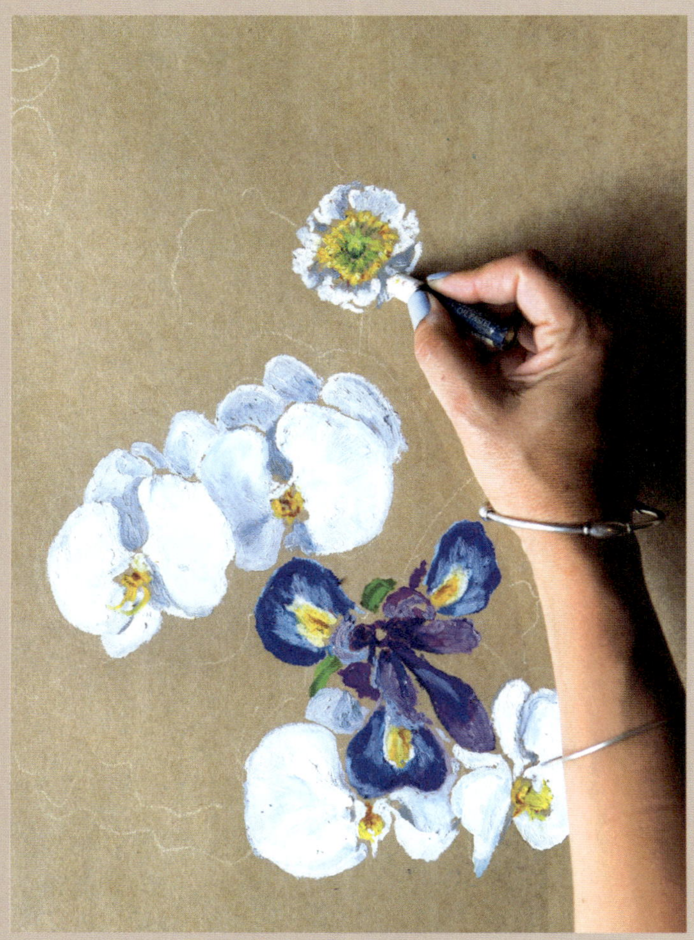
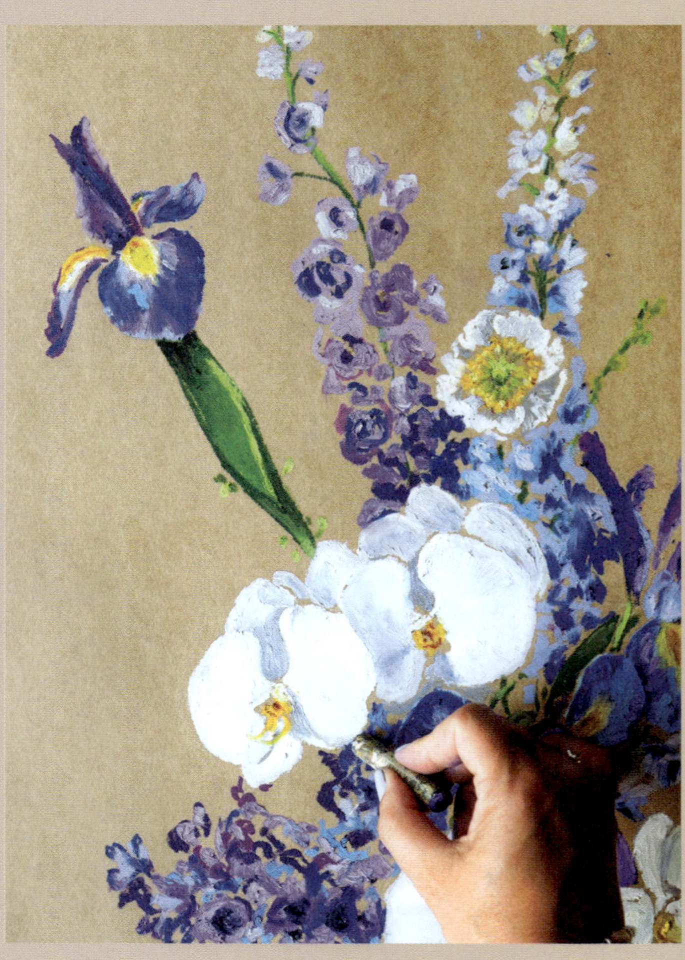

1

Use a medium-toned colour, such as peach, to lightly map out the placement of the arrangement.

2

Begin with the front-facing iris in the bottom-right corner. Closely look at its shapes and colours and draw what you see. Notice how the sepals, style arms and standards are a darker, more intense colour than the petals: use a stronger pressure on the pastels when building up these. Draw the signals, noticing how they fade out to white before blending into the purple tones.

3

Move on to the moth orchids and the Iceland poppy. Use white and shades of grey to represent the layering of the orchid petals and sepals and the cupped shape of the poppy. Shadows in grey will help define the shape of each petal. Blend the pastels depicting the orchid petals with your finger to get a smooth appearance. Use an orange yellow to give an indication of the orchids' throats, columns and lips. Look closely at the centre of the poppy and the colours within the seed pod and stamens.

4

Draw the remaining two iris flowers, observing the shapes made by their various elements. Blend the iris stems using varying shades of green. Add the delphinium petals popping out behind the longer iris.

5

Work on the delphiniums. Notice how the higher the flowers are positioned on the stem, the lighter they become. Use a blend of purple, indigo, lilac and pale blue to represent the flowers abstractly, as flowing and organic shapes. Draw in the buds at the top with white and a hint of green.

MATERIALS

Kraft paper, A2
Oil pastels

TIP

Take care to look at proportions when beginning this project, noting the sizes of the flowers and the relationships between the shapes.

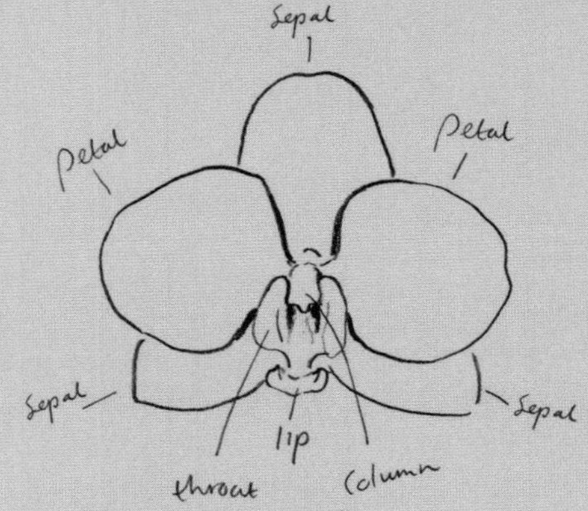

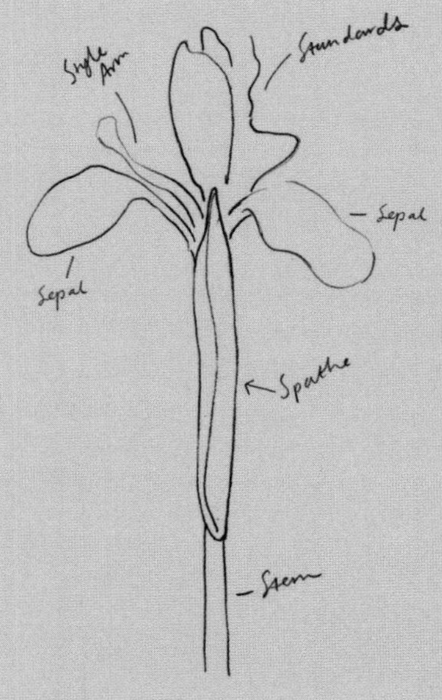

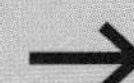

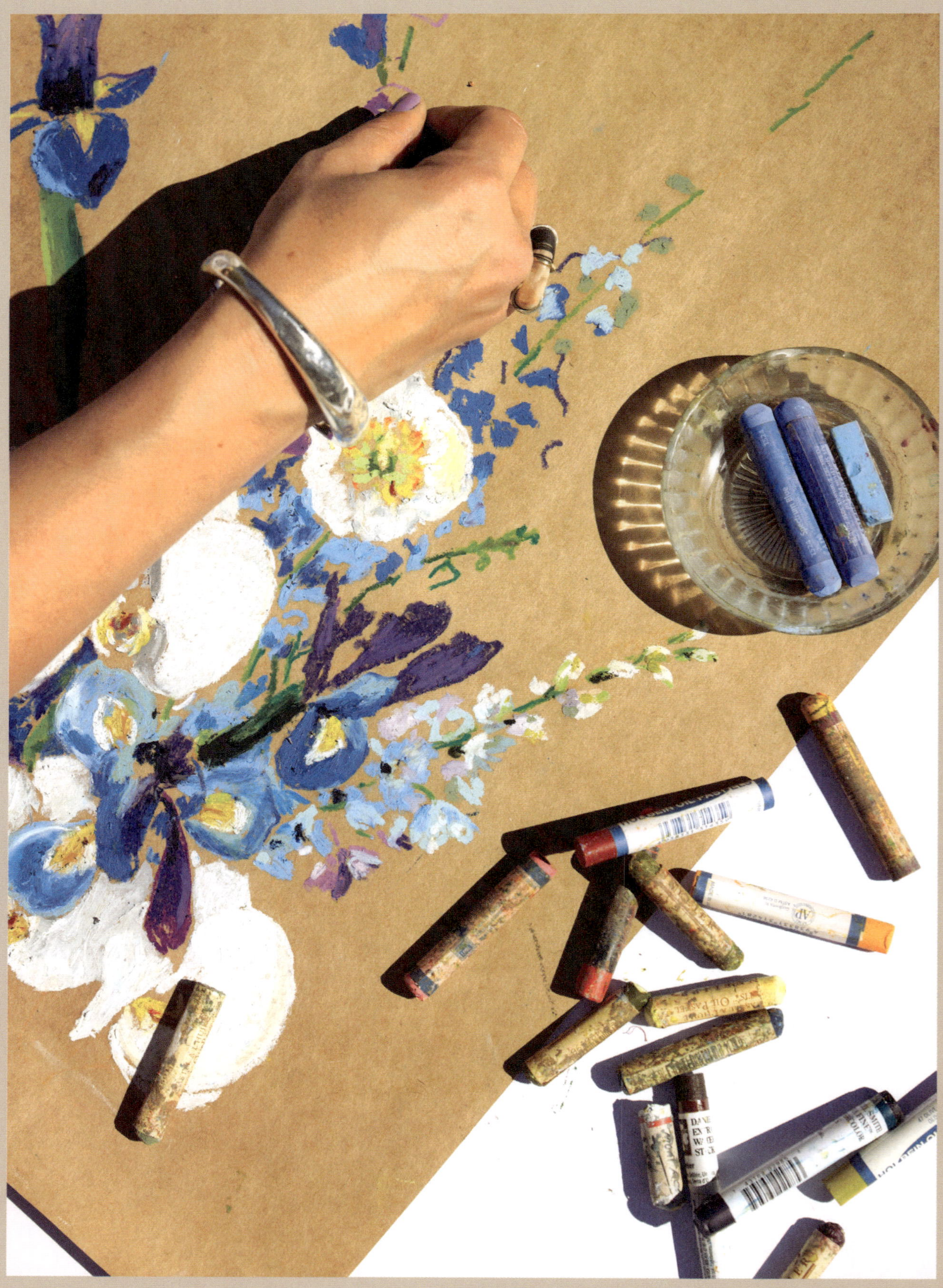

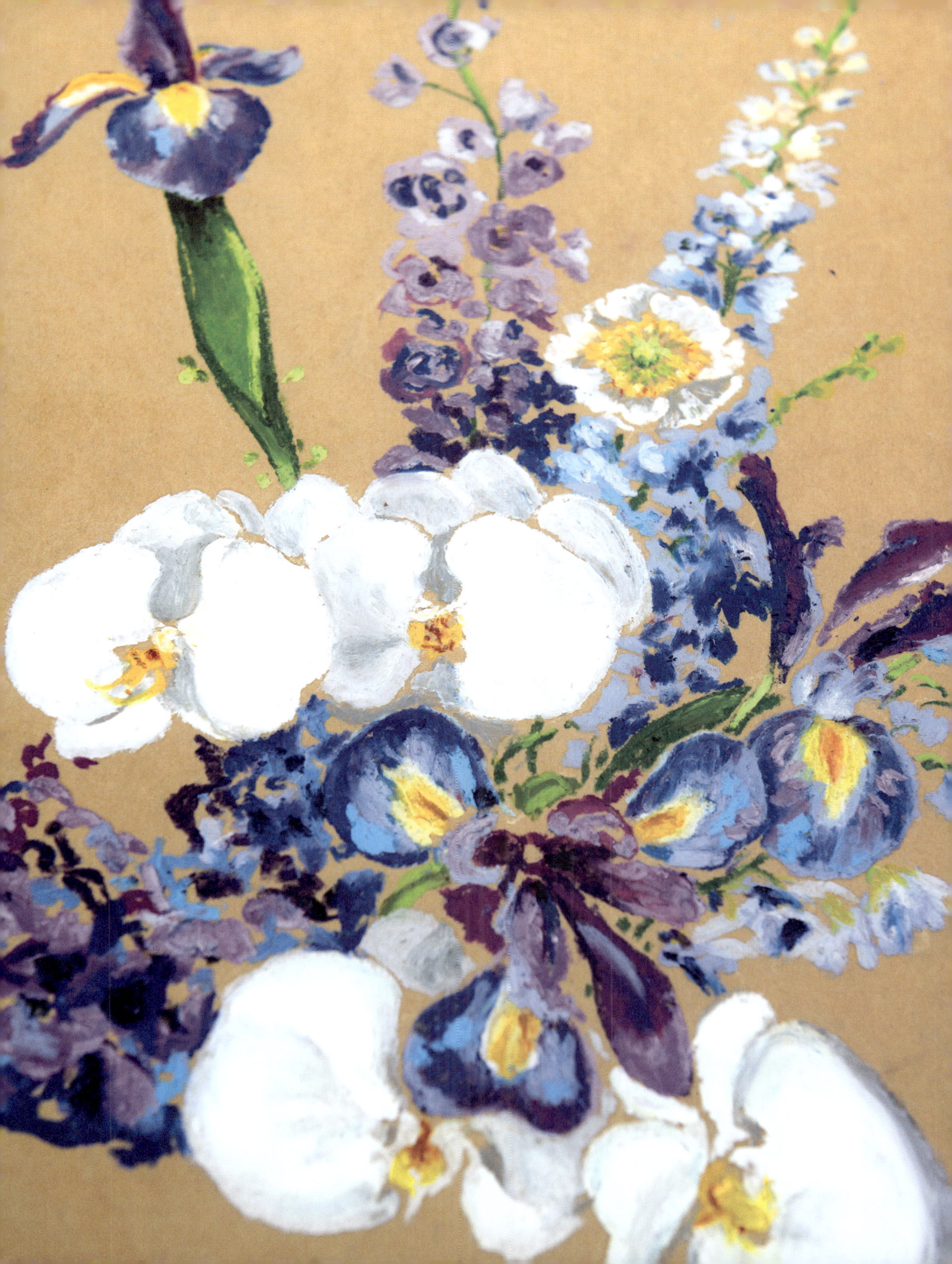

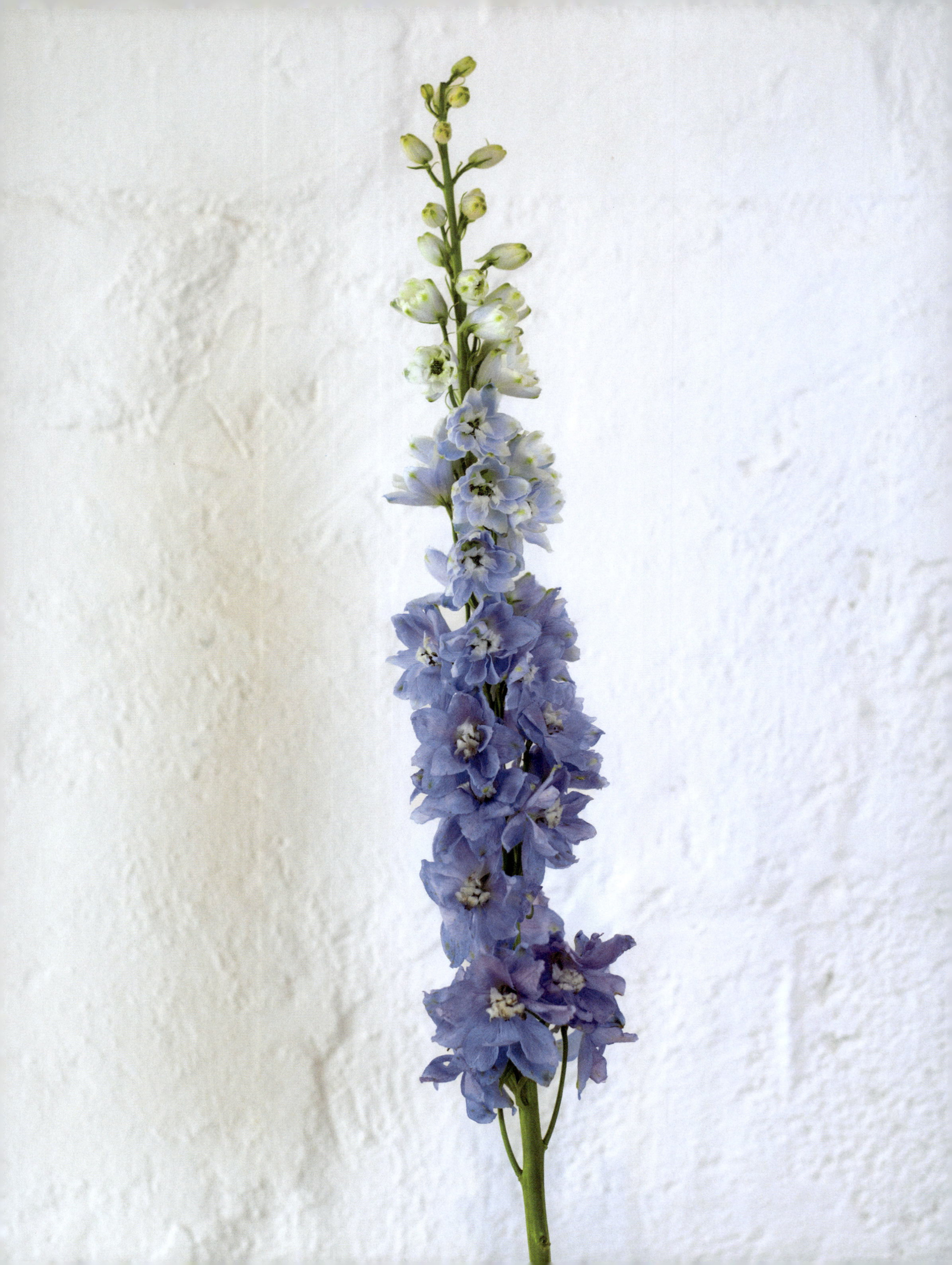

Delphinium

Delphiniums are known for their tall spires of vibrant, clustered flowers that present in a gradient of colour. The name is derived from the Greek word *delphinion*, meaning dolphin, as it was thought the shape of the flower bud with its spur resembled that of a dolphin.

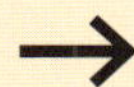

MATERIALS

Smooth watercolour paper, A4
Soft pastels and pastel pencils

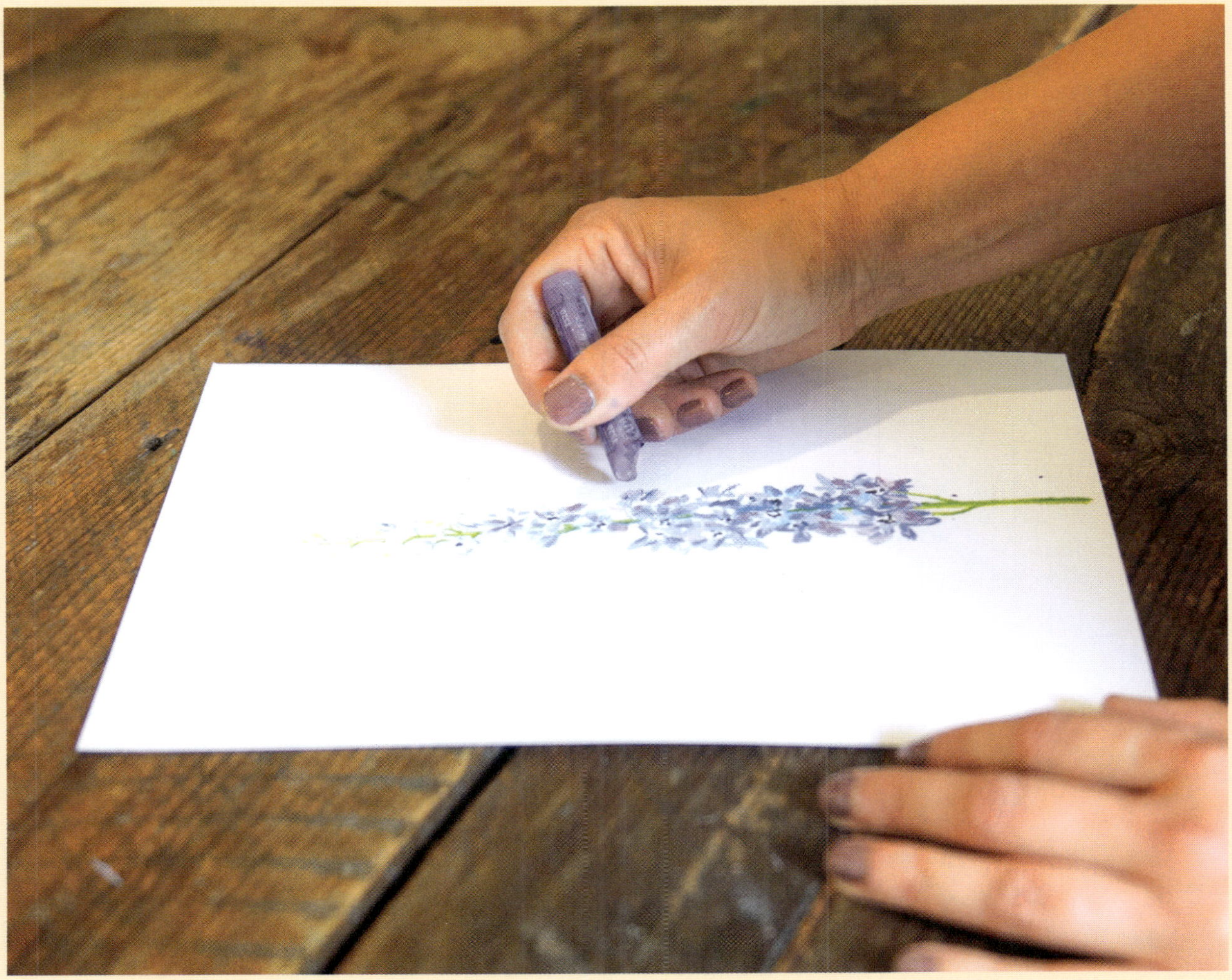

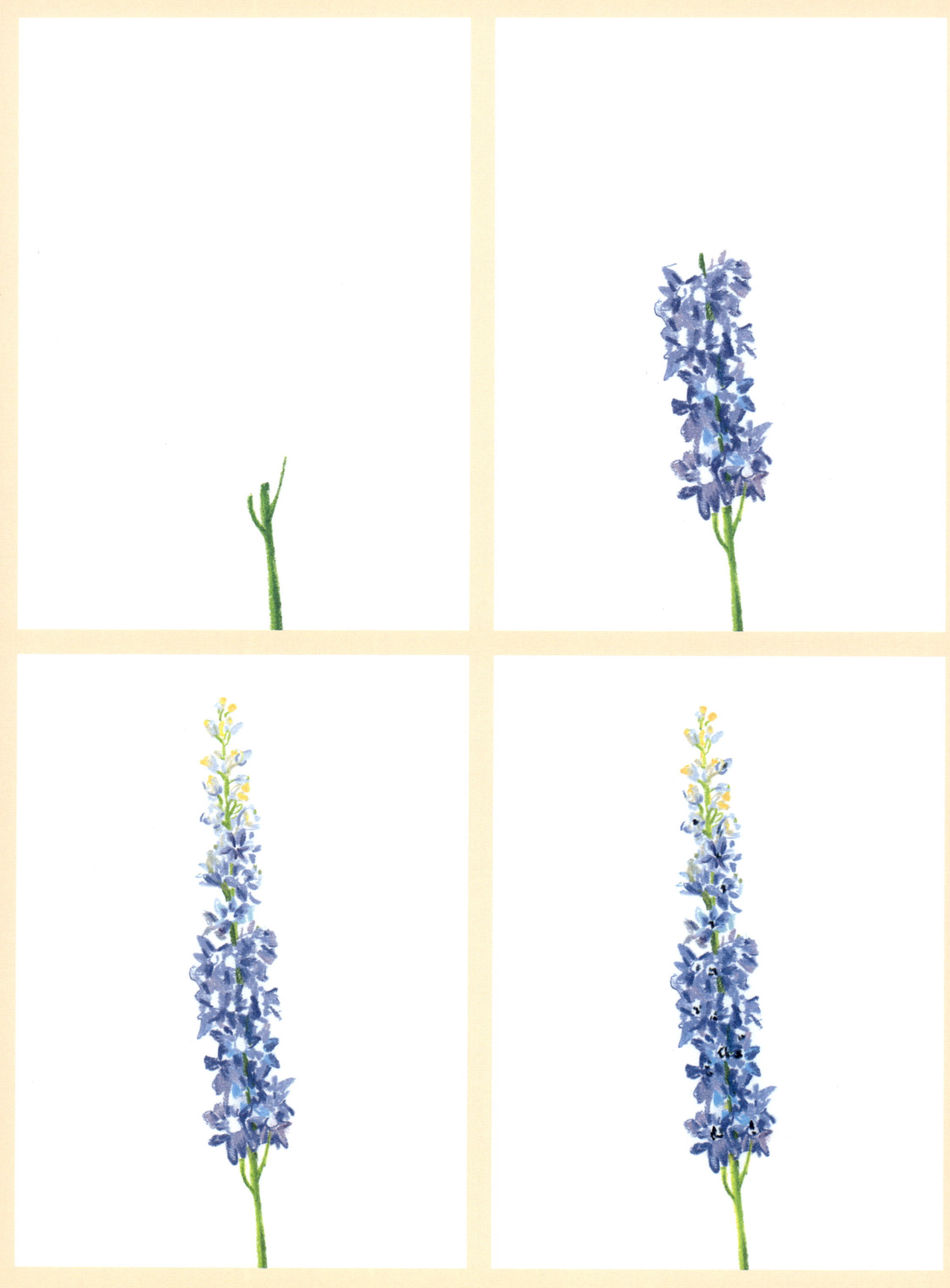

1

Leaving enough room for the clusters of flowers, draw the bottom part of the stem in the direction it grows in, moving your pastel up the page. Note that the stem is highlighted on the left-hand side and shadowed on the right, so represent this by using lighter and darker shades of green and by adding pale yellow green for the highlight.

2

Observe the irregularity and different angles in the flowerheads' star shapes. Starting at the base and leaving the centre pistil areas blank, draw the petals using a mix of lilac, purple, blue, pale blue and off white. Continue up the stem to where the flowers end, gradually using more pale blue and white.

3

Draw in the green of the stem where it is visible through the flowers, taking care to keep it on the same trajectory as the lower section. Add the remaining stem through to its topmost point. Draw the small buds, beginning with a blue base, blending to white and finishing with yellow at the tip.

4

Use a dark blue-grey to irregularly dot in the pistil areas and leave empty space for the pistil ends.

●

If you don't have pastel pencils, you can just use soft pastels for this piece.

The project will also work well on Kraft paper. Use white, rather than empty space, to highlight the pistil ends.

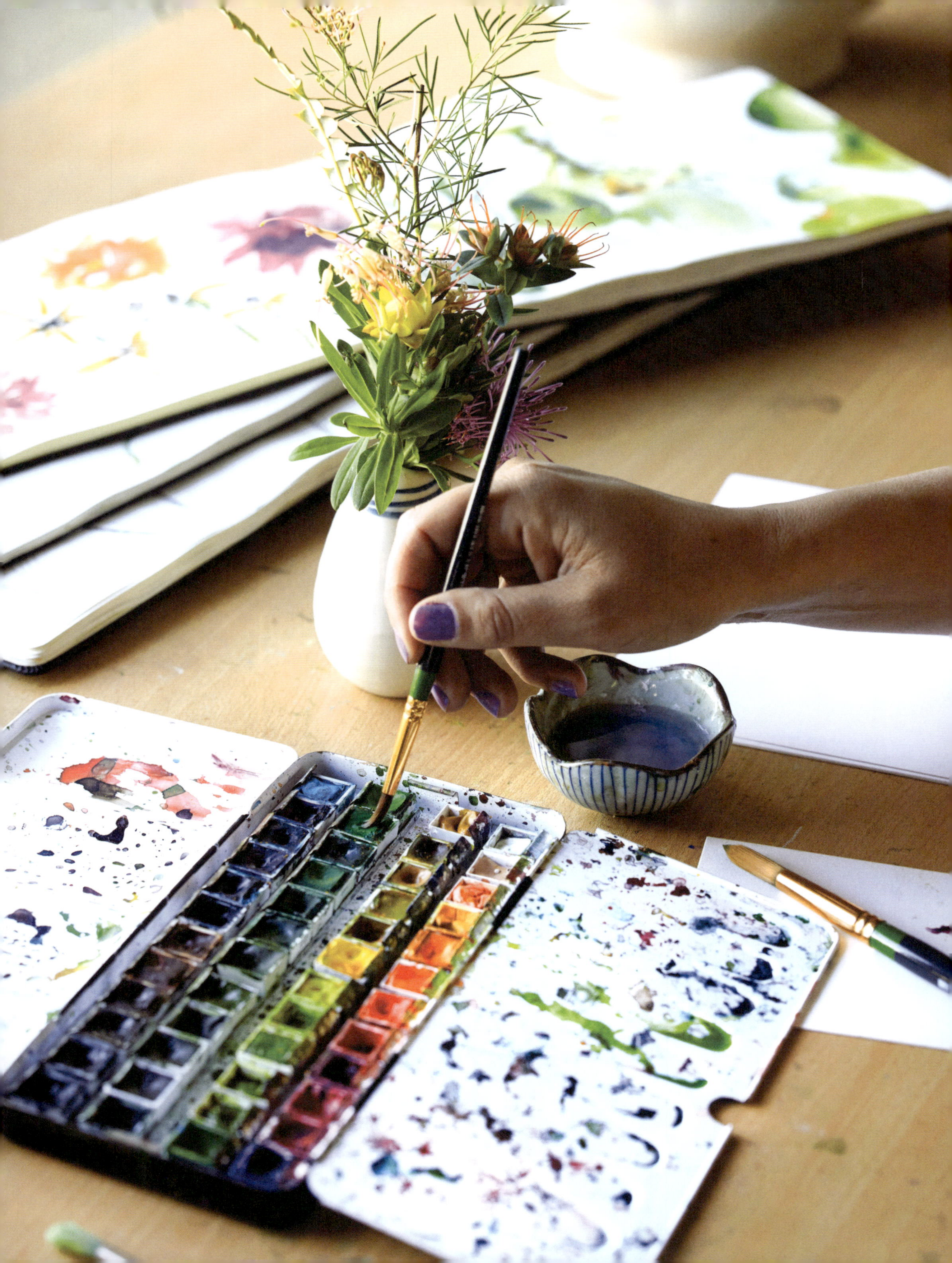

Watercolour

Watercolour is a highly expressive medium that is used to create majestic, beautiful artworks. To use watercolour, you need to let go of perfectionism and embrace unpredictability. It has a mind of its own, but while the results can be unplanned, they are usually wonderful. Watercolour is transparent, which means light bounces through the paint and off the paper, giving works luminous, bright qualities.

There is so much variation in the way you can use watercolour. Traditionally, watercolour artists would layer tones gradually to create a realistic result; however, a more modern application is the gestural wet-on-wet technique, which is how I predominantly work. Wet-on-wet is a technique that uses wet paint on top of a layer of wet paint or wet paper. It is a style of working that is unique to watercolour and gives a beautiful result of blooms and bleeding colours. In the projects that follow, you will use the wet-on-wet technique as well as the wet-on-dry technique. These techniques can be practised with the exercises on pages 52 and 55.

Working with watercolour is all about giving an impression and capturing an essence: watercolour botanical art does not need to be photorealistic. Don't be afraid to work quickly and spontaneously, using lots of water and pigment. Vary the pressure when making brushstrokes and experiment with the amount of colour and water you use, in order to change the intensity and value of the colours. Enjoy the application of watercolour and watching it bleed, morph, blend and dry. It can be mesmerising and even meditative.

A great way to buy watercolour paints is in half pans that come in a tin. Half pan or pan watercolours are intensely pigmented so last a really long time. You could start off with a small set that includes primary colours and mix your own shades.

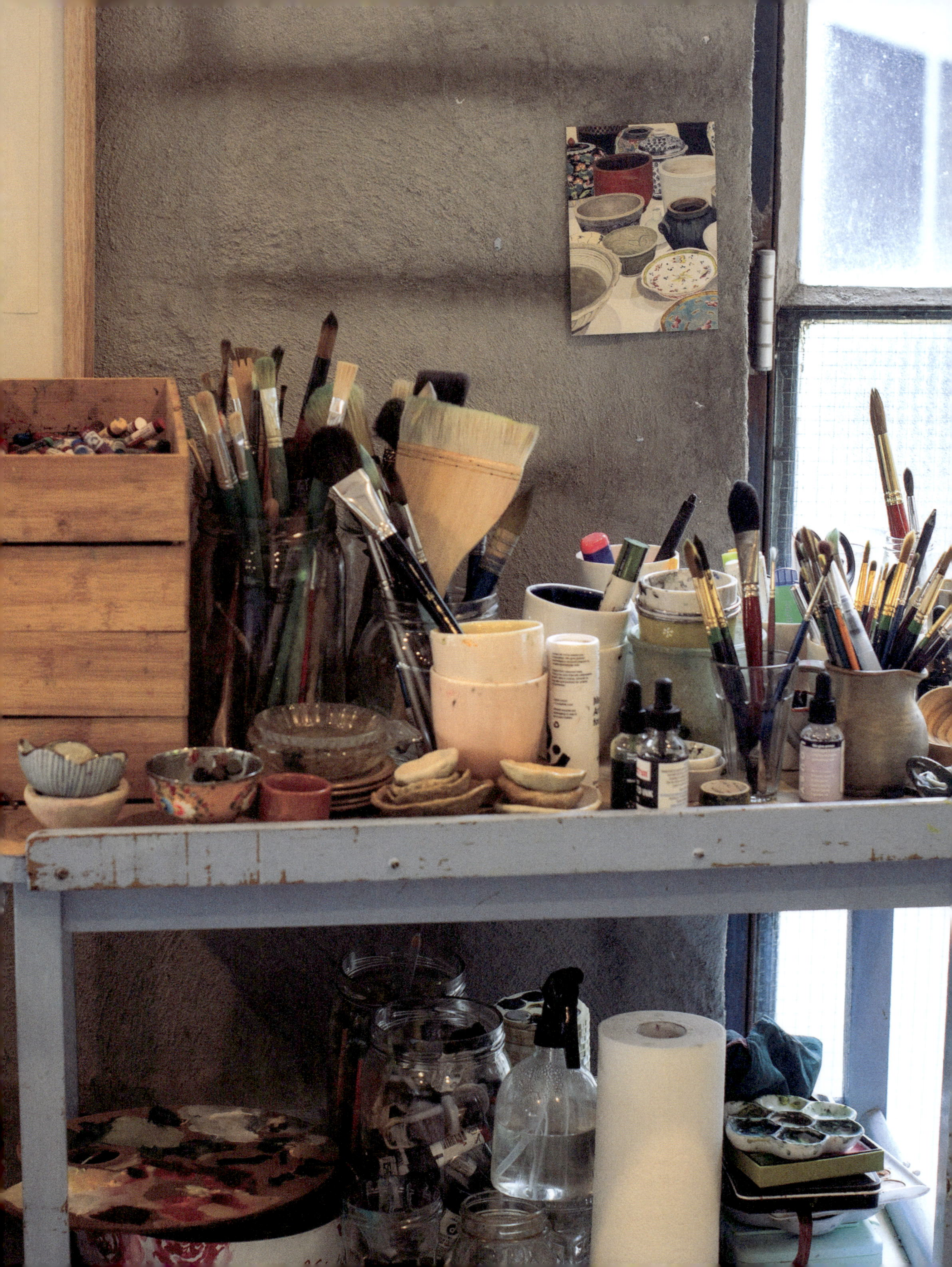

Watercolour materials

WATER VESSELS • Anything that holds water will do. I use old jars or ceramics I pick up from op shops.

PALETTE • If you don't have an artist palette, you could use a dinner plate or porcelain/ceramic tile for mixing colours.

SCRAP PIECES OF WATERCOLOUR PAPER • These are handy for mixing and testing colours.

PAPER TOWEL OR RAG • Keep something at hand for quick brush cleaning.

TIPS

It's a good idea to make a colour chart of all your watercolour shades. In the pan, they can look different from how they appear on paper.

There's not much pure black in nature, and black watercolour can look harsh and can flatten your work by diminishing the vibrancy of other colours. Instead, try combining dark umber and Prussian blue if you have a particularly dark area to paint.

Poppy

This project features ephemeral Iceland poppies in different stages of growth – one in bloom and one a bud. Iceland poppies are native to subpolar regions of Asia, North America and the mountains of Central Asia and are grown as ornamental flowers throughout the world. They are known for their leafless stems, paper-like petals and bowl-shaped flowerheads. In this project, you will be using a mix of wet-on-wet and wet-on-dry techniques (see pages 52 and 55) to paint these delicate flowers.

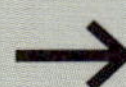

MATERIALS

Watercolour paper, A4 or A3, your choice of texture

Watercolours

Round brushes, sizes 8 and 12

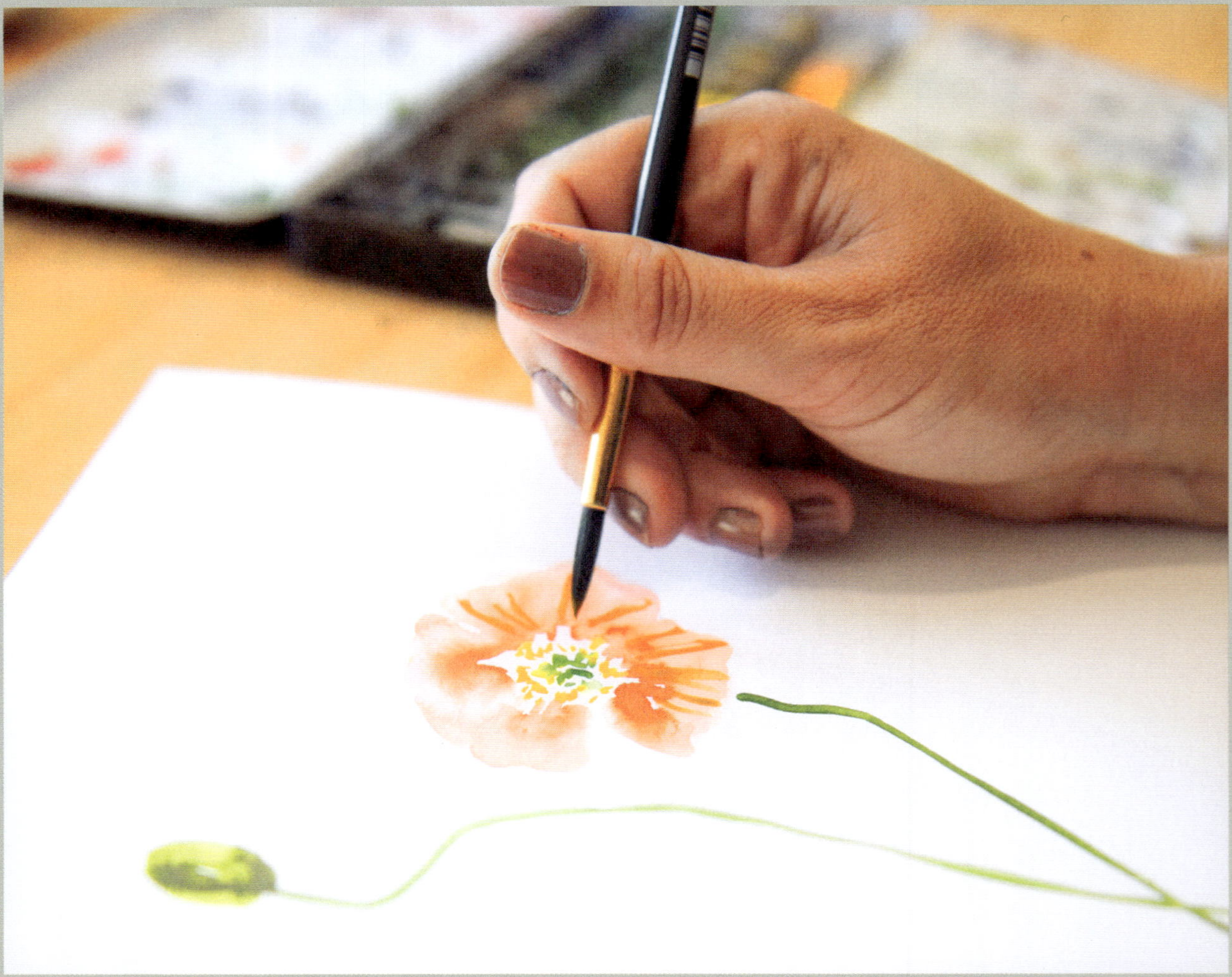

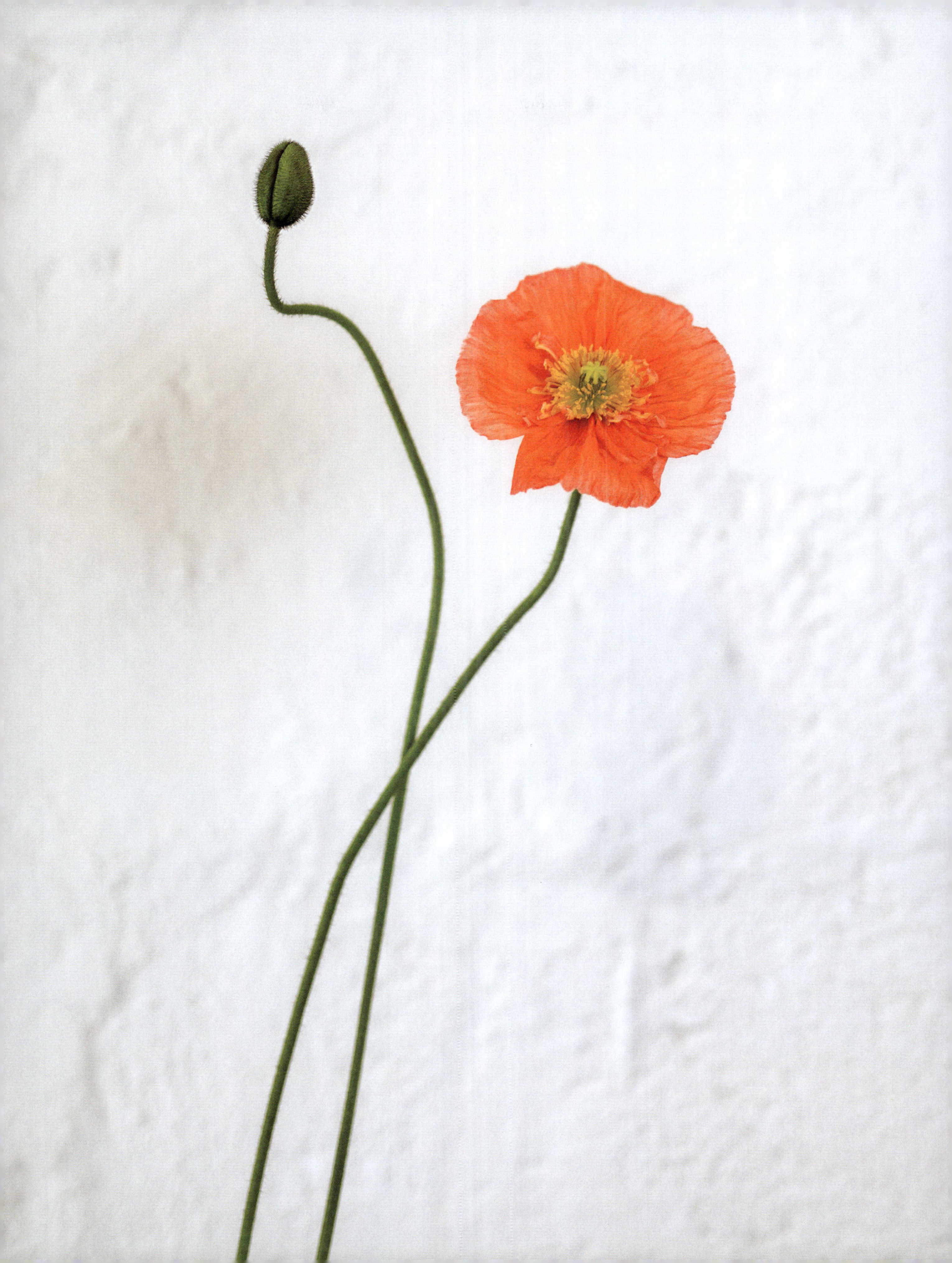

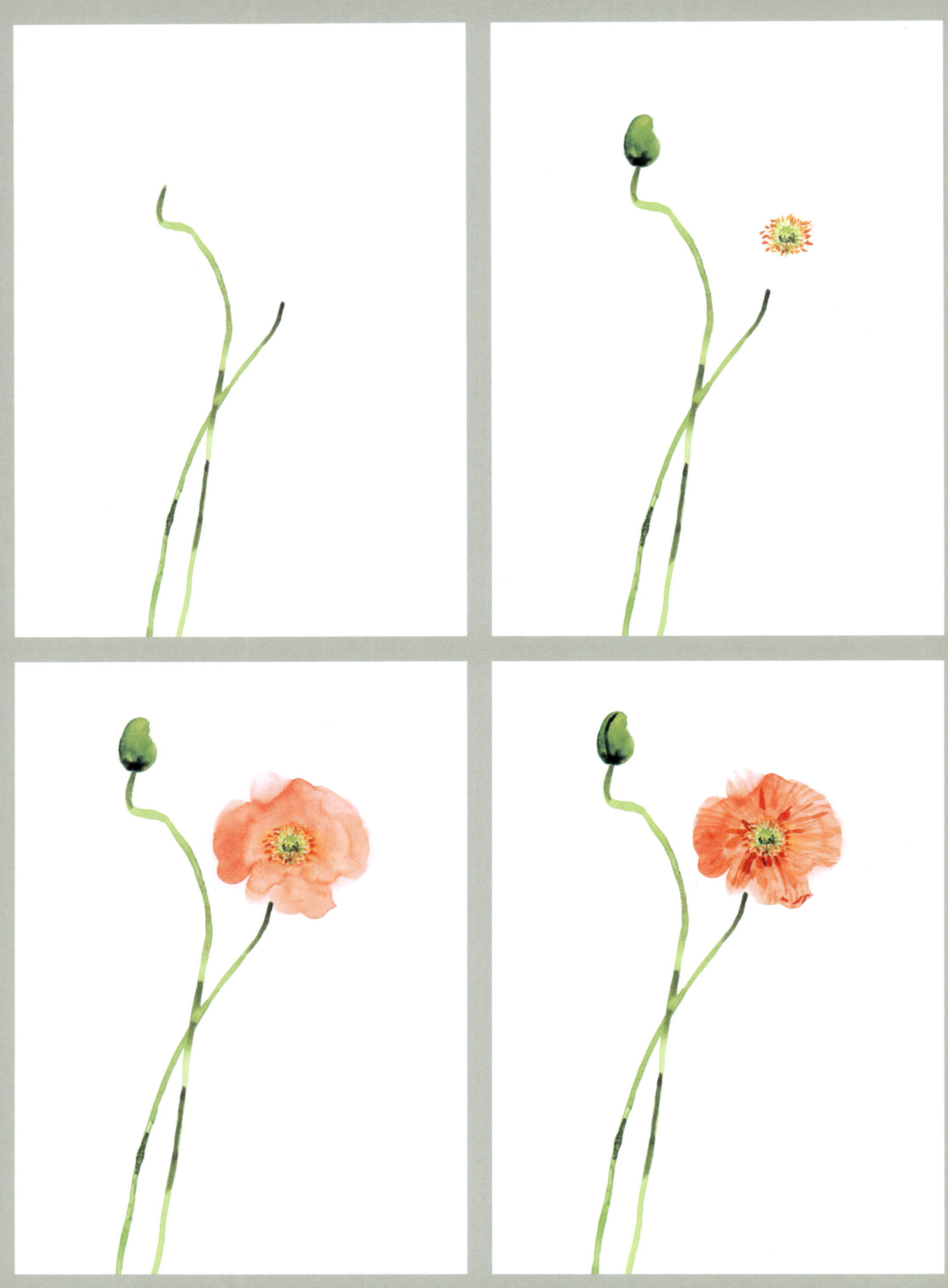

1

Mix a mid-green with yellow on your palette for a yellow-green colour. Using the size-8 brush, paint in the poppy stems lightly, with the tip of the brush to get a fine line, noting how they curve as they extend upwards. While the stems are still wet, dab a darker green into shaded areas, such as where the stems cross over and just below the bud and flower.

2

Using a light-green colour mixed with water, paint the poppy bud. While it's wet, dab in a darker green at the base and a yellow at the top to blend. Let the colours bleed into each other.

3

Paint the pistil of the open poppy. Note the starfish shape of the stigma at the top of the seed pod, the darker style and the orange-yellow stamens.

4

When the pistil is dry, switch to the size-12 brush and use a watered-down mid-orange red to paint the petals, taking care to leave some areas lighter and more watered down.

5

When the petals are dry, switch back to the size-8 brush and paint in the creases on the petals, noting the darker areas, particularly those under the pistil.

6

Add dark-green shading to the length of the bud to represent the gap between the sepals.

•

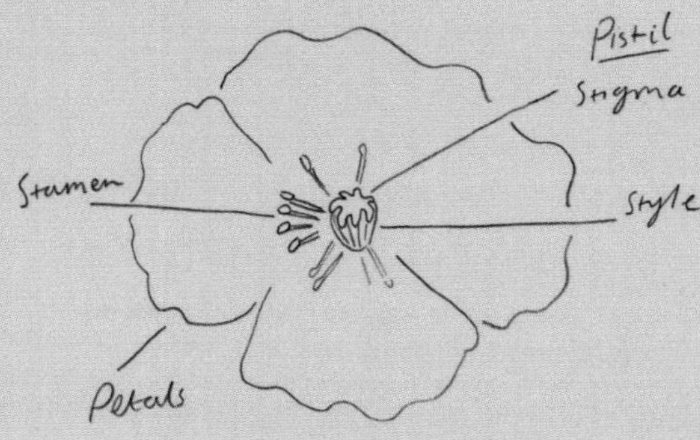

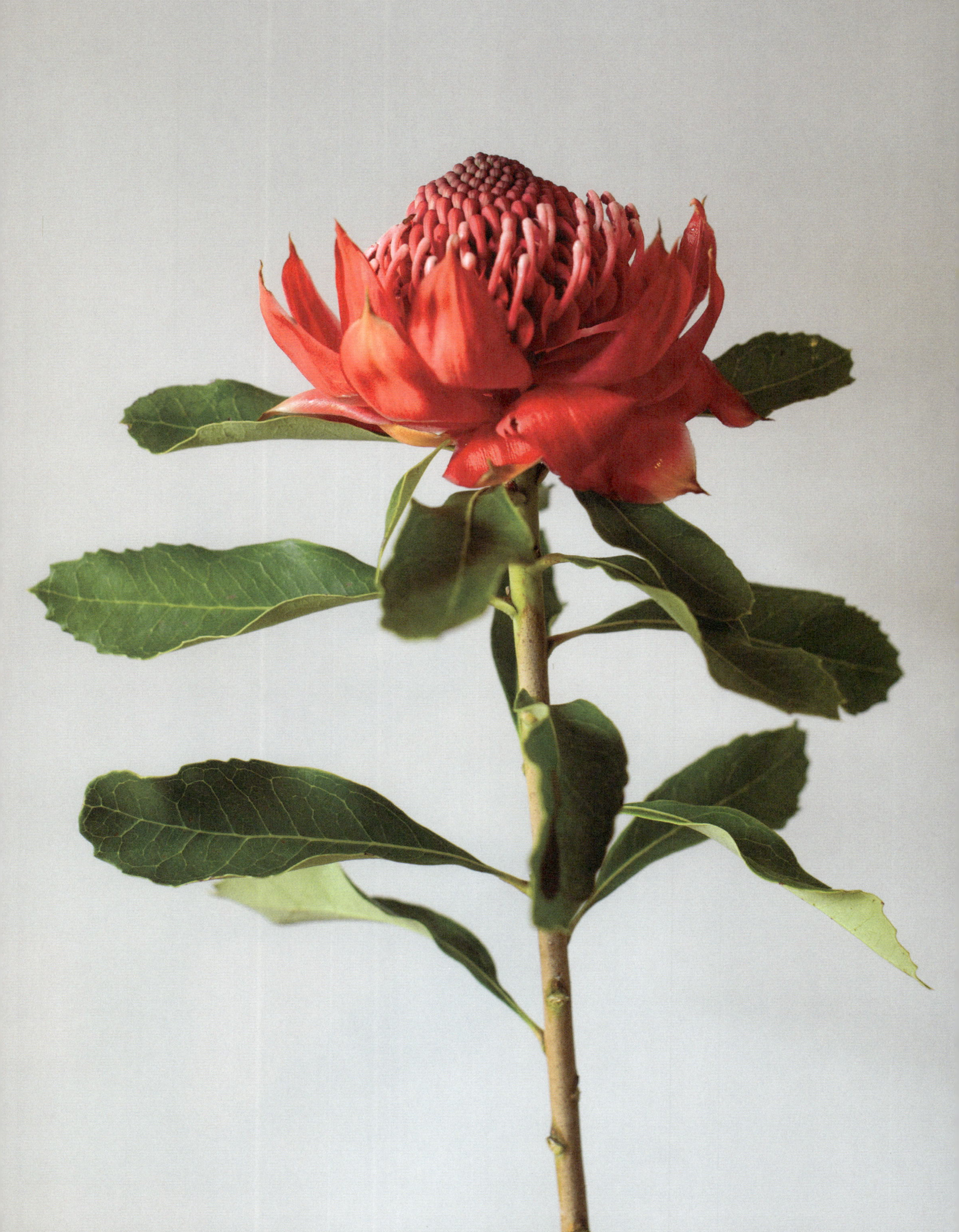

Waratah

The waratah is a much-loved native Australian flower. The common name comes from warada, the Dharug word for waratah. The botanical name is *Telopea speciosissima* and comes from the Greek word *telopos*, meaning 'seen from afar', in reference to the distinctive flower head that is recognisable from a distance.

This project uses a wet-on-wet technique. Play with adding more colour to the paint after you have applied it, experimenting with how the colours interact while still wet. Also, experiment with the pressure you put on the brush, from using the point for a fine line to pressing down for a much thicker line.

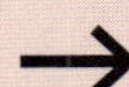

MATERIALS

Watercolour paper, A4, your choice of texture

Watercolours

Round brush, size 12

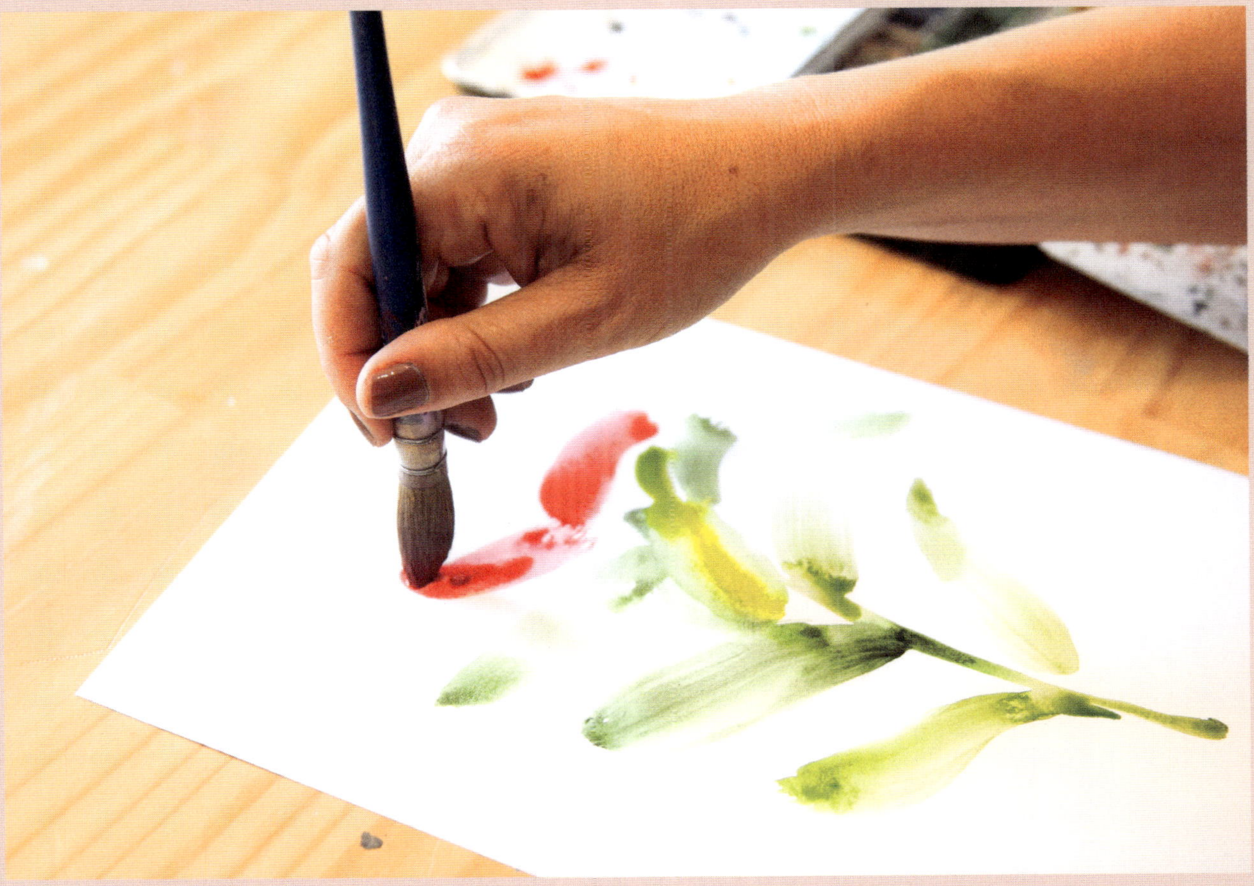

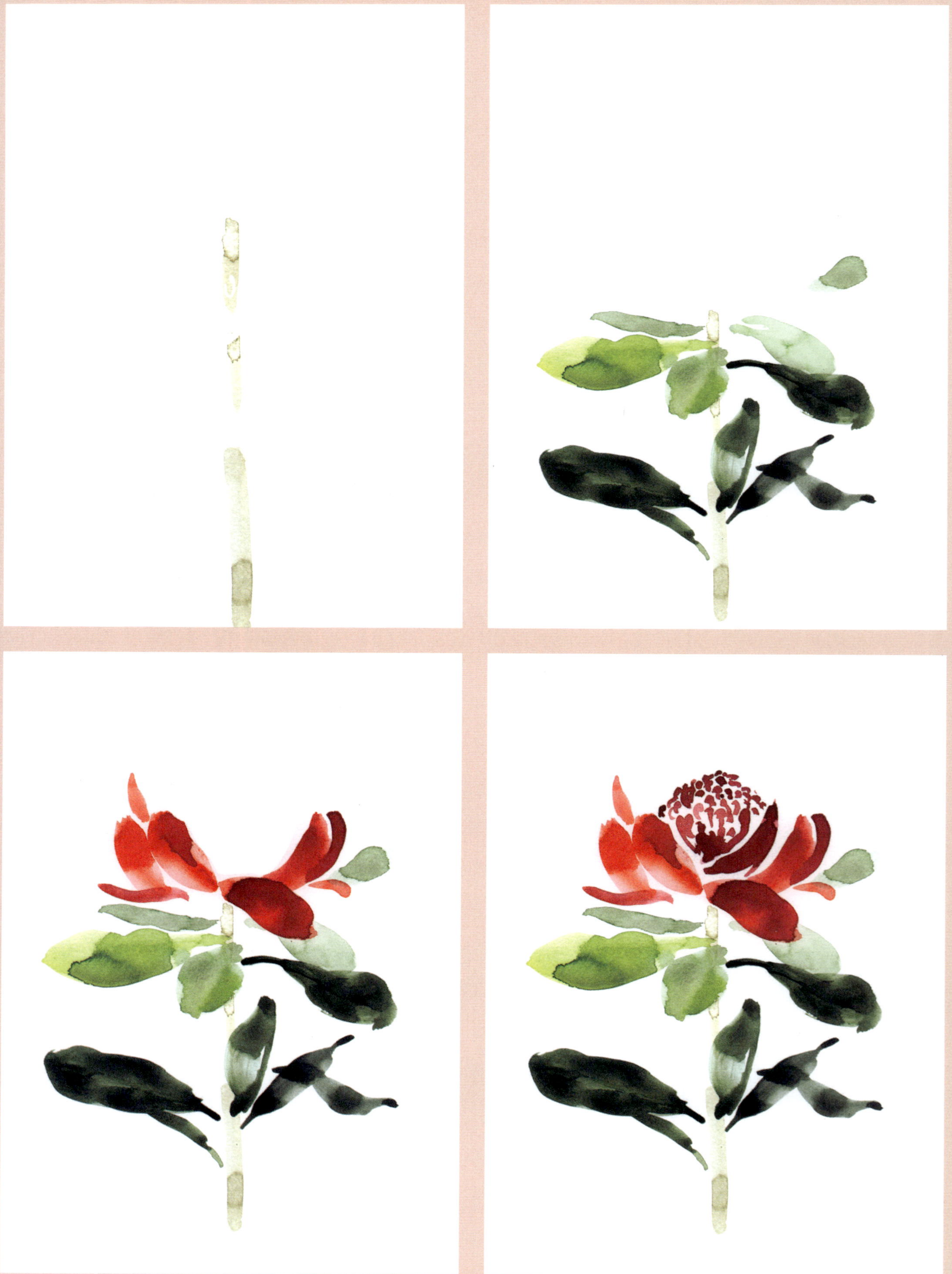

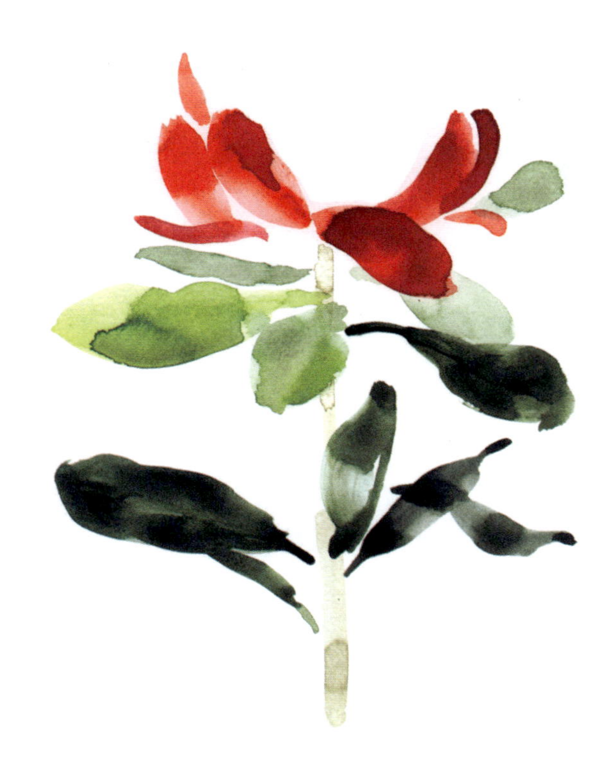
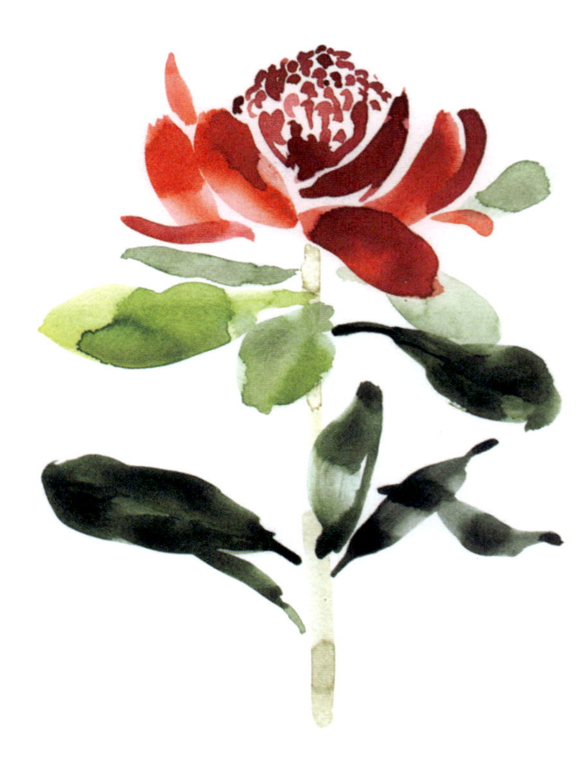

1

Use a watered-down sienna brown to lightly
paint the straight line of the stem. Leave a
gap wherever a leaf will join the stem.

2

Use a mid-green to paint the leaves. Don't worry
about accuracy but try to capture their dynamic
gestures. While the leaves are still wet, add a
darker green and yellow to create a variation
of tones bleeding together.

3

With a mix of red colours, ranging from pink- to
orange-based tones, paint the bracts gesturally,
starting at the bottom and extending upwards
while tapering away to the points. When painting
the bracts, ensure that you have picked up
enough paint on your brush to make your strokes
bold and vibrant.

4

Using the tip of the brush, paint in the flower
buds in a pyramid configuration, noting how
they become more circular in shape as they
near the top.

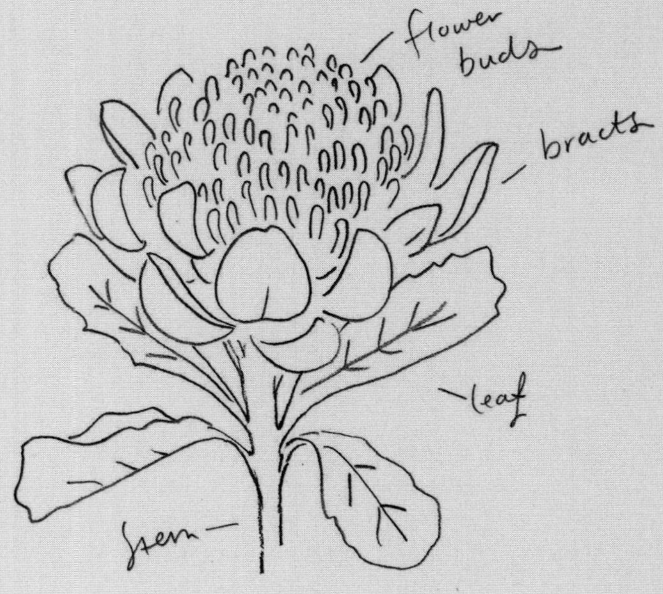

Orchid

These vibrant blue vandas (also known as blue orchids) are native to India, Burma and Thailand. Their colours intensify from pale purple to rich indigo over the course of ten days.

In this project you will be working wet-on-wet and will really see watercolours bloom. Keep the paint wet as you work, pick up lots of pigment on the brush and let the colours bleed. This artwork is more abstract than the other projects in this book.

MATERIALS

Rough watercolour paper, A3
Watercolours
Palette
Round brush, size 36

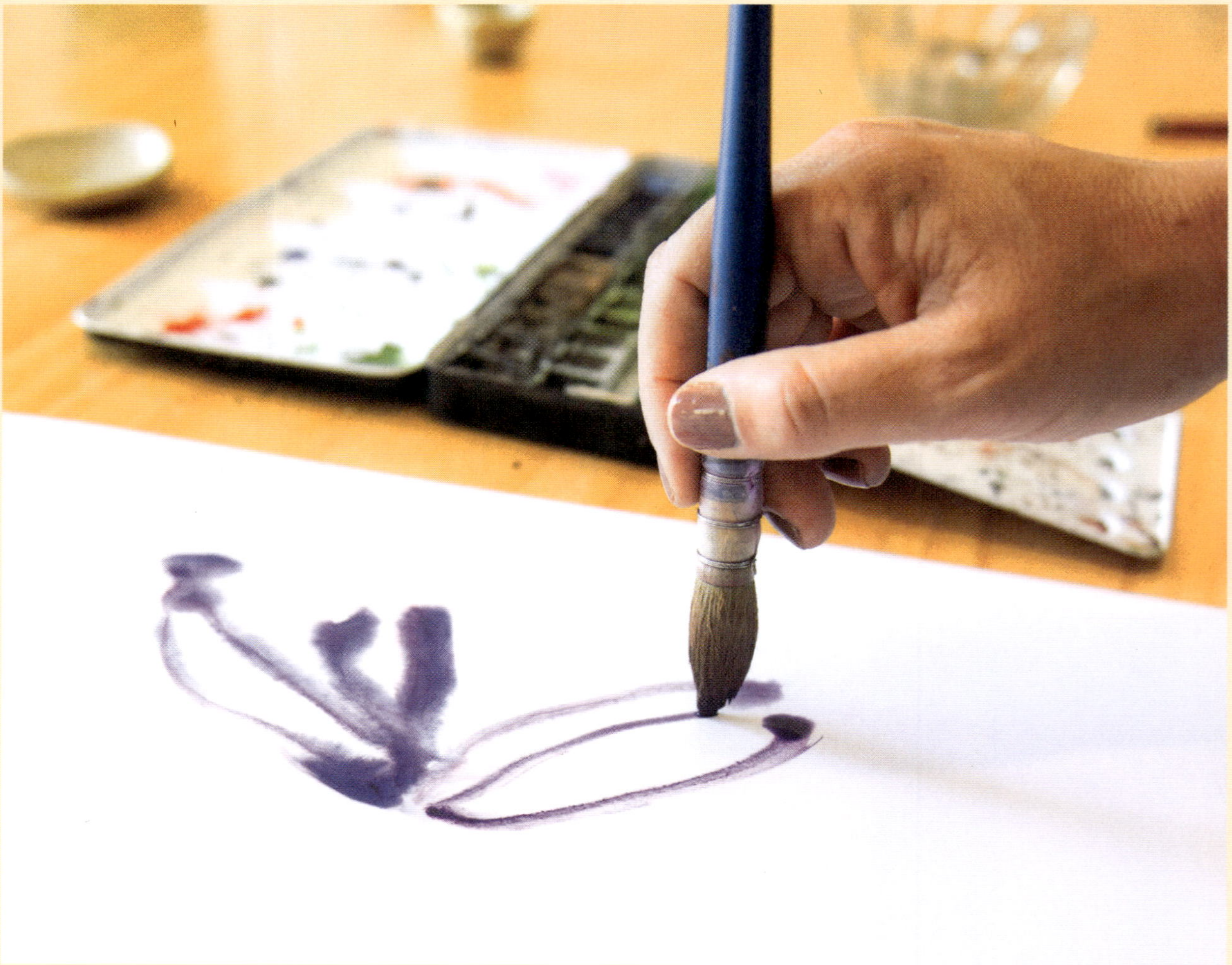

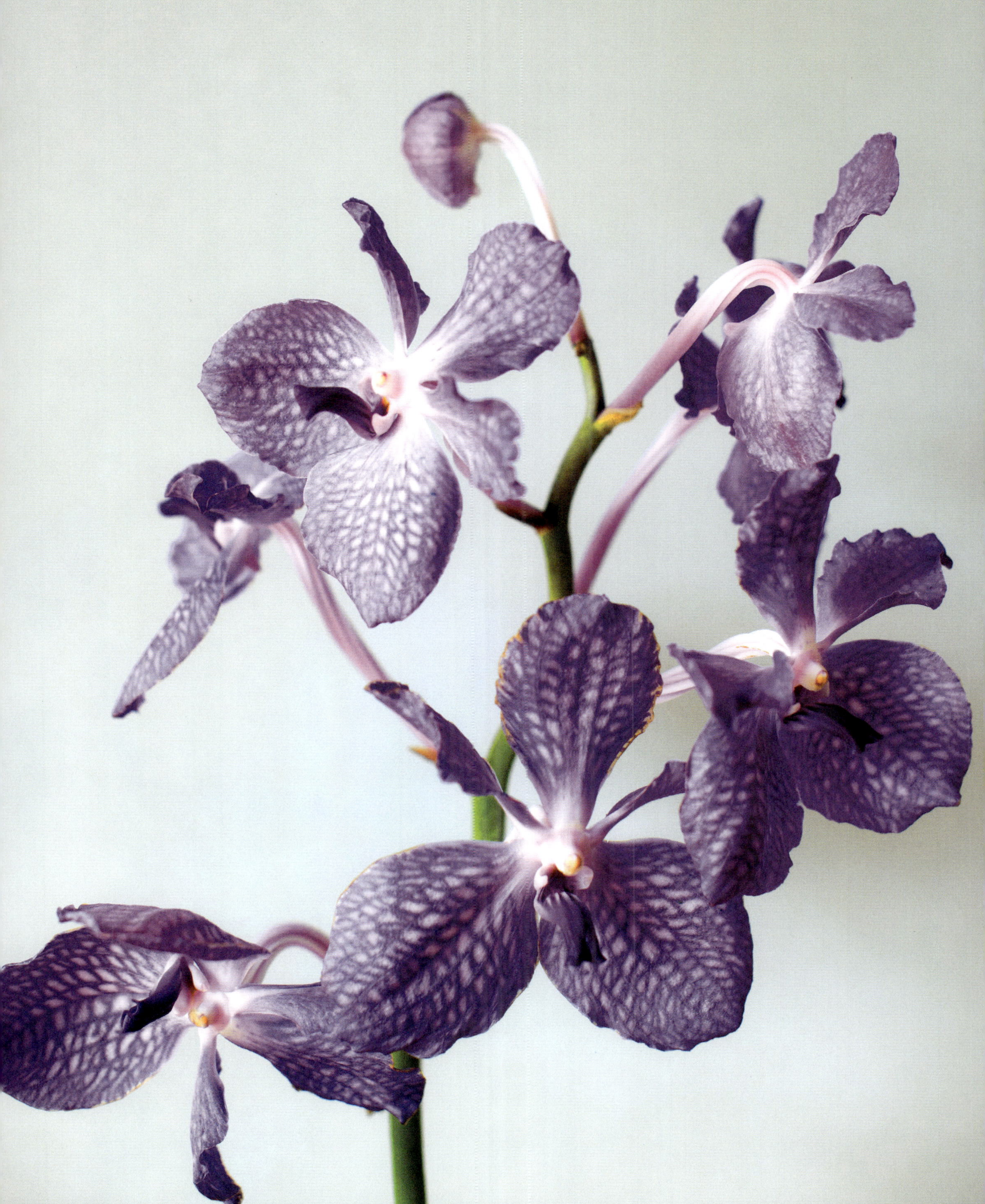

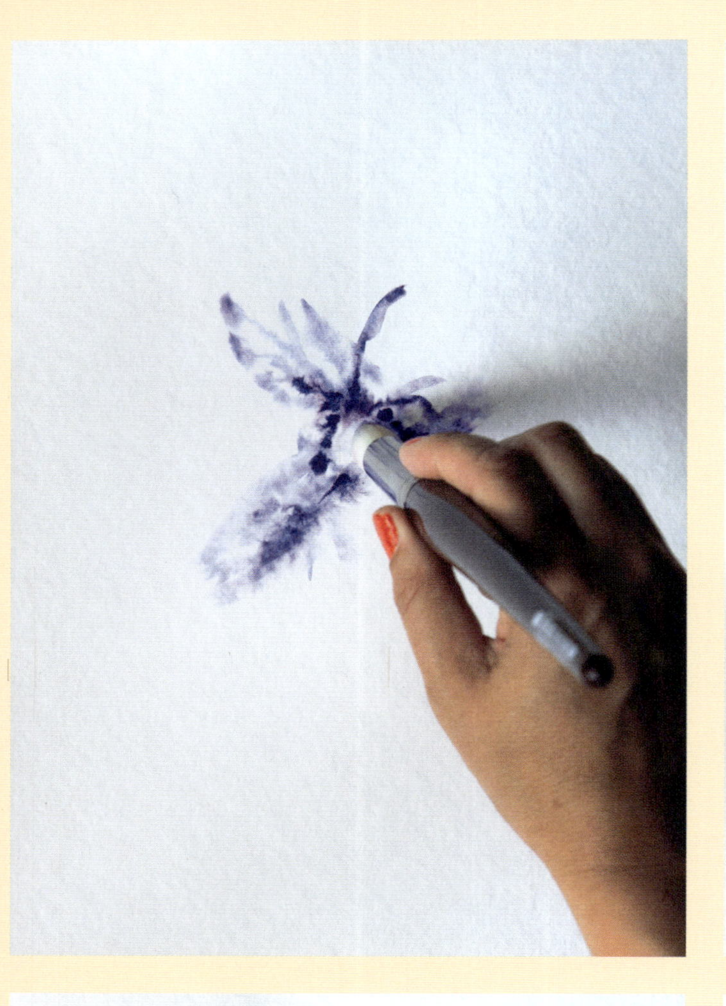
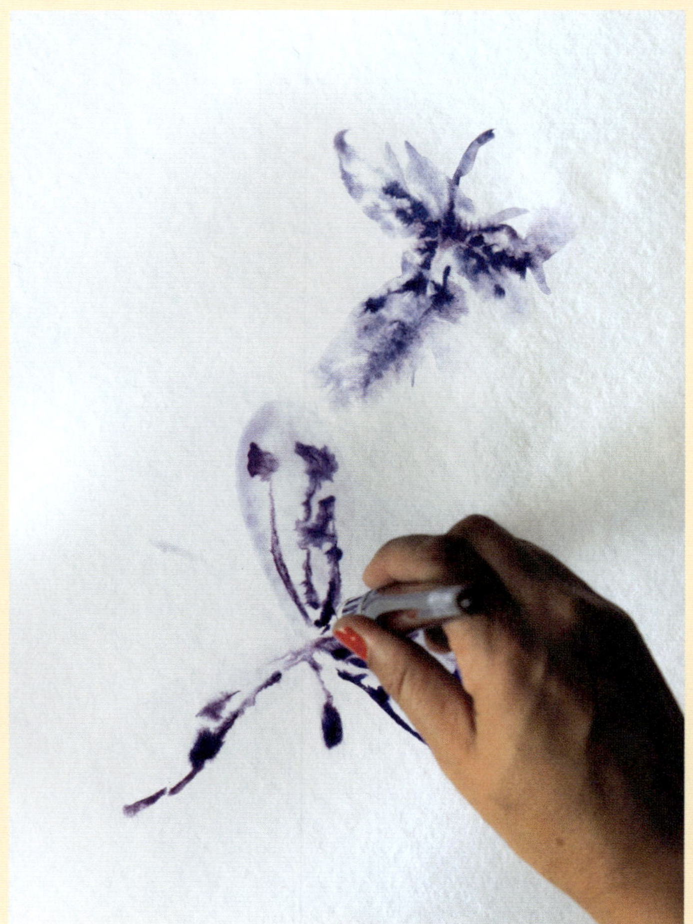
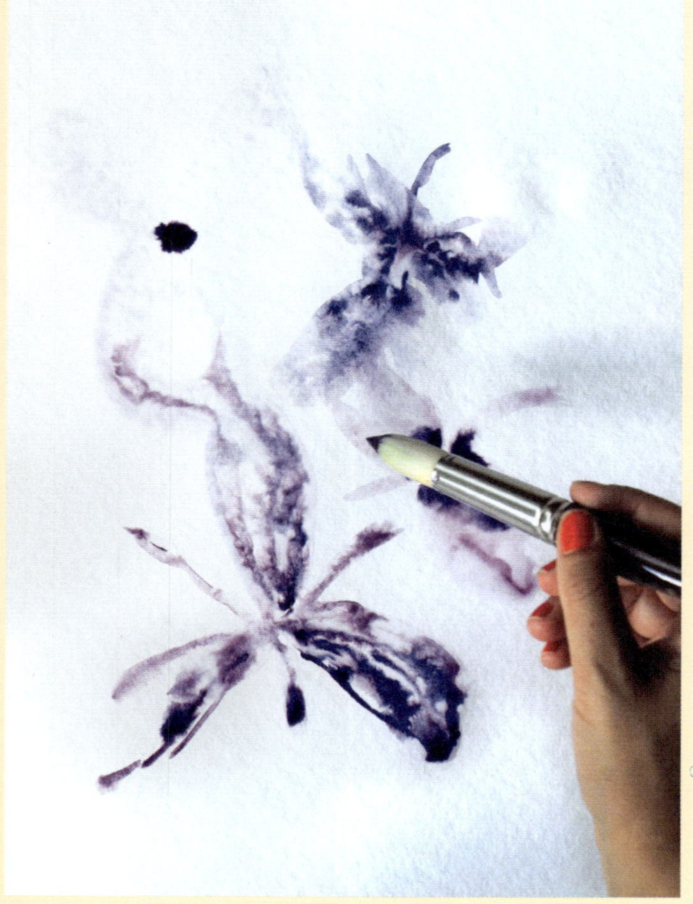
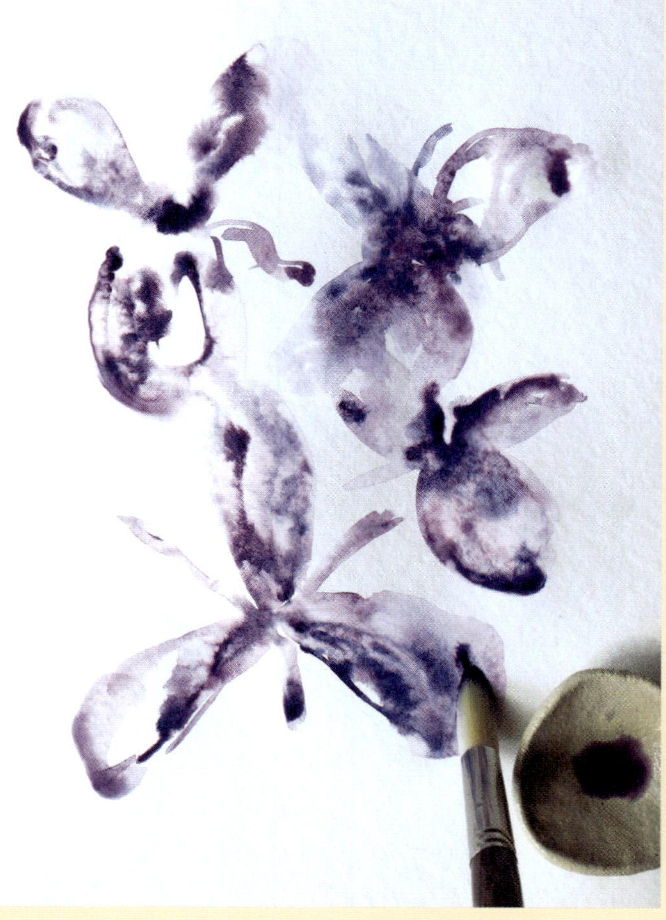

1

Load up your brush with water and abundantly
and gesturally paint the shapes of the flowers.
Because you are just using water, you will
barely be able to see what you have painted,
so don't be caught up in painting perfect shapes.

2

On your palette create a deep-purple and
indigo colour by mixing purple and blue.

3

Working quickly so the water shapes don't dry,
swish the brush around in the watercolour mix
you have made to really load up the brush. Gently
touch the tip of the brush to the centre of one
of the flower shapes and watch the colour bleed
out into the water.

4

Observe the patterns on the petals of the blue
vandas and use your brush to gesturally paint
these patterns in your petal shapes.

●

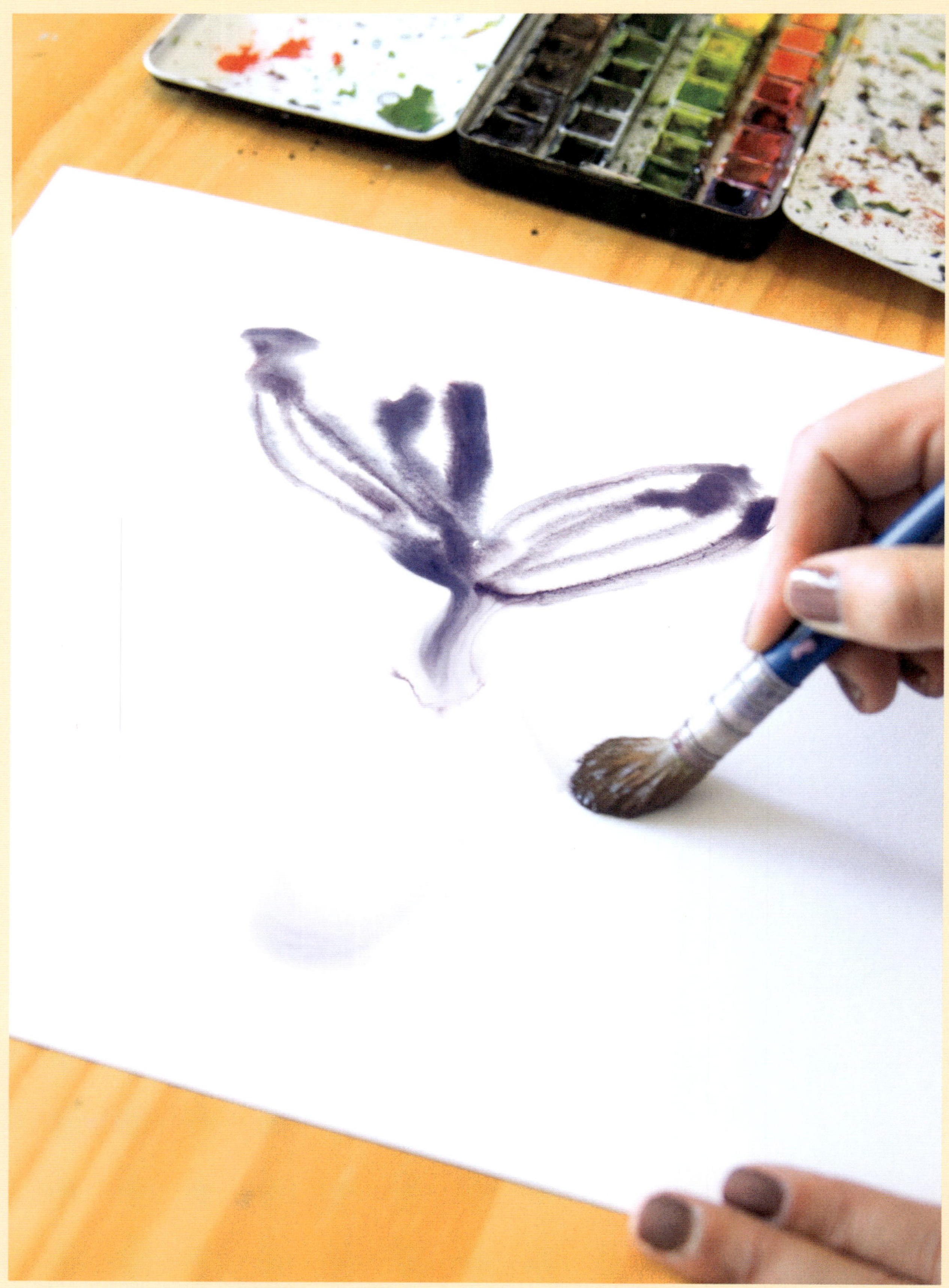

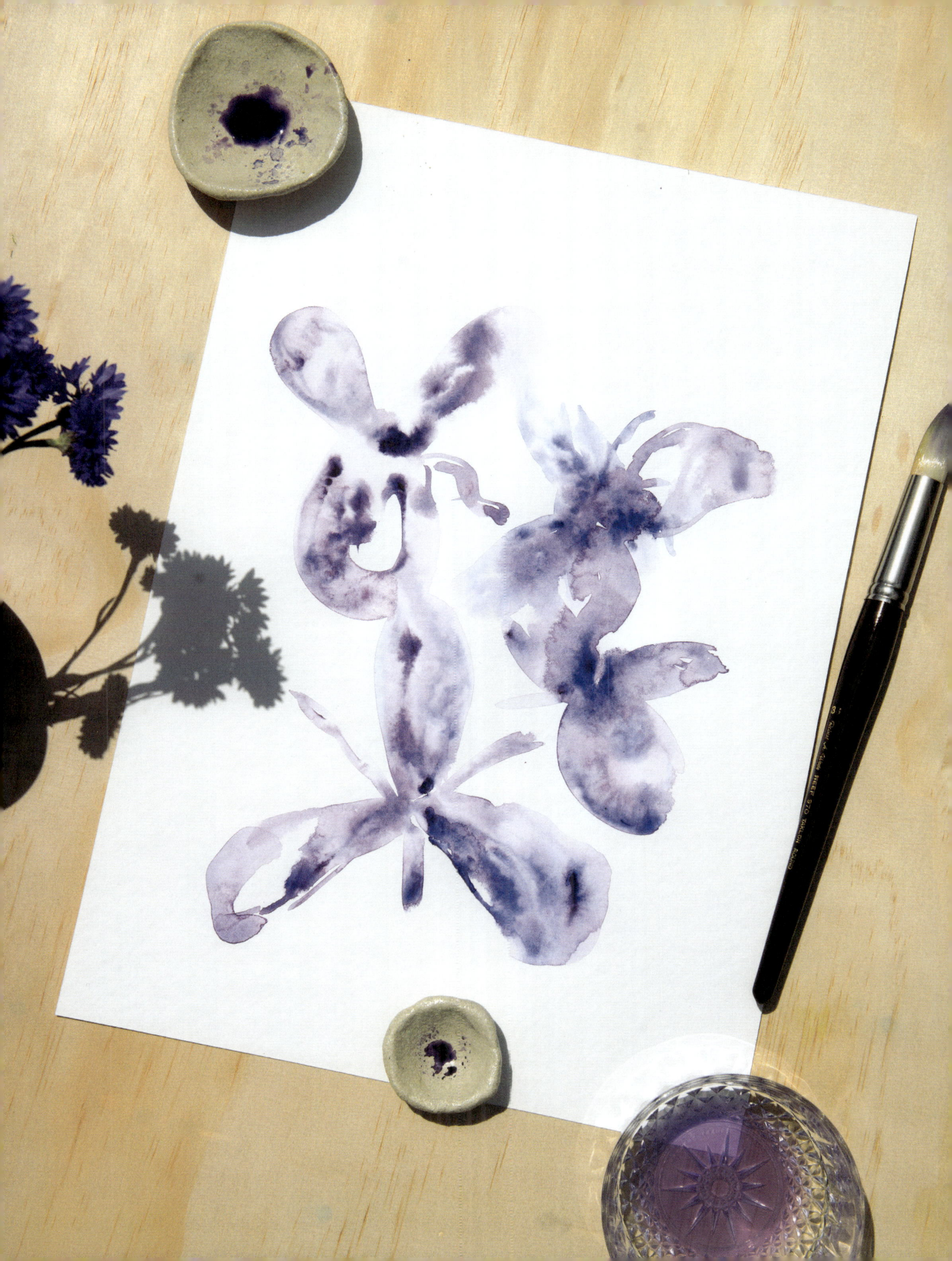

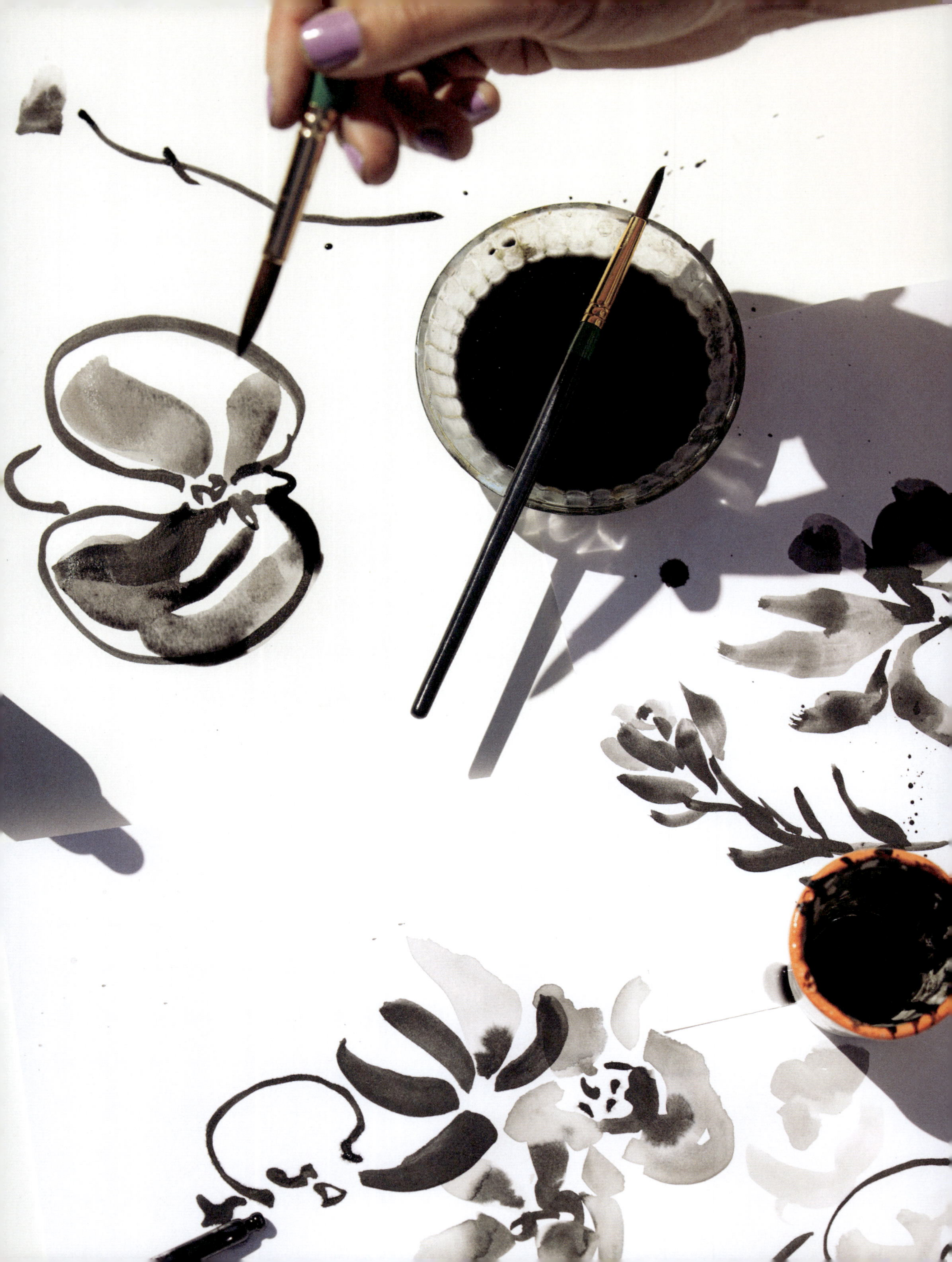

Ink

Ink comes in liquid form and is made from pigment including lampblack (a fine black soot), water and a binder. I use Indian ink, also known as Chinese ink or India ink. It is deep, velvety, rich and intense in its blackness. You can create such strong contrasts and drama with ink. Indian ink is permanent, meaning it is water resistant when dry so won't re-wet or smudge, and you can wash over an existing layer without any bleeding occurring.

Ink is a great medium for practising different values, or tones, ranging from transparent to opaque. Using ink straight from the bottle will result in strong black marks, while diluting it with water will change its opacity so it becomes more transparent.

It can be helpful to experiment with making your own value chart with ink. Do this by using a palette or ice cube tray and filling each well with water except the last, which should stay empty for now. Leaving the first well with just water in it, add a drop of ink to the second well and then move along the wells, gradually increasing the number of drops you put in each. Finish by filling the last well with pure ink. Paint a swatch from each well and notice the differences in the values as you move along the scale from transparent to opaque, or light to dark.

I work quickly and gesturally with ink, so I often make multiple versions of the one artwork and choose which I like the most. If an artwork isn't feeling right, rather than trying to fix it I keep making new versions until I'm happy with one. Try not to be fussy about creating a precise artwork; instead, be gestural, expressive and energetic to capture the essence of the botanicals in sweeping lines and marks. Don't try to control the ink; let it work with you.

While working with ink, I suggest keeping these extra materials close by:

WATER VESSELS • Anything that holds water will do. I use old jars or ceramics I pick up from op shops.

PALETTE OR ICE CUBE TRAY • This is particularly useful when you need multiple opacity washes ready to use.

PAPER TOWEL OR RAG • Keep something at hand for quick brush cleaning.

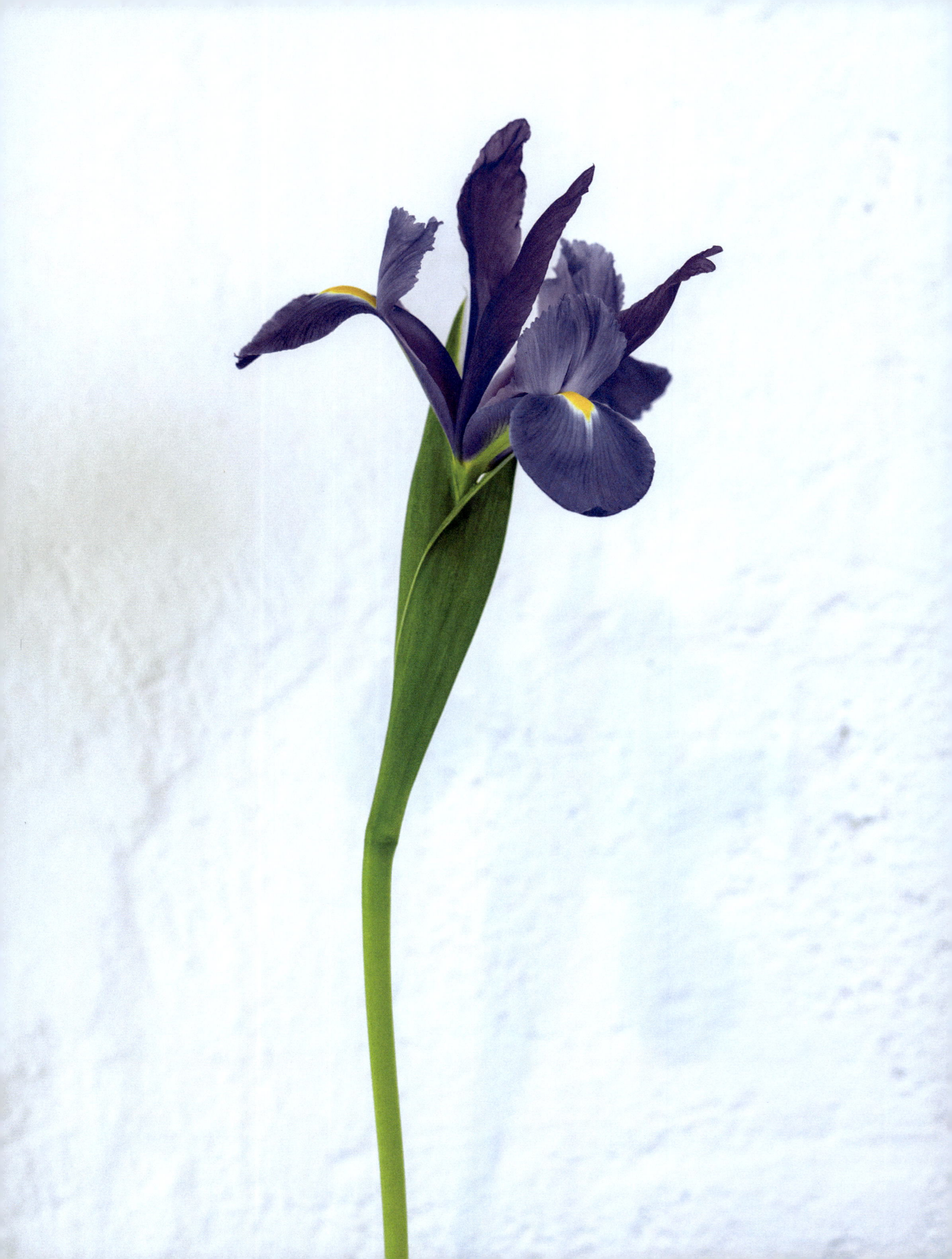

Iris

The iris flower, with its luminous array of colours, takes its name from the Greek word for rainbow. In Greek mythology, the goddess Iris was a brilliantly hued embodiment of the rainbow and a messenger of the gods.

In this project, you will be using ink to block in the iris as a silhouette. Use bold, thick, fluid strokes and don't be concerned with accuracy to the reference image; instead focus on capturing the flower's dynamic shape. You will need two vessels of ink – one with pure ink and the other with diluted wash – as well as a vessel with clean water for washing out your brush between shades.

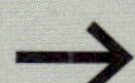

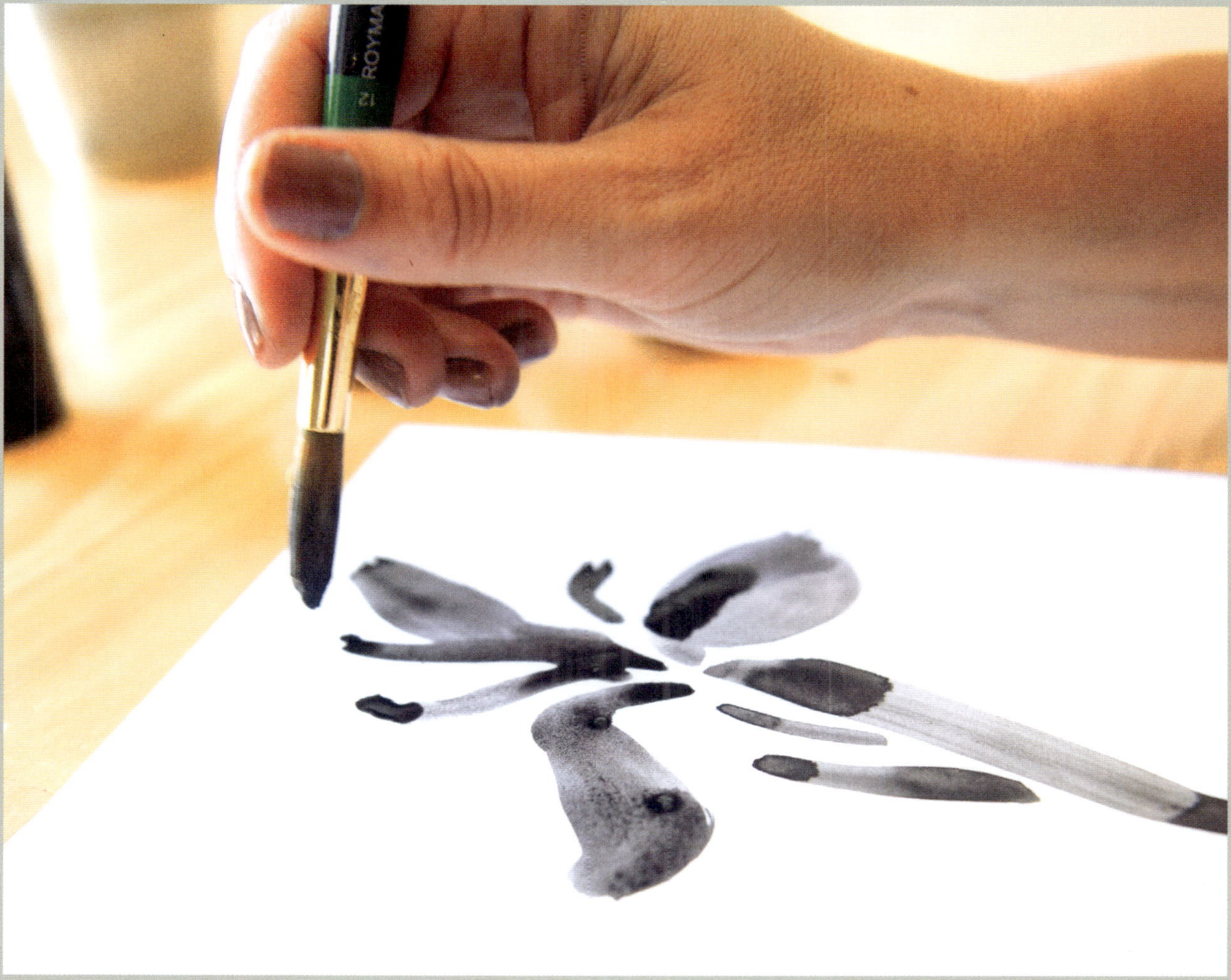

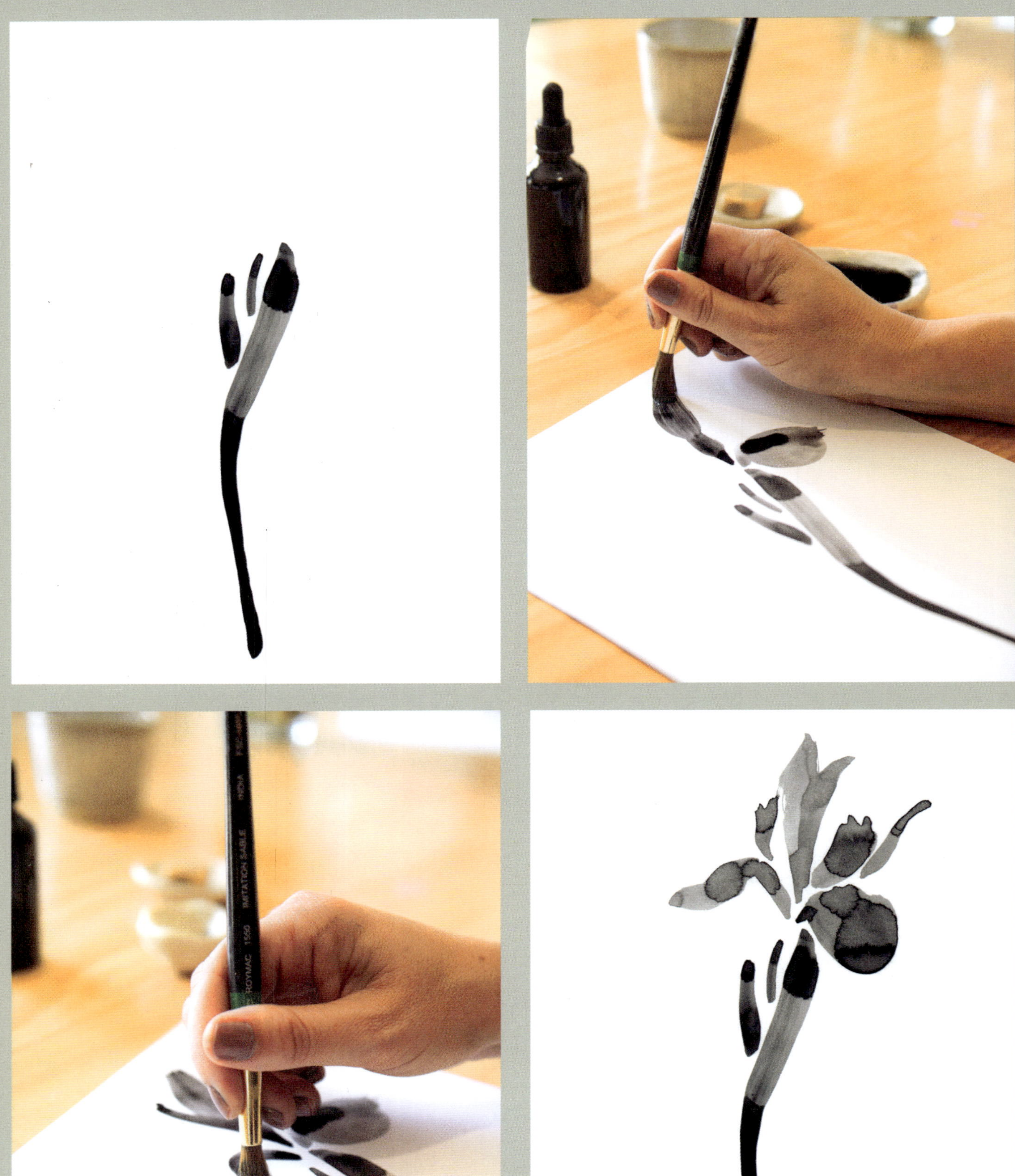

1

Dip your brush in water to soften and make it more absorbent, before dipping it in the pure ink. In a fluid, gestural motion, paint the stem from the bottom upwards, adding more pressure to thicken the line where the spathes meet the sepals. Add two small extra lines to show the spathe to the left side.

2

Clean your brush and then use the diluted ink to paint the sepals, style arms and standards rising boldly up and out from the end of the spathe, noting and capturing the unique shapes.

●

MATERIALS

Smooth watercolour paper, A4

Ink in two vessels: one with pure ink, the other with a diluted wash

Round brush, size 12

TIP

You may like to experiment with textured and rough watercolour paper to see how the different surfaces lead to diverse results.

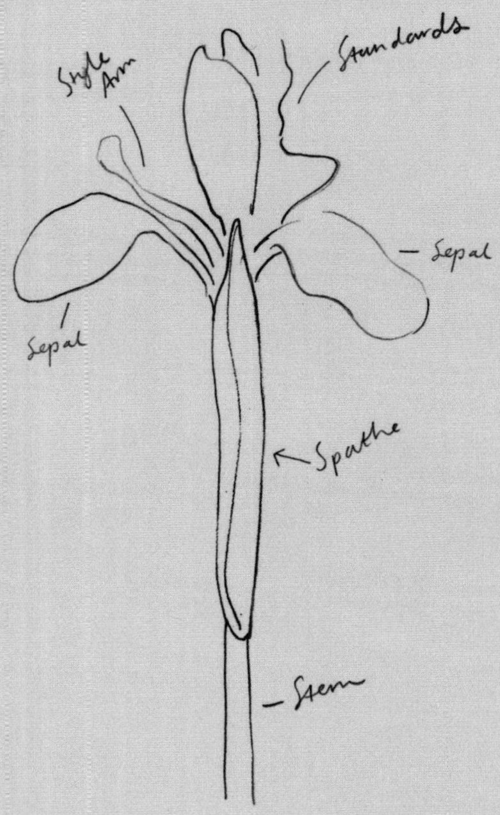

Orchid

The cymbidium orchid, or boat orchid, is said to be the oldest cultivated orchid. It was first praised 2500 years ago in writings by the Chinese philosopher Confucius. It is known for its elegant, colourful and often patterned, long-lasting blooms and features multiple flowers on a single spike. It is renowned for its resilience and adaptability, thriving in a range of climates.

You will be painting the cymbidium orchid branch with an ink outline and washes. Be gestural and confident with your mark making for this piece and work quickly, so you can make areas bleed out while lines are still wet. You are not aiming for precision but for an impression of the joyful and exuberant flower. Have three vessels for ink – one with pure ink, one with a 60 per cent dilution and the other with a 40 per cent dilution – as well as a vessel with water for washing your brush between shades. The ink is heavily pigmented, so you won't need much to give the water a light tone.

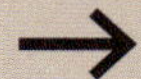

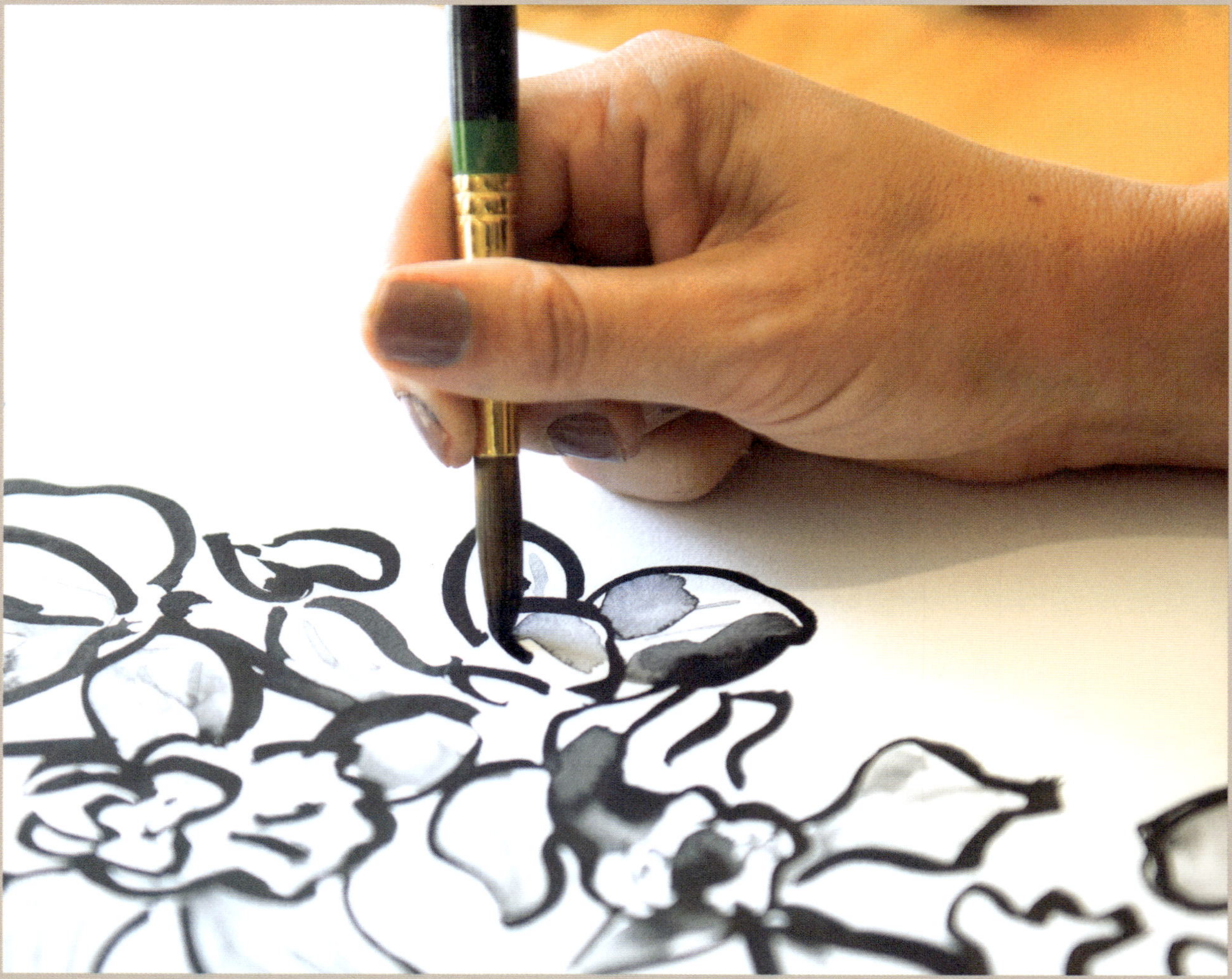

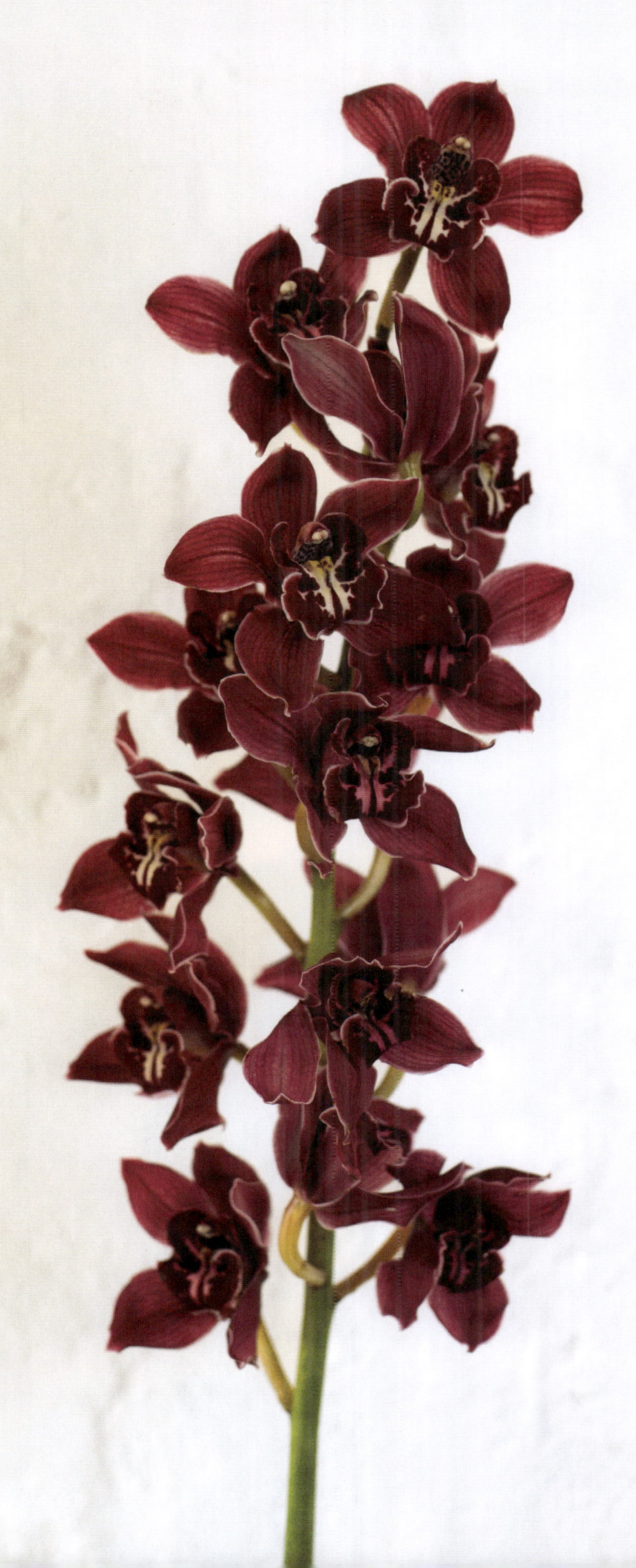

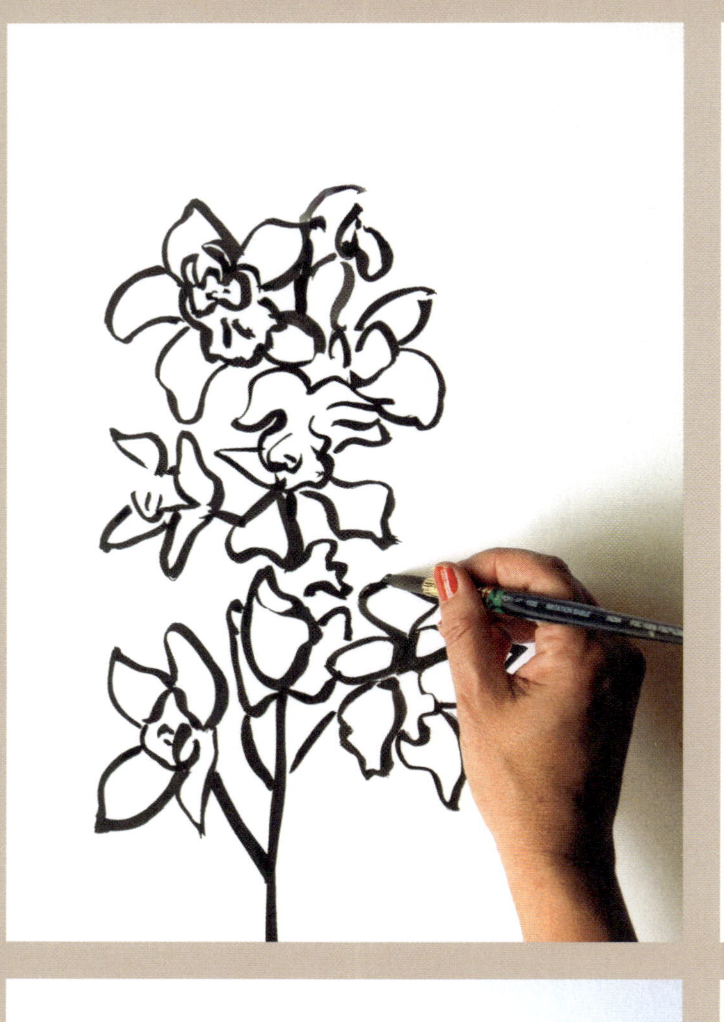
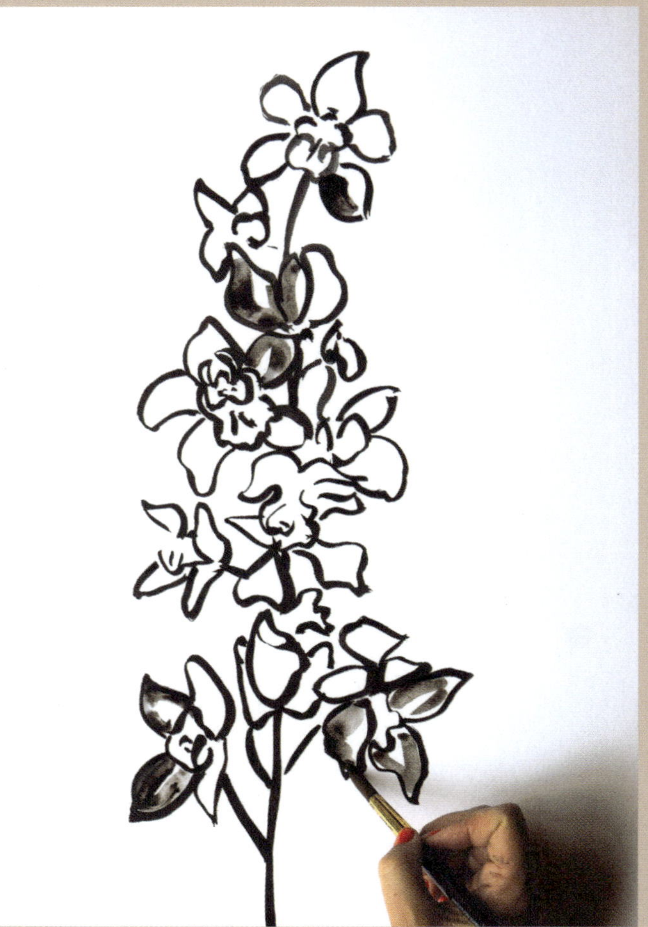
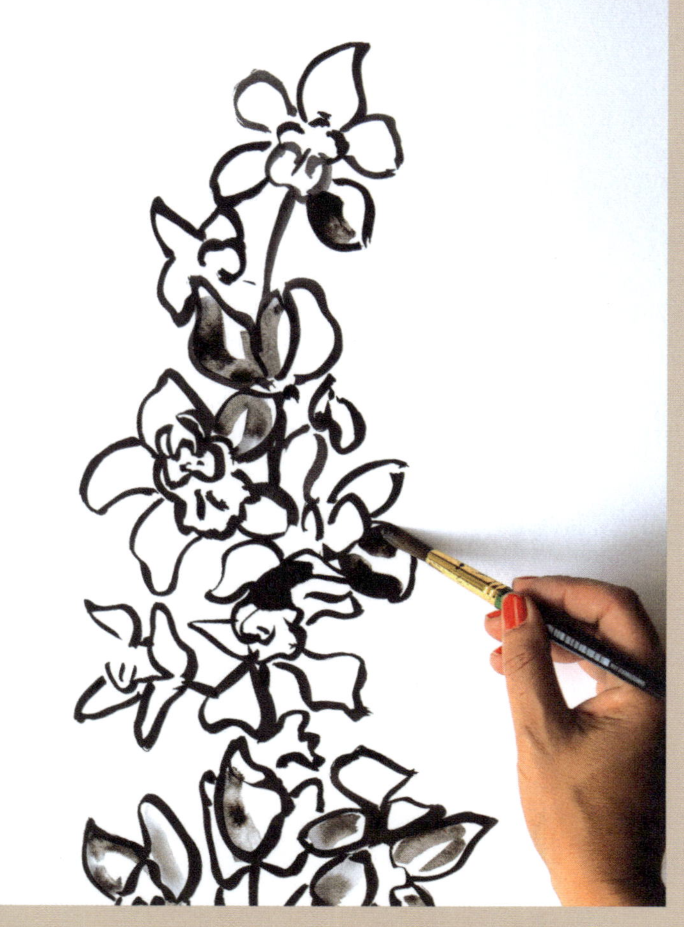
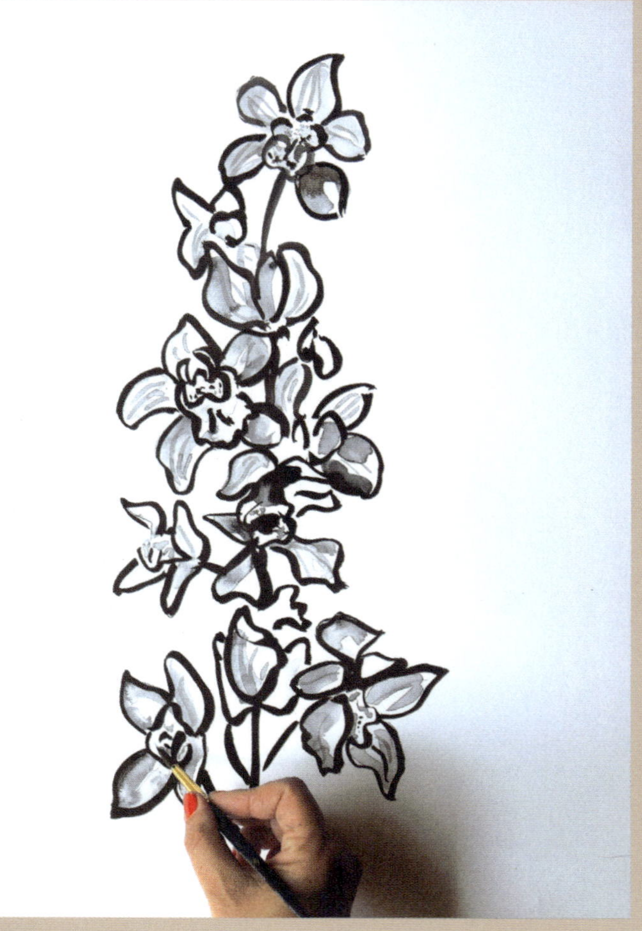

1

Dip the size-12 brush in water, to make it more absorbent, and then in the pure ink. Use the brush tip to draw the overall outline of the branch and flowers, noting how the flowerheads overlap each other. Re-wet and ink the brush as needed.

2

While the outline is still wet, use the 40 per cent dilution to fill the petals and sepals, letting the outline bleed into the wash.

3

When the outline and wash are almost dry, switch to the size-8 brush and use the 60 per cent wash to add areas of detail and bring more definition to the flowers, including fine lines in the petals and shadows in the lips, throats and columns.

●

MATERIALS

Smooth watercolour paper, A2

Waterproof ink in three vessels: pure ink, 60 per cent dilution and 40 per cent dilution

Round brushes, sizes 8 and 12

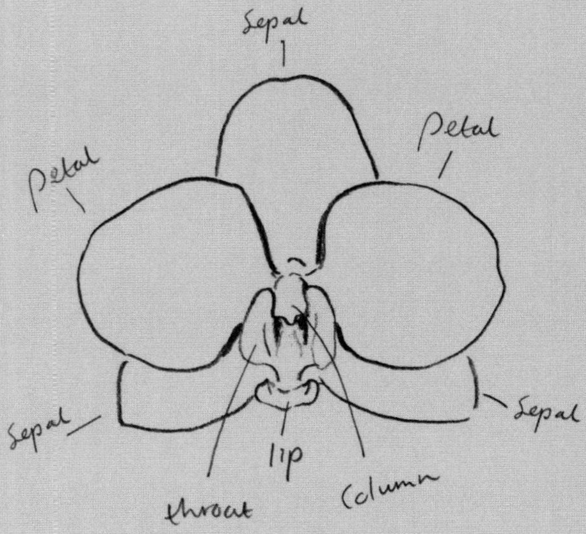

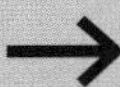

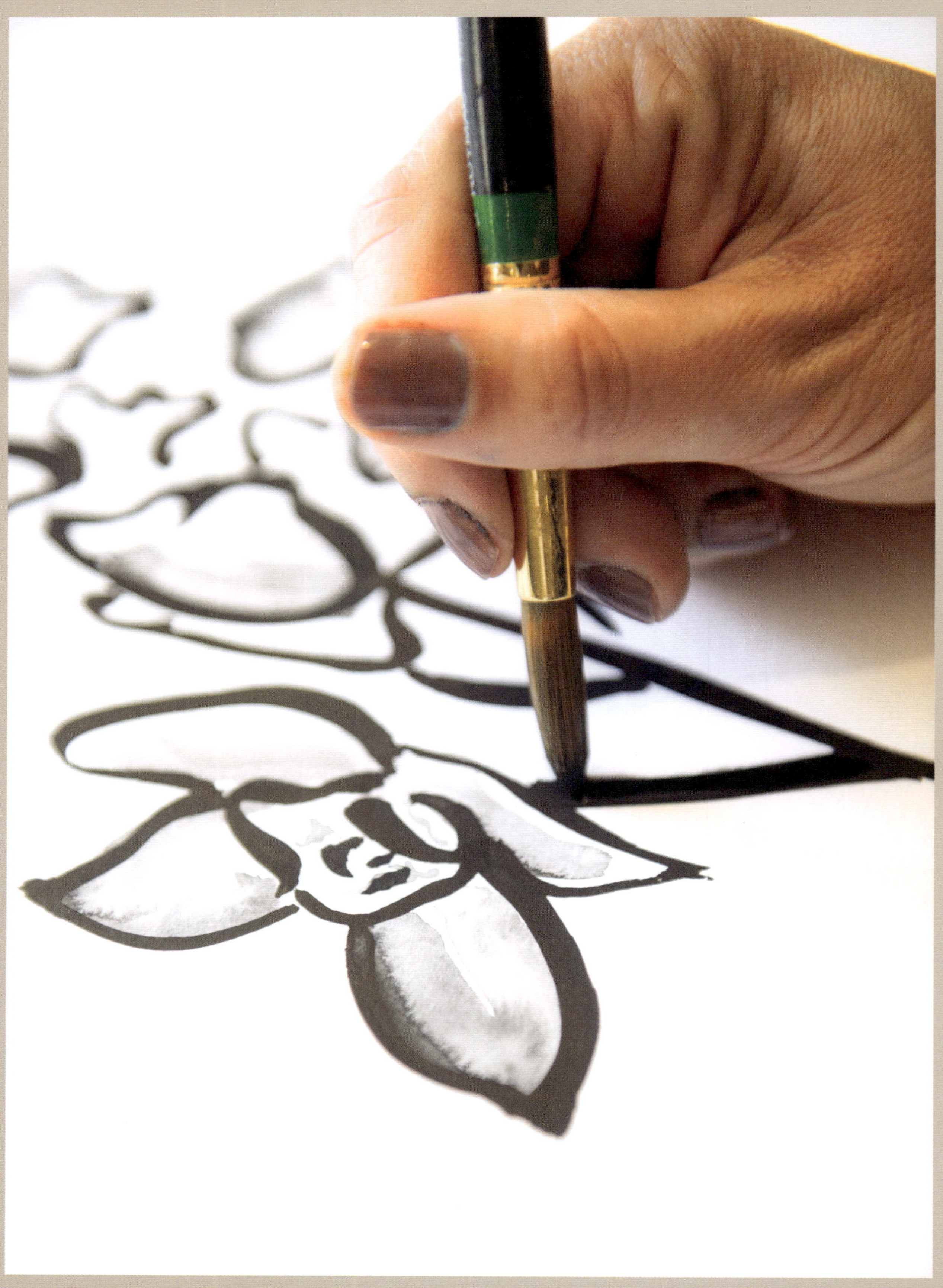

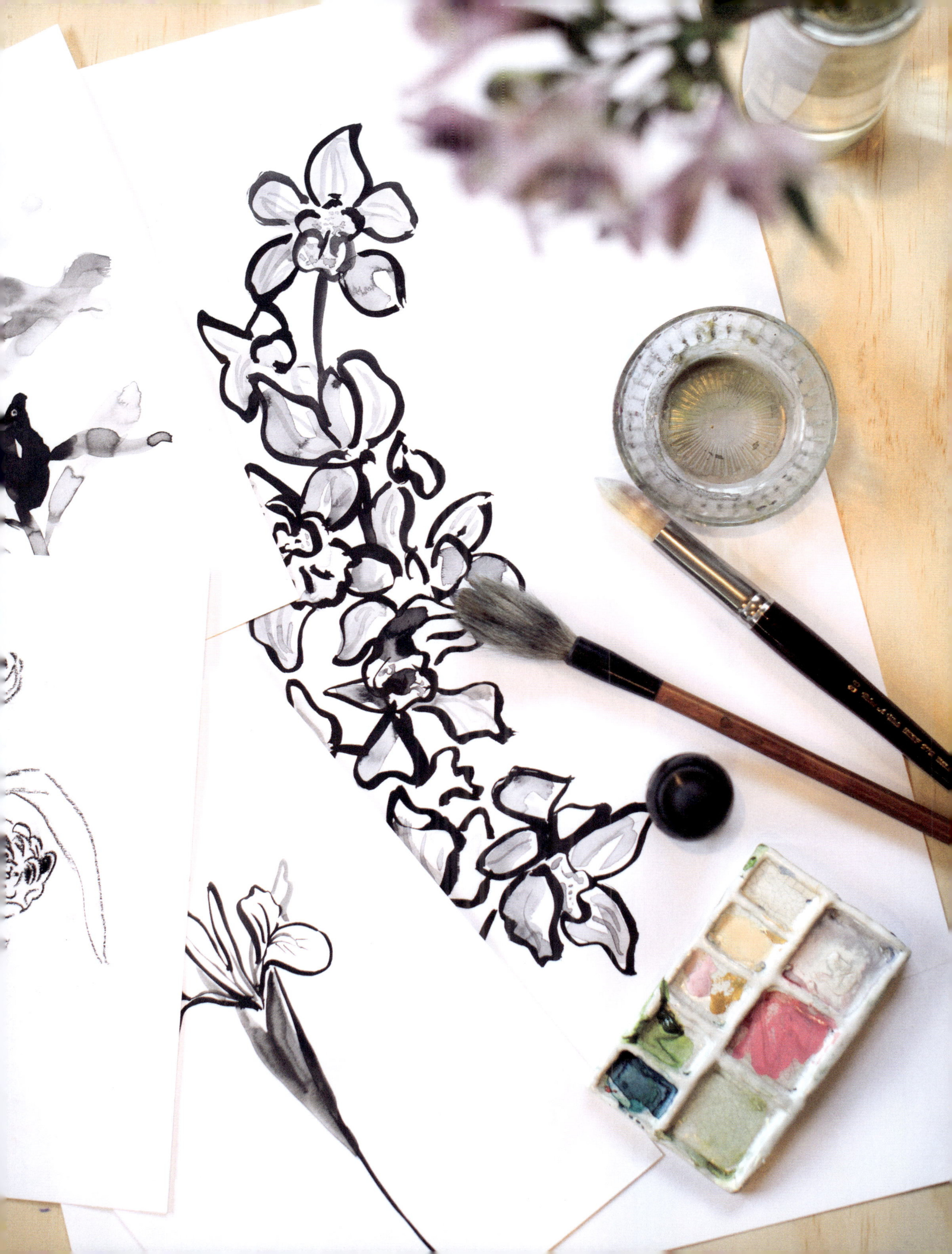

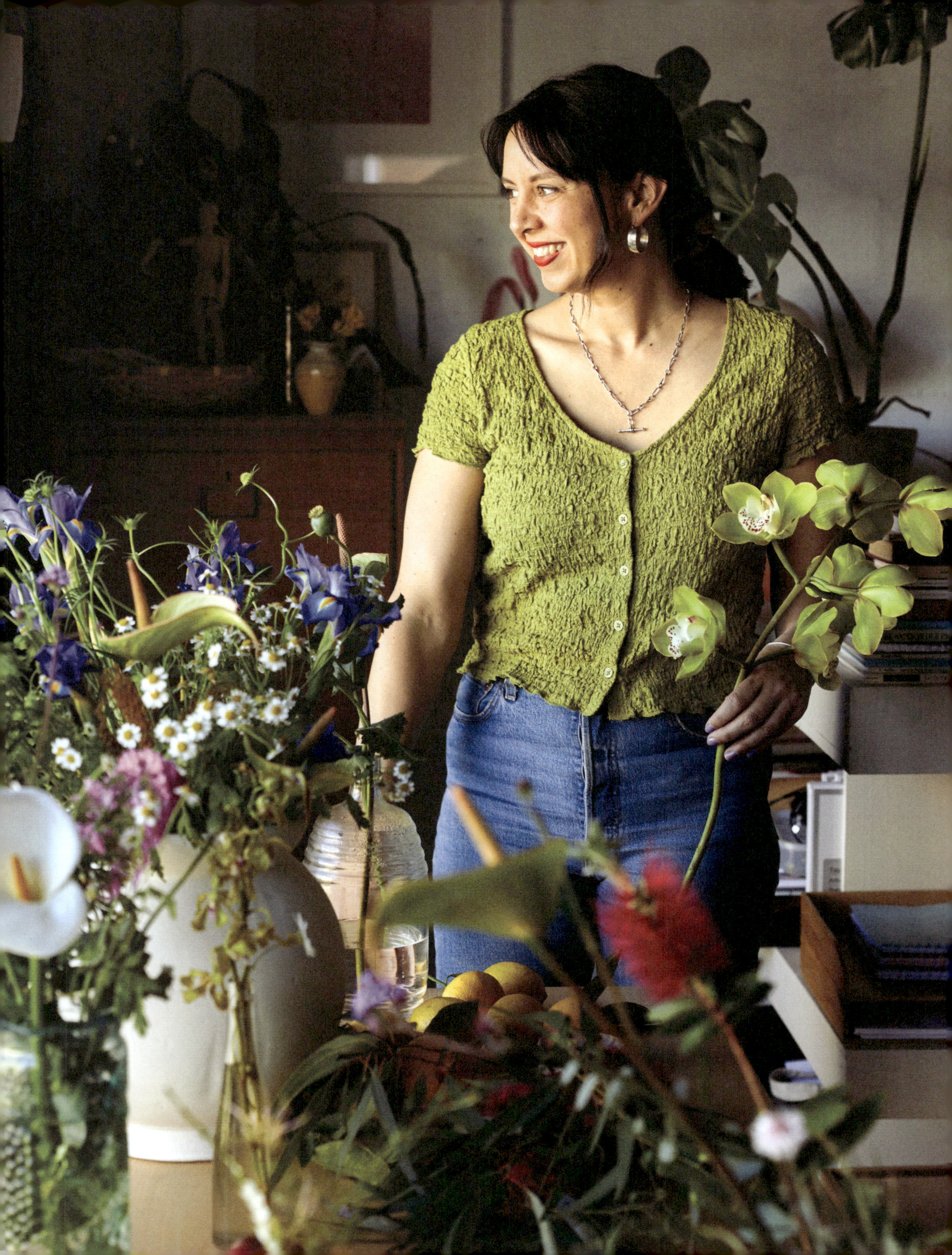

ABOUT THE AUTHOR

Sarah Hankinson is a Melbourne-based artist and illustrator with over fifteen years' experience in commercial illustration. Recently, she has combined her skills and artistry to create a practice based in the fine arts.

Inspired by the natural world, Sarah has a passion for botanical, landscape and still-life painting and drawing. In focusing on our natural surrounds, she illuminates the fragility of our environment and prompts us to delve deeper into an understanding of our sense of place. Her work encourages us to foster a deeper appreciation of and connection to the wonders of nature by slowing down and taking notice. Her pieces are visual odes to the profound beauty of the everyday, which can be easily overlooked. They express the richness of the intricacies that make life bountiful and abundant.

Sarah utilises a range of mediums, from rich, layered oil pastels to dynamic ink washes, harmonising traditional and modern techniques. With her delicate lines, bold use of colour and unique style, Sarah brings her subjects to life.

ABOUT THE FLORAL DESIGN STUDIO

Sour Sunflower is a floral design studio in Melbourne created by Alyssa Trenerry in 2018. Its style puts an emphasis on the colours and textures of flowers and turns them into thoughtful, sculptural arrangements that break the traditional binds of floristry. Each arrangement is an ode to the seasons of nature and the beauty of flowers.

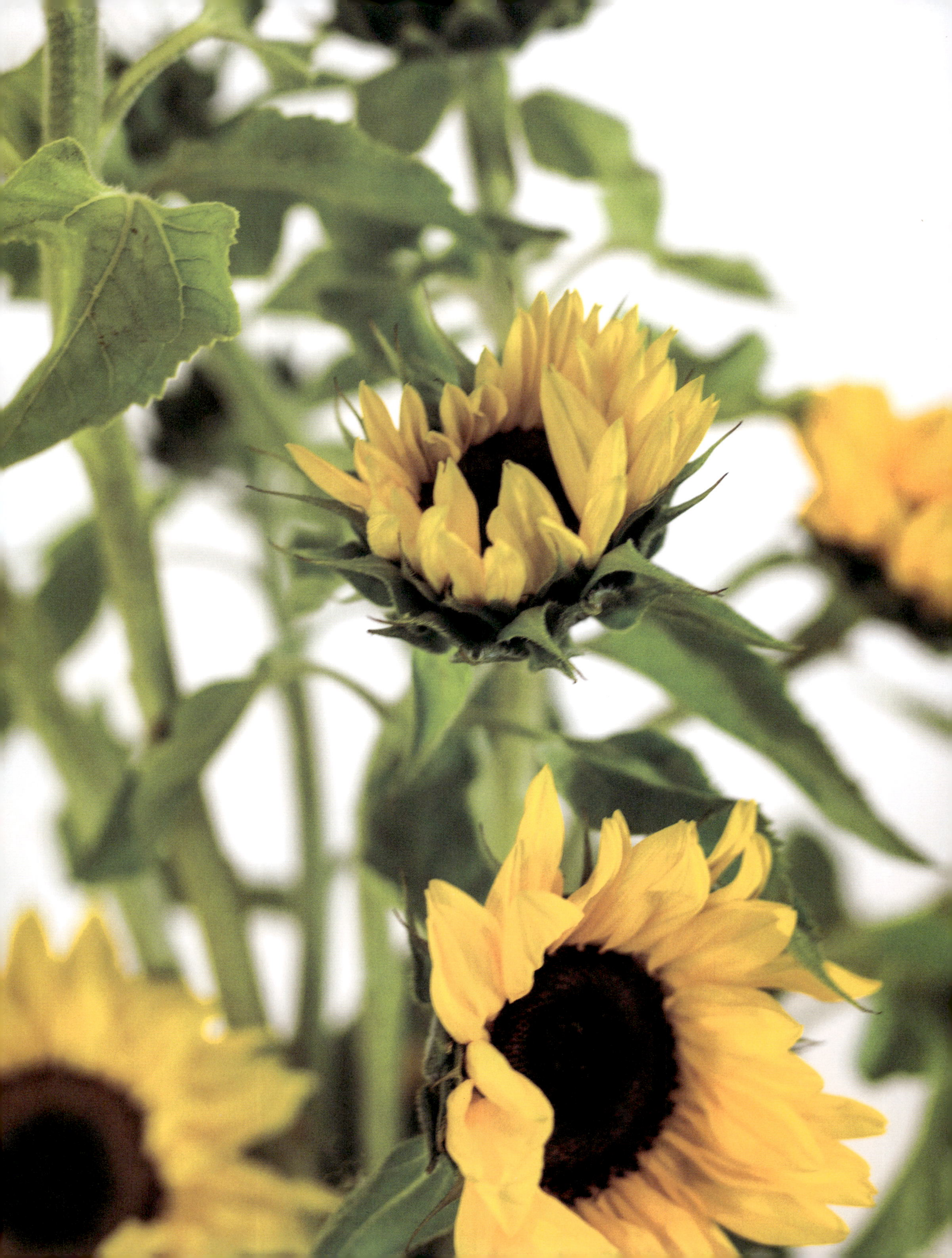

ACKNOWLEDGEMENTS

Thank you to:

Alyssa, Janna and Becca – working with creative wonder-women doing great work! Thank you for being part of the book. I feel so lucky to have had you all involved.

The Windsor Workshop family and co-workers, particularly Belinda and Bree, for everything always. Two amazing women who I am so fortunate to have as business partners in work and life. So many laughs and so much support.

Thank you always to Mike who multitasks as my partner, photographer, advisor and all-round great guy.

My sons Bobby and Pip, nieces Avie and Lulu and nephew Buddy – love you all.

Mum and Dad for supporting me in my journey as an artist. Thank you for encouraging me to pursue my passion without any pressure to get a real job!

Jess, Bree, Kenny, my extended family here and in New Zealand, thank you for all your support.

Lisa, Kirsten, Casey and Penny for having faith in me and pulling everything together. Thank you! Writing and creating the artworks for this book has been a career highlight – and so much fun.

My illustration agent, Katie, for the years of management, encouragement and support.

And thank you to anyone who has bought this book, my calendars, artwork or commissioned me for illustration work. I feel so fortunate to work as an artist.

I hope this book encourages readers to pick up a pencil and draw. Having an art practice has given me the opportunity to notice more beauty in the world, which can only be a good thing.

ACKNOWLEDGEMENT OF COUNTRY

I acknowledge and pay my respects to the Boon Wurrung people, the traditional custodians and First Peoples of the land on which I make my art, live and love. I acknowledge the important role that art has played on these lands for thousands of years and acknowledge First Peoples of Australia as the first artists and first creators of culture.

First published in Australia in 2024
by Thames & Hudson Australia Pty Ltd
Wurundjeri Country, 132A Gwynne Street,
Cremorne, Victoria 3121

First published in the United Kingdom in 2025
by Thames & Hudson Ltd
181a High Holborn, London WC1V 7QX

ISBN 978-1-760-76434-0

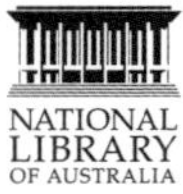 A catalogue record for this
book is available from the
National Library of Australia

British Library Cataloguing-in-Publication Data
A catalogue record for this book is available
from the British Library

Design: Casey Schuurman
Editing: Penny Mansley

Printed and bound in China by 1010
Printing International Limited

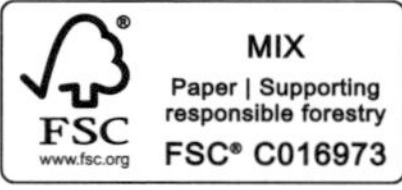

Thames & Hudson Australia wishes to acknowledge that
Aboriginal and Torres Strait Islander peoples are the first
storytellers of this nation and the Traditional Custodians
of the land on which we live and work. We acknowledge
their continuing culture and pay respect to Elders past
and present.

thamesandhudson.com.au

Image credits

Becca Crawford: 2, 5–8, 10–2, 14, 16, 19, 21, 23,
27–9, 32, 50, 62, 66–8, 80, 92, 103, 110, 128, 140
Janna Bennett/Sour Sunflower: 24, 34, 43, 46, 49,
70, 77, 82, 100, 101, 106, 115, 130, 132, 135, 142
Michael James: 37–8, 40, 53–4, 57–8, 64, 71, 74–6,
78, 86–9, 94–5, 98–9, 104, 107, 112, 114, 118, 122–3,
126–7, 131, 134, 138–9
Sarah Hankinson: 30, 35–6, 39, 41–2, 45, 48, 51, 61,
83–4, 96, 102, 124, 136